Structural Reforms for Growth and Cohesion

Structural Reforms for Growth and Cohesion

Lessons and Challenges for CESEE Countries and a Modern Europe

Edited by

Ewald Nowotny

Governor, Oesterreichische Nationalbank, Austria

Doris Ritzberger-Grünwald

Director, Oesterreichische Nationalbank, Austria

Helene Schuberth

Head of Division, Oesterreichische Nationalbank, Austria

Cheltenham, UK • Northampton, MA, USA

Published by
Edward Elgar Publishing Limited
The Lypiatts
15 Lansdown Road
Cheltenham
Glos GL50 2JA
UK

Edward Elgar Publishing, Inc.
William Pratt House
9 Dewey Court
Northampton
Massachusetts 01060
USA

A catalogue record for this book
is available from the British Library

Library of Congress Control Number: 2018945221

This book is available electronically in the **Elgar**online
Economics subject collection
DOI 10.4337/9781788971140

ISBN 978 1 78897 113 3 (cased)
ISBN 978 1 78897 114 0 (eBook)

Typeset by Servis Filmsetting Ltd, Stockport, Cheshire
Printed and bound in Great Britain by TJ International Ltd, Padstow

Contents

Contributors

Orsetta Causa, Senior Economist, Inclusive Growth and Well-being Unit, Structural Surveillance Division, OECD Economics Department.

László Csaba, Distinguished Professor of International Political Economy, Central European University and Member of the Hungarian Academy of Sciences.

Oliver Dreute, Adviser on the Multi-Annual Financial Framework, European Political Strategy Centre, European Commission.

Georg Fischer, Senior Research Associate, Vienna Institute for International Economic Studies; former Director for Social Affairs, European Commission Brussels.

Jan-Martin Frie, Analyst Economics Team, European Political Strategy Centre, European Commission.

Hubert Gabrisch, Research Associate, Wiesbaden Institute for Law and Economics.

Mahdi Ghodsi, Economist, Vienna Institute for International Economic Studies – wiiw.

Julia Gruebler, Economist, Vienna Institute for International Economic Studies – wiiw.

Sergei Guriev, Chief Economist, European Bank of Reconstruction and Development.

Vladimir Isaila, Analyst Economics Team, European Political Strategy Centre, European Commission.

Jozef Makúch, Governor, National Bank of Slovakia.

Alina Mungiu-Pippidi, Professor, Democracy Studies at the Hertie School of Governance, Berlin.

Ewald Nowotny, Governor, Oesterreichische Nationalbank.

Sonja Puntscher Riekmann, Jean Monnet Professor and Director of Salzburg Centre of European Union Studies.

Paul Ramskogler, Principal Economist, Foreign Research Division, Oesterreichische Nationalbank.

Oliver Reiter, Research Assistant, Vienna Institute for International Economic Studies – wiiw.

Doris Ritzberger-Grünwald, Director, Economic and Research Department, Oesterreichische Nationalbank.

Jiří Rusnok, Governor, Czech National Bank.

Helene Schuberth, Head of the Foreign Research Division, Oesterreichische Nationalbank.

Helena Schweiger, Associate Director, Senior Economist, European Bank for Reconstruction and Development.

Robert Stehrer, Scientific Director, Vienna Institute for International Economic Studies – wiiw.

Paweł A. Strzelecki, Economist, Narodowy Bank Polski.

Daria Taglioni, Lead Economist, World Bank.

Lúcio Vinhas de Souza, Leader Economics Team, European Political Strategy Centre, European Commission.

Barnabás Virág, Executive Director, Magyar Nemzeti Bank.

PART I

A modern take on structural reforms

1. Past and future reform challenges for CESEE and Europe at large

Ewald Nowotny, Doris Ritzberger-Grünwald and Helene Schuberth

The aim of this book is to collect assessments of achievements and failures of past structural policies with a view to adapting them so that such policies help us to address the remaining or newly emerging challenges more effectively. The book has also been designed to depart from the beaten track and to shed some light on more inclusive growth strategies. Moreover, this book has a specific, albeit not exclusive, focus on the area of Central, Eastern and Southeastern Europe (CESEE), not least because this region has – by and large successfully – gone through a profound transition period. By transforming their economic and political systems, the CESEE countries have, so to speak, implemented the basis, or the 'mother' of all structural reforms.

Now, what is meant by 'structural reforms'? The term 'structure' refers to an arrangement of individual elements that form a complex phenomenon. In the case of an economy, structural reform could thus relate to any deliberate change within or between its sectors, factors or institutions. However, in the 1950s, this term acquired specific significance when the International Monetary Fund (IMF) and the World Bank introduced the notion of 'structural adjustment' to describe preconditions for receiving emergency loans, including trade liberalization, fiscal consolidation and the elimination of price controls as well as attracting foreign direct investment (FDI) and fighting corruption. Over the years, 'structural reforms' has more generally become a code for deregulation, liberalization and privatization.

Looking back, structural policies appear to have been advocated as a panacea for growth in Europe rather often, while monetary and fiscal policies were considered as having a stimulating effect on the economy in the short term only. But the experience since the onset of the financial and economic crisis in 2007–2008 seems to indicate that the better performance of the United States of America (USA) in terms of economic growth compared with the euro area might partly be attributed to different degrees of responses in terms of macroeconomic policy instruments. This divergence may reflect the fact that the monetary and fiscal policy reaction to the crisis came at a faster pace in the United States than in Europe, and that policy-makers took more decisive action in the United States than in Europe – which happened for a number of reasons. At the same time, however, we should not underestimate the macro effects that ensue from differences in the governance of the two monetary unions and effects stemming from divergent structures of the economies in general. With that in mind, institutional reform of Economic and Monetary Union (EMU) as a whole is a structural reform project that is crucial for the euro area, in particular with regard to complementing it with a Fiscal Union. This is a long-term project, but efforts to further deepen the European Monetary Union have been stepped up following the outbreak of the financial and economic crisis in Europe in 2008. Although we central bankers are more involved in the no less important completion of the Banking Union, we certainly welcome proposals toward more fiscal risk-sharing, that is, through a kind of macroeconomic stabilization function. As such, this book will also contribute to the institutional debate on the state of EMU (Gabrisch, Chapter 16). European institutions have made important headway since the crisis, with the crisis being an important contributing factor to the reform momentum. In order to receive support for necessary integration steps, social aspects need to be addressed with great care (Puntscher Riekmann, Chapter 3; Csaba, Chapter 15). Europe faces new social and economic challenges, such as globalization, digitization, demographic change, inequality and divergence. Institutionally, the European Union's 'Pillar of Social Rights' provides a vision for the rights of workers and citizens (Fischer, Chapter 4). Additionally, the European Commission has raised the idea of providing financial incentives for structural reforms, recognizing their short-term costs while accruing their positive spillovers to the rest of the Union. Naturally, for reforms to be sustainable and efficient over the long run, domestic factors come into play. As such, the European Commission has addressed this issue through an overhaul of its surveillance tools to better monitor vulnerabilities in the member states (Vinhas de Souza et al., Chapter 17).

Both monetary and fiscal policies rely on economic structures that are capable of absorbing any given stimulus. After all, macroeconomic measures can only exploit the long-term growth potential shaped by microeconomic conditions. In other words, structural reforms ensure the functioning of the monetary transmission mechanism and thus help to create fiscal space. In turn, monetary and fiscal expansion provide some flexibility in dealing with the short-term costs of structural reforms such as contractionary and unwanted distributional effects.

Moreover, in a Monetary Union, structural policies that keep costs and wages flexible and production factors mobile enable the economies of individual member states to swiftly adjust to asymmetric shocks. However, flexibility does not necessarily imply a decentralized structure. Just take the Austrian wage bargaining system as an example. With a collective bargaining coverage rate of 98 per cent, the system is certainly among the most centralized in the world. Yet, in terms of outcome, Austrian employees' wages are sufficiently flexible so as to enable comparably low unemployment rates in Europe. There is a simple explanation for this puzzle: strong umbrella organizations of trade unions and employer associations make sure that sectoral wage agreements always take nationwide rather than sector-wide productivity increases into account. What is more, this tried and tested consensual practice extends far beyond wage bargaining. The Austrian Social Partnership might not be the fastest-moving organization, but it certainly provides the ownership needed for pragmatic and sustainable structural reforms. In contrast, labour market regimes with very little employment protection, for instance, tend to be less conducive to the long-run accumulation of firm-specific knowledge. As research has shown, this type of productivity-enhancing innovation is, however, vital for a substantial industrial sector to survive in a high-wage economy (see Kleinknecht et al. 2014).

Overall, the CESEE region experienced a remarkable convergence process, which has been resumed after having been temporarily stalled by the crisis. Structural reforms definitely played an important role alongside macroeconomic stabilization, deep economic integration and a solid human capital base. Contributions to this book by colleagues from CESEE central banks shed light on the different experiences with such reforms and the additional reform needs, which only the crisis had revealed. What appears to be common to all is that synergies between sound fiscal and monetary policies have helped to overcome the downturn (see Makúch, Chapter 10; Virág, Chapter 11; Rusnok, Chapter 12; Strzelecki, Chapter 13). Of course, some countries have the advantage of being closer to European centres of industrial gravity. At the same time, differing country paths can also be explained by gaps in institutional quality. The European Union continues to be an important anchor for institutional reform, which can only be successful, however, in an environment of strong democracy and sound governance that works against corruption and 'state capture' (Mungiu-Pippidi, Chapter 14). After all, lack of trust in the government reduces political support for the next generation of reforms, which are to address challenges such as demographic headwinds (low fertility rates, emigration and brain drain) as well as technological innovation, energy efficiency and social fairness.

One area where convergence has been less convincing is real wages, even if we take account of slower productivity change, sinking unemployment rates and weaker wage growth in the rest of Europe (see Galgóczi 2017). On the one hand, low wages are not only a factor of competitiveness; on the other hand, low wages also dampen aggregate demand. With the skill component in production increasing, one wonders why the wage shares are still so low in the region. As evidenced by one of the contributions to this book (Ramskogler, Chapter 9), labour market dualities – given increased competition between temporary and permanent labour – have dampened wage growth in Europe overall and especially in CESEE.

Ultimately, we have learned quite a few lessons from the crisis (Draghi 2017): reforming labour markets without also reforming product markets intensifies deflationary pressures, in particular at the zero lower bound. Hence, comprehensive packaging of reforms is needed to reap the benefits intended. Trade-offs between growth and equality can be observed particularly in social and labour market reforms, rather than in product market reforms, which are addressed in Chapter 8 of this book (Causa). Ideally, reforms should also encompass attempts to make public administration more efficient and include a supportive macroeconomic policy mix (Arce et al. 2016). Furthermore, the right timing and sequencing of reform steps is equally important. In many instances, reforms create winners and losers, and ways to compensate the latter have to be implemented in the reform package.

Finally, this book also discusses the emerging protectionist attitudes and trade barriers, which could hamper the functioning of modern product markets, whereas sound standardization and regulations also appear to have beneficial effects if well designed (Taglioni, Chapter 6; Ghodsi et al., Chapter 7). Furthermore the book addresses the empirical evidence for the supposed growth effects of reforms (Bordon et al. 2016) as well as the conditions under which long-run gains may outpace likely short-run pain. Then there is the perennial question of whether there is a one-size-fits-all structure for economies. Of course, economic structures evolve hand in hand with the stage and path of economic development. As reflected by the World Bank's Doing Business ranking, which aims at measuring the outcome of business regulation, the European economies have been undergoing structural convergence, and have been becoming more and more similar. In the longer run, it remains to be seen whether these trends have been borne out by fundamentals. So far the good news is that 'structural laggards' are gradually catching up; some of the CESEE economies have even come to rank among the 'structural leaders' by certain standards.

REFERENCES

Arce, O., S. Hurtado and C. Thomas (2016), 'Policy spillovers and synergies in a monetary union', *International Journal of Central Banking*, **12** (3), 219–77.

Bordon, A.R., C. Ebeke and K. Shirono (2016), 'When do structural reforms work? On the role of the business cycle and macroeconomic policies', IMF Working Paper, WP/16/62.

Draghi, M. (2017), 'Structural reforms in the euro area', Introductory remarks by Mario Draghi, President of the European Central Bank, at the ECB conference Structural Reforms in the Euro Area, Frankfurt am Main, 18 October.

Galgóczi, B. (2017), 'Why Central and Eastern Europe needs a pay rise', European Trade Union Institute Working Paper 2017.01.

Kleinknecht, A., F.N. van Schaik and H. Zhou (2014), 'Is flexible labour good for innovation?', *Cambridge Journal of Economics*, **38** (5), 1207–19.

2.   Revisiting transition reform

Sergei Guriev

2.1   DOCUMENTING THE POST-CRISIS SLOWDOWN

As the European Bank for Reconstruction and Development (EBRD) showed in its Transition Report 2013, *Stuck in Transition?* (EBRD 2013), the first two decades of transition from plan to market produced strikingly different outcomes. Two decades on, some countries (mostly in Central and Eastern Europe and in the Baltics) had built consolidated democracies and functioning market economies integrated in the global value chains and the international financial system; while these countries were found to be still behind their Western peers in terms of per capita gross domestic product (GDP), they have continued to catch up. Others (mostly post-Soviet) countries got stuck with stagnating political and economic institutions.

More recently, however, the process of convergence in Central Europe and Southern-Eastern Europe (CESEE) has also slowed down. In the EBRD's Transition Report 2017–18, *Sustaining Growth* (EBRD 2017), a synthetic control panel is constructed for each EBRD country of operation (by selecting at least 15 countries of similar size and at the similar level of development) and growth rates in EBRD countries and comparator emerging markets are compared. EBRD countries used to outperform their comparators before 2008, but have underperformed their comparators ever since (Figure 2.1). The cumulative loss of gross domestic product (GDP), relative to comparator countries, since 2008 is 9 per cent of GDP. The picture for the CESEE region is very similar (Figure 2.2).

In order to understand this slowdown, the sources of growth before and after the Great Recession in EBRD countries and other emerging markets are decomposed. Figure 2.3 presents the growth accounting for the EBRD countries, their comparators, CESEE countries and other major emerging markets regions. Before the crisis, the outperformance of transition countries was driven by the growth in total factor productivity (TFP) rather than the accumulation of factors of production. This is intuitive: these countries were already industrialized and educated when

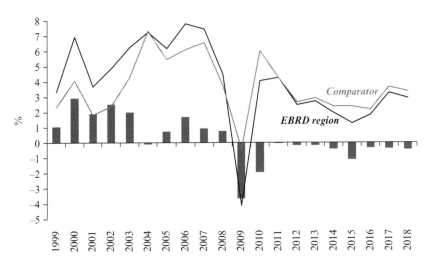

Notes: The darker line represents EBRD countries, the lighter line indicates comparators. Bars represent the difference between EBRD countries and comparators.

Source: EBRD (2017).

Figure 2.1   Growth rates in EBRD countries and their comparators

they started transition. Also, they have already completed the demographic transition, so that a further demographic dividend was unlikely to materialize. However, while these countries did have factors of production in place, due to the legacy of the command economy these factors were not efficiently utilized. Transition to market and integration into the global economy helped to raise the efficiency of factor use, which is reflected in TFP growth.

At the same time, Figure 2.4 shows that after the crisis TFP growth disappeared. In fact, the cumulative TFP growth since 2008 was negative: transition countries have not yet reached the pre-crisis TFP level. Most of the growth came from capital investment. However, in terms of investment, transition countries have also underperformed their competitors.

2.2   MIDDLE-INCOME TRAP?

Are the transition countries stuck in the middle-income trap? The concept of the middle-income trap – a slowdown in convergence experienced by countries reaching middle-income status – was proposed in Gill and

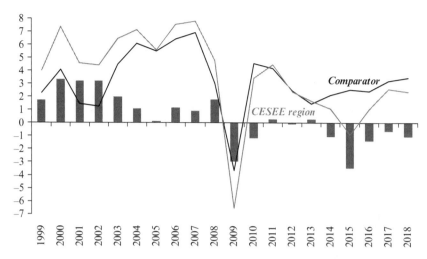

Notes: The lighter line represents EBRD countries, the darker line indicates comparators.
Bars represent the difference between EBRD countries and comparators.

Source: EBRD (2017).

Figure 2.2   Growth rates in CESEE and comparator countries

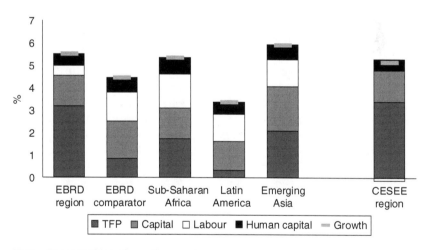

Note: Decomposition of growth, percentage per annum.

Source: EBRD (2017).

*Figure 2.3   Growth decomposition in EBRD region, CESEE and
              comparator countries, 1998–2008*

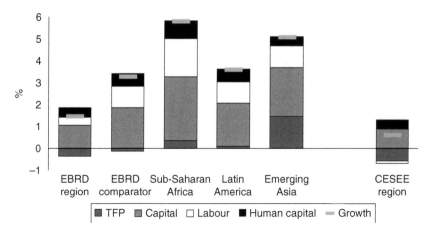

Note: Decomposition of growth, percentage per annum.

Source: EBRD (2017).

Figure 2.4 *Growth decomposition in EBRD region, CESEE and comparator countries, 2008–2014*

Kharas (2007). While there is still no consensus regarding the empirical relevance of this concept (Gill and Kharas 2015), the middle-income trap debate has helped to bring forward the main growth challenge faced by the middle-income countries. Essentially, they have to switch from a growth model based on low-wage manufacturing, investment and factor accumulation, to another model based on human capital, skill-intensive services and innovation. The concept of the middle-income trap is also in line with the neo-Schumpeterian framework that has recently taken centre stage in modern growth theory (Aghion and Howitt 1998; Aghion et al. 2013; Aghion and Bircan 2017). This framework is based on the idea of creative destruction. In such a setting, the pay-off to innovation versus adoption of existing technology depends on the distance to the technological frontier. The advanced economies are better off innovating; indeed, if they imitate existing technologies, they lose time and effort and therefore lag behind their competitors. At the same time, the benefits of imitation are not large, as their existing technology is not far behind the frontier. However, for poor countries imitation of currently frontier technologies pays off, as the benefits of adopting existing technology brings much more sizeable relative benefits. The problem is to switch from an imitation-based model to an innovation-based one once the country gets closer to the frontier. At this point, the country's political economy may be dominated by interest groups who benefit from the status quo and prefer to avoid the transition to the innovation-based model.

As argued above, the slowdown in convergence in transition countries is more pronounced than in other middle-income countries, and has a special nature. Unlike the developing countries, they have come to their current position not through factor accumulation but through a more efficient use of factors accumulated under the Soviet system. However, nowadays they face a similar problem: their existing growth model has served them well but has eventually exhausted its potential; they now need to move to a new model. This new model must be based on innovation and TFP growth.

The challenge is the same as in the other middle-income economies: these countries need to address the political economy of the status quo, they need to reform the institutions defended by those who benefit from the old growth model, and build the institutions promoting innovation-based growth. These reforms involve further international openness, financial development (especially development of equity markets), improved investment climate, competition policies, labour mobility, incentives for investment in postgraduate education and research and development.

2.3 THE (LACK OF) DEMAND FOR REFORMS

The problem with promoting further economic and political reforms is that – unlike in the late 1980s and early 1990s – reforms are no longer popular. Figures 2.5 and 2.6 report key results from the EBRD and the World Bank's Life in Transition Survey (LiTS) series (EBRD 2016b). In most middle-income transition countries, the market economy is supported by a minority of households; support for the democratic political system is higher, but at the same time well below the levels in Germany or Greece.

2.4 WHAT WENT WRONG?

Why have the residents of transition countries lost confidence in market reforms? Analysis points to the importance of (the lack of) inclusion and fairness. First, while reforms have delivered impressive economic growth on average, the benefits of this growth have not been shared broadly. Figure 2.7 presents Branko Milanovic's famous 'elephant curve' (Milanovic 2016) for the post-communist countries. Since the beginning of reforms, real incomes in these countries have grown at about 2 per

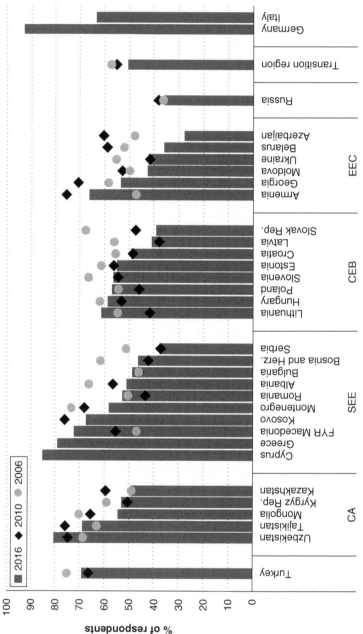

Source: Life in Transition Survey (LiTS) I (2006), LiTS II (2010), LiTS III (2016).

Figure 2.5 Percentage of respondents supporting the market economy

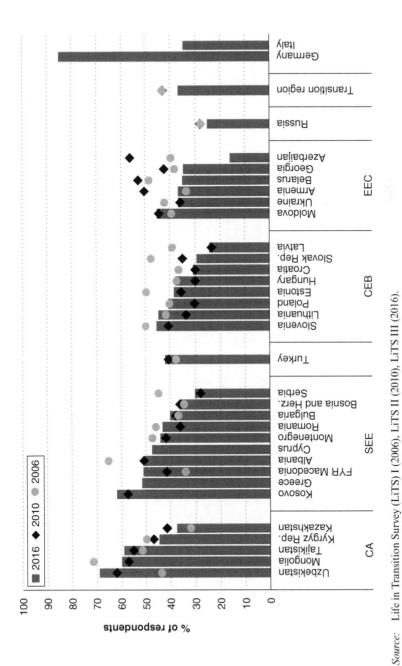

Source: Life in Transition Survey (LiTS) I (2006), LiTS II (2010), LiTS III (2016).

Figure 2.6   Percentage of respondents supporting democracy

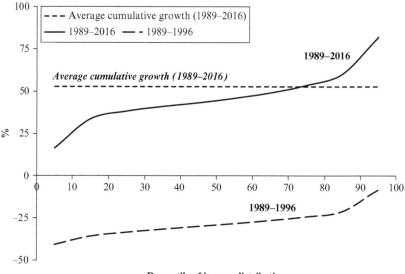

Source: EBRD (2016a).

Figure 2.7   *Post-communist countries: cumulative growth in income since 1989 depending on initial income*

cent per year on average. However, for the bottom 75 per cent of the population incomes grew at slower rates, while the real beneficiaries of this growth were the top 10 per cent of the households. As Milanovic's analysis may produce different results for country groups and individual countries, within-country elephant curves are also looked at, and for the vast majority of them the results are similar. Figure 2.8 shows the results for Russia, where the top 20 per cent have seen growth at or above the average rate (which in the case of Russia was about 3 per cent per year), while the bottom 80 per cent have experienced growth rates below average. Moreover, the bottom 10 per cent have seen their incomes actually fall. In order to put these results in a perspective, the chart for the United States is also presented (Figure 2.9). There, the top 10 per cent have also done very well; however, the bottom 90 per cent have not fallen too far below the average. In this sense, the issue of those 'left behind' is much larger in the transition countries than in the modern United States (or other Western countries).

These problems look even more striking when exploring the households for which the reforms have reduced the gap between their incomes

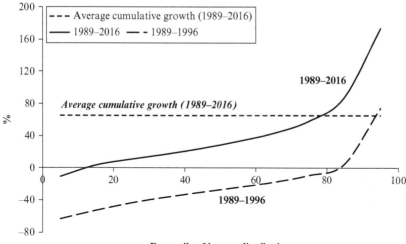

Source: EBRD (2016a).

Figure 2.8 *Russia: cumulative growth in income since 1989 depending on initial income*

and incomes of the advanced economies. It turns out that this income convergence has taken place *on average*, but not for the majority of households. Only 44 per cent of post-communist households have seen incomes catching up with those of G7 (Group of Seven) countries. As for the other 56 per cent, their incomes have further fallen behind those of rich countries' residents.

Increase in inequality per se is not necessarily a negative development. After all, socialist economies were 'too egalitarian' (at least in terms of nominal incomes); the socialist equality was unfair in the sense that talent and effort were not being rewarded with higher pay. Reforms were actually meant to introduce 'fair' inequality, creating market-based meritocratic incentives. However, in many countries we have also seen a dramatic increase in 'unfair' inequality, where success was based on circumstances of birth, connections and even breaking the law, rather than on effort and skills.

This brings up the second source of the low popularity of reforms: the view that reforms have not been carried out in a fair way; instead, they have brought inequality of opportunity and corruption. In order to test this hypothesis, the correlation between the perception of corruption and trust in government is checked (controlling for income, education, employment

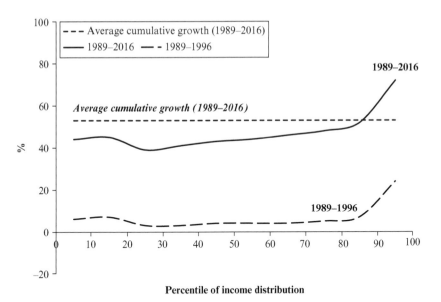

Source: EBRD (2016a).

*Figure 2.9　US: cumulative growth in income since 1989 depending on
　　　　　　initial income*

status, age, gender and town fixed effects). Table 2A.1 in the Appendix shows that perception that corruption is growing has a strong negative effect on trust in government. Results for other measures of government approval and of corruption perceptions (as well as experience of corruption) are very similar. Importantly, the views on corruption affect government approval more than economic variables such as respondents' income and unemployment. Once perceptions of corruption are included in the regression, the coefficients at the economic variables become insignificant. This is not the case in other countries (Guriev and Treisman 2017).

In order to understand the role of 'fairness' of inequality, income inequality is decomposed into two components: (1) 'unfair' inequality, or inequality of opportunity (the part of inequality that is explained by gender, race, place of birth and parental background); and (2) 'fair' inequality (the residual, explained by effort). It is found (EBRD 2016a) that in many transition countries inequality of opportunity accounts for about half of the total income inequality.

Table 2A.2 in the Appendix shows that support for the market economy is negatively correlated only with the inequality of opportunity (the 'unfair' component of inequality), while the 'fair' component of inequality is positively correlated with support for markets.[1] This shows that it is the unfairness of the inequality, rather than inequality per se, that drives lower support for reforms in transition countries.

2.5 RETHINKING TRANSITION

The importance of inclusion and fairness for the political legitimacy of market reforms prompted the EBRD to rethink the destination of the transition process. In November 2016, the EBRD Board approved the new 'Transition Concept', defining the success of transition as a sustainable market economy characterized by six qualities: (1) competitive; (2) well-governed; (3) green; (4) inclusive; (5) resilient; and (6) integrated. While (1) – related to creating competitive markets and private ownership – has always been an essential part of the Bank's mandate, qualities (2) and (4) are directly linked to the political sustainability of market reforms. Good governance is critical for fairness, and inclusion is understood by the EBRD precisely as equality of opportunity (in a sense, the 'green' quality is also related to inclusion, namely to sharing the benefits of today's economic growth with future generations).

2.6 LIGHT AT THE END OF THE TUNNEL

Given the update of the Transition Concept, the EBRD has also redesigned its conceptual framework for measuring the transition progress. The good news is that the indicators of reforms alongside the six dimensions above (EBRD 2017, Chapter 5) shows the pick-up in the speed of the (fair and inclusive) reforms in 2017. This may be related to recent growth in the global economy and in the euro area in particular, which creates growth opportunities and thus eases the fiscal burden in the transition countries as well. The positive developments in 2017 may also be related to the wake-up call delivered by the 2016 rise in populism in the West. Learning from past mistakes, mainstream politicians may now understand that in order to withstand populists' offensive, their countries need growth, which in turn implies the necessity of reforms – and these reforms should be fair and inclusive.

NOTE

1. This is consistent with Starmans et al. (2017) who show that people generally prefer 'fair' inequality to 'unfair' equality. The results are also consistent with the earlier analysis by Denisova et al. (2009), who show that support for privatization in transition countries is higher among skilled (and thus better-off) individuals in countries with stronger democratic institutions and better governance.

REFERENCES

Aghion, P., U. Akcigit and P. Howitt (2013), 'What Do We Learn From Schumpeterian Growth Theory?', in P. Aghion and S. Durlauf (eds), *Handbook of Economic Growth 2B* (pp. 515–63), Elsevier, Amsterdam.

Aghion, P. and C. Bircan (2017), 'Middle-Income Trap from a Schumpeterian Perspective', EBRD Working Paper 205, European Bank for Reconstruction and Development, London.

Aghion, P. and P. Howitt (1998), *Endogenous Growth Theory*, MIT Press, Cambridge, MA.

Denisova, I., M. Eller, T. Frye and E. Zhuravskaya (2009), 'Who Wants To Revise Privatization? The Complementarity of Market Skills and Institutions', *American Political Science Review*, **103** (2), 284–304.

EBRD (2013), *Stuck in Transition? Transition Report 2013*, European Bank for Reconstruction and Development, London.

EBRD (2016a), *Transition for All: Promoting Equal Opportunity in an Unequal World. Transition Report 2016–17*, European Bank for Reconstruction and Development, London.

EBRD (2016b), *Life in Transition: A Decade of Measuring Transition*, European Bank for Reconstruction and Development, London.

EBRD (2017), *Sustaining Growth. Transition Report 2017–18*, European Bank for Reconstruction and Development, London.

Gill, I.S. and H. Kharas (2007), *An East Asian Renaissance: Ideas for Economic Growth*, World Bank, Washington, DC.

Gill, I.S. and H. Kharas (2015), 'The Middle-Income Trap Turns Ten', Policy Research Working Paper 7403, World Bank, Washington, DC.

Guriev, S. and D. Treisman (2017), 'The Popularity of Authoritarian Leaders: An Empirical Investigation', Mimeo, UCLA.

Milanovic, B. (2016), *Global Inequality: A New Approach for the Age of Globalization*, Harvard University Press, Cambridge, MA.

Starmans, C., M. Sheskin and P. Bloom (2017), 'Why People Prefer Unequal Societies', *Nature Human Behavior*, **1**, http://christinastarmans.com/papers/2017%20Starmans%20Sheskin%20Bloom%20Inequality.pdf.

APPENDIX

Table 2A.1   OLS regressions for trust in government

	Trust in president	Trust in government	Trust in parliament
There is less	0.178***	0.200***	0.194***
corruption now	(0.016)	(0.017)	(0.020)
than 4 years ago			
Unemployment	−0.029*	−0.019	−0.012
	(0.017)	(0.013)	(0.009)
Log income	0.025	0.007	−0.005
	(0.016)	(0.012)	(0.007)
R-squared	0.38	0.39	0.40
Number of	13,544	13,779	13,636
households			
Number of PSUs	1489	1489	1489

Notes: Individual-level socio-demographic controls are included but not reported. The specification also controls for primary sampling units' (PSUs') fixed effects. OLS = ordinary least squares.

Sources: Life in Transition Survey (LiTS) II (2010), LiTS III (2016).

Table 2A.2   Support for markets as a function of 'fair' and 'unfair' income inequality

	Linear probability model		Logit model	
'Unfair' income inequality	−1.093*	−1.012*	−4.508*	−4.169*
	(0.480)	(0.473)	(2.112)	(2.085)
'Fair' income inequality	1.046**	1.064**	4.424**	4.516**
	(0.354)	(0.356)	(1.587)	(1.600)
Perception of relative economic well-being		0.017**		0.077***
		(0.005)		(0.022)
Income decile	0.010***	0.008**	0.042***	0.035**
	(0.003)	(0.002)	(0.011)	(0.011)
Observations	12,258	12,185	12,258	12,185

Notes: Dependent variable: support for market economy. Perception of economic well-being is the self-perceived income decile (1 corresponds to the poorest decile). The income decile is the objective decile in the income distribution based on respondents' income. Additional controls include gender, education level, age and life satisfaction, region dummies, inequality of opportunity with respect to jobs and education, country inflation, unemployment and per capita GDP. Standard errors are clustered at the country level and are shown in parentheses. *, ** and *** indicate statistical significance at the 10, 5 and 1 per cent levels, respectively.

Sources: Life in Transition Survey (LiTS) III (2016), World Economic Outlook, World Development Indicators, and author's calculations.

3. Europe's moments of truth: wicked crises, good and bad consequences

Sonja Puntscher Riekmann

The twenty-first century seemed to bode well for the European Union (EU). The establishment of the Economic and Monetary Union (EMU) and the single currency, the constitutional turn, the big enlargement of 12 mostly post-communist states and thus the healing of the decade-long fissure of the continent, were instances of success. An atmosphere of departure seemed to prevail; which was, however, delusive and in any case short-lived. The constitutional moment turned sour in the French and Dutch negative referenda on the Constitutional Treaty (2005); the very existence of the euro was challenged in the financial crisis unleashed by the bankruptcy of Lehman Brothers in the United States (2008), and exacerbated by the ensuing fiscal crisis of eurozone members; the enlargement (2004 and 2007) that should have consolidated the democratic and socio-economic transformation of the new members developed less smoothly than presaged. Under the brilliant surface a host of problems were slumbering: the Union had cultivated the illusion that centralized monetary policy was viable, despite leaving economic and fiscal policy in the hands of the member states because they were bound to the common rules of fiscal discipline; in the constitutional debate the Union failed to gain a solid consensus of citizens who were captured by Eurosceptic elites and parties; with regard to enlargement it believed that Europeanization would somehow automatically emerge from implementation of the *acquis communautaire*. Most remarkably, it neglected the nascent turmoil in its neighbourhood that resulted in social upheaval, war and refugee movements. Last but not least, it was overwhelmed by the politicization of European politics, whereas Brexit became the epitome of reflections on European integration that could no longer evade the notion of disintegration (Vollaard 2014; Rosamond 2016). These phenomena caused a sentiment of frustration and an all-pervading discourse of crisis. Indeed, 'crisis' is the term dominating the political rhetoric and academic work on the Union from 2010 onwards (e.g., Laffan 2016).

This, however, is only part of the story. A less pessimistic account questions the dramatic overtones of the crisis discourse by pointing to the Union's history as one that since its inception has been characterized by institutional innovation and policy adaptation because of crises. In an experimental spirit the Union has created a new governance architecture that accommodates diversity and is capable of learning by comparison (Zeitlin 2016). As a matter of fact, the Constitutional Treaty was by and large integrated into the Treaty of Lisbon. Contrary to the prophecy of doom, the eurozone did not disintegrate; while the euro was stabilized by non-standard monetary measures, and bolstered by stricter rules for fiscal discipline and surveillance of states and banks. Brexit has (so far) not found followers; whereas the rise of Eurosceptic parties in 2017 has been curtailed either by the electoral success of pro-European actors, as in France, the Netherlands and Germany, or by declarations of a European commitment, as in Austria. The refugee movements have gradually been contained, and the consequences more appropriately tackled than in 2015. Finally, strategies to deal with the multiple crises in the neighbourhood are also emerging in terms of foreign, security and development policies.

So all is well? Not quite. Serious and multiple challenges loom large: first, with regard to the Union's institutional architecture that owing to the crisis measures has increased its hybrid nature and redefined the horizontal and vertical balance of powers, while more sweeping reforms to forestall further financial crises are still under discussion in 2018; second, with regard to the socio-economic diversity that may pose threats of disintegration in case of new asymmetric shocks; third, despite the return of economic growth we witness the rise of inequality of income and societal chances that belies the European welfare credo and thus furthers politicization and the questioning of the Union's legitimacy; and fourth, with regard to the Union's external relations in the fields of trade, where liberalism is yielding to protectionism and security where Europe is still too divided to perform as a powerful actor.

It is, of course, beyond the scope of this chapter to tackle all problems mentioned. Its focus is on the EU's institutional reordering in the wake of the financial and fiscal crisis and on the feasibility of selected reform proposals tabled for a deeper EMU. It starts with a brief discussion of the main strands of political science literature on the crisis and their assessments of how far the EU changed over the last decade; it then evaluates the formal and informal outcome of institutional change; and finally, discusses the chances of further deepening in pertinent fields in connection with politicization of EU decision-making.

3.1 CRISES AS MOMENTS OF TRUTH?

If crises are moments of truth, the question is: what and whose is the truth? Who decides that problems have turned into a serious crisis in which 'existing paradigms, policies, institutional roles and rules' are challenged (Laffan 2016, p. 916)? In which a whole political system may be 'tested and contested' (ibid.), traditional modes of problem-solving no longer work and new ones are yet to be found? How, and how fast, do political and economic elites recognize that 'simple' problems have become 'wicked' and that new tools and rules are needed for their resolution (Rittel and Webber 1973)? Who and what frames the cognitive approach to the problem? Last but not least: which interests prevail and which succumb?

At the beginning of the euro crisis in 2010 the capacity to define the truth certainly belonged to financial markets whose speculative actions against some member states had created a momentum of high risk and uncertainty. It is of limited avail to criticize the preceding mispricing of banks and subsequently of state creditworthiness by the same actors. Their new assessments drove banks, and then states that had saved their banks, to the brink of illiquidity if not insolvency. While financial markets were the main driving forces at the onset of the development, they just seemed to unveil a much older truth: that is, that the eurozone consisted of very diverse (political) economies which, since Maastricht and despite the pledges enshrined in that Treaty as well as in the Stability and Growth Pact (SGP), had hardly converged. While the lack of an Optimum Currency Area (OCA) and of stabilization mechanisms to compensate for the deficiency had been criticized by a number of economists at the birth of the single currency, the builders of the euro thought they could ignore such warnings because the common currency is based on clear rules about debt, deficit and inflation. Moreover, the successful start of the euro with regard to its positioning vis-à-vis other currencies, in particular the United States (US) dollar, confirmed their belief to such an extent that they considered the outbreak of the subprime crisis as a US affair against which the euro would remain immune. When this belief was shattered by real events, eurozone political elites first held on to the old rulebook. Only when with the Greek case this position became untenable did they allow for non-standard measures, and finally switched gear to prevent the disintegration of the eurozone and the possible ruin of the euro. Fears of contagion with consequences also for the core of the eurozone ended momentarily the bickering about who is to blame.

The bickering was resumed once the statement by the President of the European Central Bank (ECB), Mario Draghi, in 2012, that the ECB 'would do whatever it takes' to save the euro, had brought calm to financial markets and reduced the dangerous credit spreads between eurozone members. Now the old truths about the need for fiscal discipline and for policy change to foster competitiveness were revived with great emphasis, undergirded by ideological arguments about their effects and legitimacy and, finally, by the verdict that solidarity between the fiscal 'saints' and 'sinners' could only come at the price of austerity. While before the crisis the issue of fiscal rectitude was met in the Council meetings with an attitude of 'don't ask, don't tell' or, as in the case of France and Germany, was resolved by rule relaxation (2005), after the bail-out in the form of loans and credits conceded to the states under pressure, the new truth was to avoid moral hazard by strict conditionality and by supranational and international surveillance. Hence the battle for truth about the political, legal and economic viability of rescue mechanisms, and about their legitimacy in a policy field that had never been conceived in terms of bail-outs, automatic stabilization and redistribution. Indeed, most member states cling, at least rhetorically, to the old hegemonic truth: no transformation of the Union into a transfer union; assistance is temporary and credits have to be repaid, while the impaired or failing economy is to be restructured whatever the social costs; no fiscal union that would give more clout to supranational actors such as the Commission or the European Parliament; no change of the ECB into a lender of last resort.

Yet, beneath this truth another one slowly made its way to the surface. It is the truth that centralization of monetary policy and decentralization of fiscal, economic and social policy are an odd construction, prone to fail again in case of asymmetric shock. It finally became clear that for some members already the adoption of the euro had exposed them to an asymmetric shock. It is in the vein of this truth that the banking union with supranational and national surveillance based on common rules became possible (even if still with a number of exceptions; Kudrna and Puntscher Riekmann 2018); that the ECB legitimized by the ruling of the Court of Justice of the European Union (CJEU) on 'the OMT case' – the eurosystem's outright monetary transactions in secondary sovereign bond markets – could together with the national central banks implement a substantial and prolonged quantitative easing programme; that the European Commission gained important powers in the European Semester, the Excessive Deficit Procedure (EDP) and the Macroeconomic Imbalance Procedure (MIP) and in 2017 could produce a 'White Paper on the future of Europe' (European Commission 2017a) along with a number of reflection papers – including one on deepening of EMU – spelling out scenarios in greater detail (European Commission 2017a, 2017b).

What are interesting, though, are the language and strategies used by European actors to sell their new truth to the public. As analysed by Vivien

Schmidt (2016), the ECB and the Commission opted for two different ways of communication. The ECB legitimized its actions by replacing the hitherto important notion of 'credibility' of the bank by the term 'stability' of the euro – thus feeding particularly into the German idiosyncrasy of stability – and managed to transform itself into a quasi-lender of last resort 'by hiding in plain view' (Schmidt 2016, p. 1042). The Commission went from 'governing by rules and numbers to greater flexibility' (ibid., p. 1044), without admitting to do so. It justified its flexibility – which also led to imputations about arbitrariness and calls for a more independent surveillance agency – with the successful reforms of states implementing austerity measures that allowed for it (ibid., p. 1046). It would, however, be mistaken to attribute the success of ECB or Commission activities in and after the crisis to these linguistic shifts and strategies of communication alone: the change of personnel (in the ECB board of governors the German hardliners were replaced, whereas in 2014 a new Commission took office) ushered in the reinterpretation of rules and a more functionalist approach to the wicked problems by disentangling and converting them into resolvable ones. Hence, a neo-functionalist reading (Schimmelfennig 2014) of what happened is still appropriate even if intergovernmentalism had given a forceful sign of life. Indeed, member states' governments had taken the driver's seat by transforming the European Council into the 'main venue for debating how the EU should respond to the Eurozone crisis' (Puetter 2012; Becker et al. 2016). The theory of new intergovernmentalism (Bickerton et al. 2015) assumes national governments to be entrapped in their European decisions – the creation of the euro in this case – that can only be sustained by more European decisions. In this reading it is less surprising that in the state of emergency the German Chancellor Angela Merkel advocated the costly assistance to Greece in the reluctant Bundestag by stating 'There is no alternative' and conjuring up the future of the EU (*Frankfurter Allgemeine Zeitung*, 5 May 2010).

The story of the eurozone crisis is but another instance of actors shifting truths under pressure. This general wisdom notwithstanding, however, it is difficult to foresee when actors are capable of such shifts (in the euro crisis it took almost two years from problem recognition in late 2009 to Draghi's announcement in mid-2012), as these are hard to communicate to the electorate (Merkel's statement occurred only after an important regional election). Much depends on whether an integrative or disintegrative framing of crisis interpretation prevails (Falkner 2016, p. 965), whether actors have a common purpose (for example, saving the euro) or at least sufficiently overlapping interests (for example, the failure of the euro may be detrimental for the whole eurozone). Finally, it remains to be seen whether the change of mindset is irreversible once the crisis has subsided.

3.2   WHAT HAS ACTUALLY CHANGED?

In the euro crisis, European political elites finally seemed prepared to change their previous positions in order to rescue banks and member states in dire straits. However, they did not embark on major Treaty revisions, but rather created new institutions outside the Treaty. Only Article 136 of the Treaty on the Functioning of the European Union (TFEU) was amended in 2011 by simplified revision procedure to legitimize the installation of the European Financial Stability Facility (EFSF) and the European Stability Mechanism (ESM). It reads: 'The Member States whose currency is the euro may establish a stability mechanism to be activated if indispensable to safeguard the stability of the euro area as a whole. The granting of any required financial assistance under the mechanism will be made subject to strict conditionality.' The ESM is an international financial institution based on a treaty signed by the eurozone members in 2012 and ratified according to national constitutional law. It was accompanied by another intergovernmental Treaty on Stability, Coordination and Governance in the Economic and Monetary Union (Treaty on Stability, Coordination and Governance in the European Union – TSCG; or Fiscal Compact) signed in 2012 to impose onto its signatories stricter rules such as balanced budgets, corrective mechanisms and benchmarks for debt and deficit reduction plans.

While the ESM is conceived as a backstop to operate in times of financial instability and the Fiscal Compact as a signal to financial markets that this time member states are really taking debt and deficit issues seriously, with the so-called Six- and Two-Pack (2011 and 2013), preventive and corrective measures were established also within EU law. They strengthened the power of the Commission to assess and to influence national fiscal policy, in particular by controlling budget plans in the European Semester. Moreover, member states agreed to bind their hands by allowing for the mechanism of reversed qualified majority voting on relevant Commission recommendations addressed to single member states.

In short, the crisis opened the window of opportunity for decisions that had been skirted around in the previous years. This is, however, not the whole story, in particular not for the so-called programme countries. The loans and credits by the EFSF/ESM were conditional upon the signing of Memoranda of Understanding (MoUs) which significantly curtailed the fiscal room of manoeuvre of national governments, and encroached on their fiscal, economic and social policies that so far had largely been outside the remit of EU law (Scharpf 2011). A special institution was created to negotiate and supervise the implementation of the MoUs: the Troika, composed of representatives of the Commission, the European

Central Bank and the International Monetary Fund. As the Troika also imposed significant cuts on wages and pensions to reduce the deficit (in particular in Greece, Portugal, Spain and Ireland) and thus to restore market credibility and competitiveness, not only the citizens who suffered most started to question its legitimacy. The Troika was heavily criticized in the parliaments of affected states and the European Parliament; so much so that in 2014 the newly elected Commission President Jean Claude Juncker announced to replace it with a more democratically and legitimate structure based on European and national parliamentary control (Juncker 2014). Crisis resolution was thus also confided to an 'irregular' institution whose members were not bound to EU law. In particular the European Parliament criticized the Commission's neglect of Treaty provisions and the Charter of Fundamental Rights when acting in the Troika (European Parliament 2014).

Thus, the window of opportunity was wide open not only for necessary reforms, but also for the creation of new problems, legally and politically. Legal disputes arose in academia, and before the national and European courts, particularly with regard to the legality of the bail-out measures that were seen as infringing Article 125 TFEU (C-370/12 *Pringle*), or of non-standard measures by the ECB (C-62/14 *Gauweiler*) which the German plaintiffs considered as transgressing its mandate. In both cases of preliminary rulings the Court of Justice of the European Union legitimized the crisis measures, although attaching some conditions: in the *Pringle* case the court added that the ESM is not the guarantor for the member state's debt; whereas in the *Gauweiler* case it stated that with the OMT programme the ECB acted within its mandate provided, first, that it 'refrains from any direct involvement in the financial assistance programs . . . and complies strictly with the obligation to state its reasons and adheres to the requirements deriving from the principle of proportionality', and second, that 'the timing of its implementation permits actual formation of a market price in respect of the government bonds' (Saurugger 2016, p. 939). The CJEU framed its discourse in terms of stability of the euro and the eurozone rather than price stability alone.

Politically, the crisis shifted European power relations between creditor and debtor states, between national and EU institutions, and between EU institutions. The first divide resulted in an ugly blaming and shaming of debtors for having infringed the Maastricht debt and deficit rules and thus caused the crisis, and of creditors for imposing fiscal rules onto debtors without concern for social and economic consequences. The result was deep mutual distrust among national elites and citizens alike. Second, the power shift between national and EU institutions is epitomized by the rise of the European Council, the Eurogroup and the Economic and

Financial Affairs (ECOFIN) Council forming the centre of crisis politics, a development which further strengthened the power of national executives to the detriment of parliaments (Puntscher Riekmann and Wydra 2013). Also, the Commission and the ECB as surveillance agencies of national fiscal and financial institutions in general, and with regard to the programme countries in particular, benefited from the crisis (Becker et al. 2016), the Troika being the most conspicuous case in point. Third, power shifts between EU institutions are an intriguing case: while some scholars see the theory of intergovernmentalism validated or the emergence of a new intergovernmentalism (Bickerton et al. 2015; Schimmelfennig 2015), others advocate a more nuanced view on the presumed decline of the Commission or on judicial restraint by the CJEU (Schimmelfennig 2014; Becker et al. 2016; Saurugger 2016). However, it is plausible to assume that all interpretations hold parts of the truth: undoubtedly, at the height of the crisis the European Council, the Eurogroup and ECOFIN Council were of utmost importance, but the formal strengthening of the European Council with its permanent presidency and the formal/informal upgrading of the Eurogroup had already occurred with the Treaty of Lisbon of 2009. But it is equally beyond doubt that implementation and practical management of crisis measures could hardly work without the Commission and the ECB. Unless the Union falls apart, member states will always need supranational organs to produce knowledge about all national positions formed in the light of different political economies, and to ensure commitment to the decisions jointly taken. Finally, two important changes in the EU governance architecture are marked by the rise of the ECB to almost a lender of last resort (Schmidt 2016), but also by the sidelining of the European Parliament at defining moments of the crisis. Moreover, national parliaments became important rivals as they were to give consent to ESM bail-outs.

However, being based on international contracts rather than embedded in a strong constitutional setting, the Union is potentially always threatened by the volatility of 'obligations of good faith' by member states (Puntscher Riekmann and Wydra 2015). Such volatility is enhanced by the politicization of EU decision-making (Statham and Trenz 2015) and epitomized by the rise of challenger parties on the extreme right and left who in the new millennium are, if to a different extent, Eurosceptic. Since the onset of the crisis in 2008, mainstream parties in EU member states have lost 12 per cent of their voters (Hobolt and Tilley 2016, p. 985). In some countries they are voted out of office (for example, Greece, Portugal and Ireland); in some they are confronted with fierce opposition inside and outside parliament (for example, Austria, Germany, France, Italy, Finland, Estonia); while in others challengers enter government coalitions (for example, Greece, Austria, Finland, Poland). This at least in part explains the more cautious approach to European integration by mainstream parties, whereas the subsiding of the crisis seems to weaken their will to take bolder steps towards deepening EMU.

3.3   WHERE DO WE GO FROM HERE?

However, the wicked crisis brought about a more visionary approach of 'building a deeper and more genuine EMU' by the Commission which, at least rhetorically, is endorsed by European Council summit conclusions. The Commission was repeatedly tasked with the elaboration of pertinent proposals, which it delivered in spring 2017 (European Commission 2017a, 2017b). They are interesting documents insofar as they claim to be the result of broad consultations with national governments, and instead of advocating one path to follow they present several scenarios: five in the case of the 'White Paper on the future of Europe' (European Commission 2017a), ranging from 'more of the same' to a significant overhaul of the institutional set-up. They do, however, also point to what each scenario may entail. In his State of the Union address in September 2017, the President of the Commission Juncker added a sixth scenario that combines scenario four and five and represents significant deepening. The 'Reflection Paper' (European Commission 2017b) on a deeper EMU, on the other hand, opts for a sequencing of steps to take between 2017 and 2019, and between 2020 and 2025. For the latter period a financial and fiscal union is envisaged. Some of the proposals, such as the setting up of a European treasury and the issuing of Eurobonds or safe assets, will certainly unleash a legal and political debate about whether they necessitate Treaty revision.

While it is hard to tell whether, when and in which form these proposals will become objects of a more serious discussion by member states, many of which seem to be paused in a 'wait and see' position, the election of President Emmanuel Macron in France and the formation of a grand coalition in Germany may bode well again for the European Union. Not only has Macron, in a speech at the University of Sorbonne in September 2017, outlined his bold vision for a deepened EU and a genuine EMU in particular, but also the coalition paper of the new German government puts the evolution of the Union front and centre. Both actors reiterate their role as engines of integration. It is, though, a matter for future research what the two will agree upon; how they will convince all or most of the others; whether they will engage in piecemeal and rather stealthy reforms by secondary legislation, or take up the constitutional debate again. What is clear already is that they both consider differentiation as a viable option, and that the core of the future Union is formed by the eurozone.

REFERENCES

Becker, S., M. Bauer, S. Connolly and H. Kassim (2016), 'The Commission: boxed in and constrained, but still an engine of integration', *West European Politics*, **39** (5), 1011–31.

Bickerton, C.J., D. Hodson and U. Puetter (2015), 'The new intergovernmentalism: European integration in the post-Maastricht era', *Journal of Common Market Studies*, **53** (4), 703–22.

Draghi, M. (2012), Speech by Mario Draghi, President of the European Central Bank, at the Global Investment Conference in London, 26 July. https://www.ecb. europa.eu/press/key/date/2012/html/sp120726.en.html.

European Commission (2017a), 'White Paper on the future of Europe'.

European Commission (2017b), 'Reflection Paper on the deepening of the Economic and Monetary Union'.

European Parliament (2014), 'Report on the enquiry on the role and operations of the Troika (ECB, Commission and IMF) with regard to the programme countries' (2013/277(INI)).

Falkner, G. (2016), 'The EU's problem-solving capacity and legitimacy in a crisis context: a virtuous or vicious circle?', *West European Politics*, **39** (5), 953–70.

Hobolt, S. and J. Tilley (2016), 'Fleeing the centre: the rise of challenger parties in the aftermath of the crisis', *West European Politics*, **39** (5), 971–91.

Juncker, J.-C. (2014), 'A new start for Europe: my agenda for jobs, growth, fairness and democratic change. Political guidelines for the next European Commission', Opening Statement in the European Parliament, Strasbourg, 15 July.

Juncker, J.-C. (2017), 'President Jean-Claude Juncker's State of the Union Address 2017', European Commission, Brussels, 13 September. http://europa.eu/rapid/press-release_SPEECH-17-3165_en.htm.

Kudrna, Z. and S. Puntscher Riekmann (2018), 'Harmonizing national options and discretions in the EU banking regulation', *Journal of Economic Policy Reform*, **21** (2), Special Edition on Constructing Banking Union, 144–58.

Laffan, B. (2016), 'Europe's union in crisis: tested and contested', *West European Politics*, **39** (5), 915–32.

Puetter, U. (2012), 'Europe's deliberative intergovernmentalism: the role of the Council and European Council in EU economic governance', *Journal of European Public Policy*, **19** (2), 161–78.

Puntscher Riekmann, S. and D. Wydra (2013), 'Parliaments against governments: representation in the European state of emergency', *Journal of European Integration*, **35** (5), 565–82.

Puntscher Riekmann, S. and D. Wydra (2015), 'Obligations of good faith: on the difficulties of building US-style EU federalism', *Contemporary Politics*, **21** (2), 201–19.

Rittel, H. and M. Webber (1973), 'Dilemmas in a general theory of planning', *Policy Sciences*, **4** (2), 155–69.

Rosamond, B. (2016), 'Brexit and the problem of European disintegration', *Journal of European Political Research*, **12** (4), 865–71.

Saurugger, S. (2016), 'Politicization and integration through law: whither integration theory?', *West European Politics*, **39** (5), 933–52.

Scharpf, F.W. (2011), 'Monetary Union: fiscal crisis and the preemption of democracy', MPIfG Discussion Paper 11/11.

Schimmelfennig, F. (2014), 'European integration in the euro crisis: the limits of postfunctionalism', *Journal of European Integration*, **36** (3), 317–37.

Schimmelfennig, F. (2015), 'Liberal intergovernmentalism and the euro area crisis', *Journal of European Public Policy*, **22** (2), 177–95.

Schmidt, V.A. (2016), 'Reinterpreting the rules "by stealth" in times of crisis: a discursive institutionalist analysis of the European Central Bank and the European Commission', *West European Politics*, **39** (5), 1032–52.

Statham, P. and H.-J. Trenz (2015), 'Understanding the mechanisms of EU politicization: lessons from the eurozone crisis', *Comparative European Politics*, **13** (3), 287–306.

Vollaard, H. (2014), 'Explaining European disintegration', *Journal of Common Market Studies*, **52** (5), 1142–59.

Zeitlin, J. (2016), 'EU experimentalist governance in times of crisis', *West European Politics*, **39** (5), 1073–84.

4. Social Europe: the Pillar of Social Rights

Georg Fischer[1]

The Proclamation of the European Pillar of Social Rights (EPSR) (see Council of the European Union 2017; European Commission 2017a[2]) at the Gothenburg European Summit marks an important policy change. From the early 2000s to the mid-2010s, the European mainstream focused on two economic policy issues – competitiveness and fiscal stability – paying less attention to social challenges. With the proclamation the three European institutions – Parliament, Commission and Council – as well as the member states of the European Union (EU), commit themselves to implement the 20 principles of the pillar within their respective responsibilities. This is different from the Charter of Fundamental Rights in two respects. The charter is more committing but less wide in scope. The charter is legally binding on the European institutions and member states when implementing European Union law, while the pillar is a political declaration which requires other legal instruments or court interpretation to gain direct legal effect. The charter covers areas of EU and not national competence, while the principles of the pillar are applicable to EU and national competence.

The preamble to the pillar document recognizes the issue:

> The European Pillar of Social Rights expresses principles and rights essential for fair and well-functioning labour markets . . . It adds new principles which address the challenges arising from societal, technological and economic developments. For them to be legally enforceable the principles and rights require first dedicated measures or legislation to be adopted at the appropriate level. (recital 14 of the Interinstitutional Proclamation of the European Pillar of Social Rights – Council of the European Union 2017)

While this text underlines that the principles are not directly enforceable legislation[3] it also states that implementation legislation is needed. Two points stand out in the reasoning: 'the social consequences of the crisis have been far reaching . . . and addressing those . . . remains an urgent priority' (recital 10 of the Interinstitutional Proclamation of the European

Pillar of Social Rights – Council of the European Union 2017). Hence implementation is a serious concern.

In his contribution ahead of the Summit, the Commission President explained:

> Europe is slowly turning the page on years of economic crisis but it has not yet surmounted the biggest social crisis it has known for generations. The challenges of youth unemployment, inequality and a transforming world of work are ones we all face. In Gothenburg, we have a unique opportunity to seek out common solutions. This should be a landmark moment – with the proclamation of the European Pillar of Social Rights, we are showing our joint commitment to protect and uphold the rights of equality, fairness and opportunity that we all stand for and that all citizens are entitled to. And it must also be the first step of many in this direction.

The remainder of this chapter reviews briefly the 'biggest social crisis' and how it relates to the European project, summarizes the messages of the pillar, reviews means of implementation, and concludes with a discussion of proposals for EU measures going beyond the present framework.

4.1 THE BIGGEST SOCIAL CRISIS AND THE SUBSTANCE OF THE PILLAR DOCUMENT

As the preamble to the pillar states, there is good news in European labour markets: employment rates are rising (having exceeded the 2008 level at the time of writing), wages have picked up and unemployment is going down. However, other social data show a disappointing picture. Youth and long-term unemployment remain high. Progress on gender equality in the labour markets is slow. Many, in particular young people, work in different forms of precarious employment, most with considerable wage penalties in comparison to comparable full-time permanent jobs. Involuntary part-time work is widespread. Poverty levels, in particular child poverty, in the euro area are higher than in 2008. Ten per cent of the Europeans live in working households with income below the poverty threshold ('in-work poverty'). And 10 per cent of children grow up in households in which nobody works ('low work intensity'), with serious implications for the future of those children.

Considering these facts, the Gothenburg summit highlighted rising inequality and a lack of social convergence across the EU. One way to understand these concerns is to look at three interlinked developments: rising inequality and insecurity in most EU economies; the end of

North–South convergence in unemployment and poverty; and the pace of East–West convergence in particular in earnings.

High and rising inequalities are seen as a threat to cohesion and there is concern about the negative impacts on economic performance. The International Monetary Fund (IMF), the Organisation for Economic Co-operation and Development (OECD) and more recently the European Commission have produced converging analysis: in most member states, low income groups suffered heavily during the great recession and were the last to benefit from the emerging recovery, and this after two decades in which the highest income groups saw their income and wealth rising far more than the bottom and the middle income groups (with France being a notable exception). Rising inequality and insecurity go together. And there is a strong socio-economic bias: less well educated individuals, working women with children, migrants and the young have fewer secure employment positions, lower earnings and are less well covered by social security. Many are trapped in cycles of precarious jobs, unemployment and inactivity; and even those who move up in their careers later face disadvantages in their pension entitlements.

The spread of these atypical forms of employment started long before the crisis as a result of structural transformations in our labour markets, but the crisis accentuated the social impacts as those workers were more likely to lose jobs and to be re-employed at similar or even more precarious conditions. Both rising inequality and economic insecurity are driven by broader economic and societal trends such as globalization, digitalization and ageing. As these trends are global, and labour market and social policies are mostly national, one can ask why European leaders would articulate a concern at the level of the EU.

The first answer is rather simple: many Europeans associate their labour market prospects with Europe and expect the EU to make an effort to address unemployment and social security, as documented in many public opinion surveys.[4] Secondly, EU economies share a single market, and most of them a single currency. This increases their mutual dependency and adds to pressures for cost savings at the expense of environmental, health or labour standards. This is why an elaborated framework of single market regulation has been put in place, including regulations relating to labour issues. Often the impact of globalized markets appears as pressure from within the single market. While integration has overall positive impacts on both economic performance and well-being, social costs in terms of job losses and reduced earnings are inevitable. Similarly for trade: EU member states can defend their interests better together, but trade agreements might have negative labour market impacts in certain regions or sectors. In short: economic integration does not only produce winners, and there is always a risk of reinforcing a 'race to the bottom'-type competition. There is also the issue of perception: while benefits are usually widespread and often not seen as resulting from economic integration, social costs in one's own town or even family are perceived as linked to market opening, liberalization of services or trade agreements.

These concerns are not new. The first set of European labour legislation and the European Social Fund were included in the Treaty of Rome to support adjustment in the economic community. Later EU labour legislation reflects the recognition that the single market required common standards. In dealing with globalization and the common currency, this recognition might have got lost. This might have something to do with concerns about global competitiveness or, more generally, with the belief in markets and a fatigue with public policies.[5]

It would be incorrect to say that the EU did not react to negative impacts of globalized markets or of economic integration. The European Structural and Investment Funds (ESIF) are available for member states to fund job creation, labour market adjustment and social inclusion, and the European Globalisation Adjustment Fund (EGF) was specifically created to support workers in firms negatively affected by global economic trends. The proclamation of the pillar reflects a rethink, emphasizing the importance of labour law to deal with precarious employment, and the need to extend social protection and offer labour market support to workers in transition.[6]

While rising inequality and insecurity result from long-term economic trends and started long before the recession, the biggest shock for EU policy-makers and people alike was the collapse of North–South convergence during the great recession. This does not mean to say that the massive dispersion of performance in the great recession did not have root causes going back to economic and labour market structures and policy failures before the recession, but the facts are indeed striking. In 2007, unemployment rates across the EU and the euro area had converged to a margin of 2–3 percentage points around an average of around 7 per cent (only Slovakia had more than 10 per cent). By 2010, the differences were massive, and in 2016 after some years of recovery the difference between the average unemployment rate and the rates of Spain and Greece was over 10 percentage points, and unemployment rates in all Southern European countries were still over 10 per cent. Lasting low levels of economic activity and high unemployment have increased not only monetary poverty but also the share of households being deprived of some basic goods and services. This is typically measured as the share of households experiencing severe material deprivation.[7] The numbers for 2016 show that this share has doubled in Southern European countries since 2007, reaching over 20 per cent in Greece and over 10 per cent in Italy and Cyprus. Some Central and Eastern European countries display similar levels of severe material deprivation to Italy and Greece, but these levels have continuously declined over the crisis period, and in Poland have even halved.

Such an explosion of social divergence conflicts with the core goals of the EU on promoting social cohesion and the well-being of EU citizens, and questions thereby the overall purpose and the legitimacy of the EU project. Moreover one cannot deny that the increase in social divergence between the core of the euro area countries and the 'periphery' have something to do with the incomplete architecture of EMU, in addition to long-term structural factors and failures of public policies. The extraordinary length of the recession in the euro area forced these countries to reduce employment as well as earnings and public budgets at the same time.

There is an additional point that Jean-Claude Juncker raised in his candidacy speech to the European Parliament, commenting the financial support programmes to Greece and other countries:

> But we also made mistakes . . . I would like to see a very rigorous social impact study carried out before any adjustment programme is implemented. I would like to know how adjustment programmes impact on people's lives. In future there will be no adjustment programmes unless they are preceded by a thorough social impact assessment. (Juncker 2014, p. 18)[8]

While the pillar documents do not review crisis programmes, some principles can be seen as a response to experiences with these programmes, in particular in relation to the treatment of social partners and to the changes in wage rates, labour law provisions and in social programmes. The pillar advocates a strong social partners role in wage-setting; social and civil engagement in policy-making; it asks for adequate benefits of reasonable duration, the right to labour market support for the unemployed and for minimum income schemes and social housing, just to mention a few. The pillar principles go beyond the existing policy consensus in several respects. For example, the pillar commits its signatories to ensure that minimum income schemes allow for a life in dignity, which goes further than the existing *acquis* asking that such schemes should exist.

A number of EU support measures were taken as a response to the massive rise in unemployment and the social hardship resulting from the prolonged recession. Access to the ESIF was simplified for the states most hit by the crisis and by austerity. The Youth Guarantee as a policy commitment by all member states, and the Youth Employment Initiative as a funding instrument, were introduced in 2012. And the Fund for European

Aid to the Most Deprived (FEAD) has been used for material support and social integration since 2014. These new instruments provide help where it is urgently needed, and are seen as pilots for future social programmes to be discussed later.

There is a third convergence issue: East–West is not about divergence but about the pace of convergence, and wages are clearly at the centre of the debate. From the mid-2000s to the mid-2010s, East–West convergence in incomes and wages has continued, but not everywhere. In my view the crucial point, however, is not whether wage convergence has returned, which most recently seems to be the case almost everywhere in Central and Eastern Europe, but that many realize it will take a relatively long time for earnings and incomes in Central and Eastern Europe to come close to those of neighbouring Western European countries. It seems that the recognition of a relatively long-lasting income gap has led to two fears: firstly, of a race to the bottom undermining standards, notably in Western European countries; and secondly, of a continued outflow of the more active, better-qualified labour force, undermining the capacity for Central and Eastern European economies to catch up. The EU needs to find a way to cope with this gap in income for a comparatively long time. The recent compromise on the posting of workers directive suggests that this can be achieved. The Pillar of Social Rights is designed to provide a broader frame of social rights so that workers on both sides feel fairly treated, and agreed standards are the norm. At the same time, the different European funds help to promote convergence in productivity, and the European Social Fund in particular by developing human skills and employability of the workforce in the region.

It is this social crisis and its impact on the legitimacy of the European project against which the pillar has been developed. President Juncker and his partners at the Gothenburg Summit want to document that Europe is more than a huge integrated single market, remote from the needs of ordinary people. Indeed the principles respond to the labour market pressures resulting from globalization and digitalization, and the social impacts from the impacts of the long-lasting recession. As an example, the relevant pillar principles commit member states and the EU to more proactively help workers undergoing transitions, to provide labour rights independent of contract or employment type, prohibit abuse of atypical contracts, and to provide similar social security for similar work independently of the employment status as well as the portability of acquired social protection rights and of training entitlements when changing jobs or employment status. In relation to gender equality it broadens the language on equal rights for women and men to education, and on rights to care leave, to income support and to a return to work for carers and their rights at work.

The use of language of rights in the pillar text has the advantage of being concrete. As shown above, these rights cannot be legally reinforced as such unless they are put into European or national legislation. No wonder that many demand a clear plan for implementation,[9] referring to the Commission President's statement that the pillar adoption is a first step of many. I do, however, disagree with those who consider a declaration of principles by the European leaders as meaningless. Proclaiming basic rights and principles on what support, rights and benefits Europeans can expect when facing labour market change and life risks is important for the European Union, and can become quite powerful when used well by those advocating these rights.[10] In discussing the way the pillar principles will operate in practice, it is important to bear in mind that member states retain primary responsibility for most aspects covered under the pillar.

4.2   IMPLEMENTATION OF THE PILLAR DOCUMENT

Together with the pillar, the Commission proposed a package of concrete measures: a proposal for a directive on remunerated care leave and rights at work for carers (European Commission 2017b); and two invitations to social partners (the first step in social legislation at EU level), one on the labour contract and one on access to social protection independent of the specific employment type.[11] They refer to different principles in the pillar text and propose legally enforceable rights. Following the proclamation of the pillar, the Commission adopted a proposal on the labour contract (transparency, predictability of working hours, better coverage of precarious employment) after consulting the social partners (European Commission 2017c).

Implementation is not only about translating principles into legislation, but also about ensuring that actual legislation is followed on the ground. The Commission considers better cooperation between national labour administrations and more transparency as essential for better managing cross-border situations in the labour and social field, and has launched a public consultation on creating a European labour authority and a European social security number.

The 20 principles contain a wide range of policy areas that are largely the responsibility of member states, such as education, social services and social protection schemes. For some core domains of the pillar, such as wage-setting and training of workers, national or sectoral social partners are the main actors. Hence progress on achieving the pillar principles needs to be monitored in a holistic way, looking at several areas together and over longer periods. To monitor actual progress the Commission proposes a 'social scoreboard' (European Commission 2017f) with indicators covering employment, gender equality, income inequality, training, poverty, education and training, as well as health. The new scoreboard builds on the social scoreboard that the Commission suggested in 2013 to assess social progress in the Economic and Monetary Union (EMU), which covered trends in unemployment, youth unemployment, household disposable income, the at-risk-of-poverty rate and inequalities (the S80/S20 ratio[12]). The extended scoreboard is to be used in the European Semester to provide member states, the euro area and the Union with an assessment on progress in implementing the pillar principles.

To use the European Semester of economic policy coordination for an integrated monitoring of economic and social progress raises important questions. The pillar proclamation did not review the relationship between economic and social policies beyond general wording, such as modest economic growth being a root cause of the social challenges, and the observation that economic and social progress are intertwined. The Commission President and other members have spoken about the need to rebalance social and economic objectives. This is indeed what a full integration of the pillar principles in the European Semester would require. Perhaps the most critical aspect of such a rebalancing is to systematically consider the social implications of the economic policy advice given in the European Semester itself, and to review it accordingly.

To go beyond monitoring, the Commission suggests a benchmarking process. Benchmarking would include defining desired outcomes and policy parameters. Specific benchmarking exercises are presently under way on unemployment benefits and minimum income, reviewing coverage of those in need, with adequacy and duration of benefits, and activation requirements and support. One could go further to benchmark welfare systems more broadly, looking at the scoreboard indicators on inequality, poverty and household income, and on earnings. These indicators describe social outcomes, and they could be combined with another indicator in the scoreboard that measures the impact of social transfers on poverty reduction. Each country differs in terms of its starting point and structure, hence benchmarks would need to be interpreted in the country-specific context, but the commonly agreed parameters would allow measurement of progress in a comparable manner, to identify policy challenges and facilitate learning from each other.

The underlying logic here is coordination of national policy efforts. There is a common interest in social progress across the EU and therefore the EU institutions, governments and other stakeholders were ready to engage in the exercise of the pillar. While some commitments deal directly with rights of individuals, others contained in the pillar principles require far-reaching reforms in the organization of national labour markets, and of welfare systems and education and training. Will the combination of standards in the pillar and a benchmarking peer learning process be sufficient to carry through a convergence process? One concern already discussed is the constraints arising from the macroeconomic policy framework. Another is that member states might not have the resolve and the capacity to carry through the necessary reforms. For example, the benchmarking exercise might suggest a recalibration of social expenditures in favour of younger generations and children, and higher taxes on higher wealth and incomes. Such reforms are difficult to implement. Better training and education, as well as more effective labour market services, might require substantial capacity development including addressing vested interests. A proposal in the Five Presidents' Report (2015) is to make agreed benchmarks binding, and if constraints relate to resources and capacity, development funding could be coupled with technical assistance. This proposal builds on measures launched under the previous Commission: the Youth Guarantee and the Youth Employment Initiative that combined agreed standards for helping unemployed or excluded young people with additional funding from the EU budget.

The ESIF could be part of such an exercise; it also provides ample lessons for criteria for conditional funding: clear targeting where needs are biggest (early childhood education, gender equality, training for the low skilled, job support for the long-term unemployed), more social partners and civil society involvement, more transparency on outcomes and actual results, impact analysis and serious evaluation.

This is a form of policy coordination requiring a higher level of political consensus. Could it work? One issue is funding: would 'richer' countries see the long-term benefit from more rapid social convergence in the European Union so that they would agree to high levels of EU funding? Would poorer countries or those in greater difficulties be less inclined to gain short-term competitive advantages by lower labour and social standards? In a longer-term perspective all countries can face major difficulties and could benefit from support. More rapid social convergence could benefit everybody. The case can be made in economic terms: stronger overall growth, a better-skilled labour force and better opportunities. And there is also the prospect of reduced social tension: less risk of poverty-driven population movements, less possibility to exploit workers in emergency situations, and a better chance to retain qualified people if they see incomes and opportunities converging.

There is one more argument to be considered. The agreed principles of the Pillar of Social Rights with the demand for social convergence go beyond equal rights in a formal sense. Terms such as good-quality education, adequacy in relation to wages and income, satisfaction of needs, and life in dignity, indicate a cross-European concept of equal opportunity corresponding to the idea of promoting social convergence across the EU. It seems to me that an EU policy that combines setting standards and funding with technical support would contribute to achieving equal opportunity beyond formal rights.

4.3 SOLIDARITY AND STABILIZATION

The pillar document does not present solidarity and stabilization instruments as means of implementation, as they are considered in the parallel running discussions in the European Council on the future architecture of EMU. But is pan-European solidarity exclusively a technical issue of completing EMU? For the most important German social philosopher, Jürgen Habermas, European solidarity is a political and social necessity for the EU countries and their populations to live together in the longer run. A leading German social scientist, Claus Offe, considers major EU social programmes necessary to enable Europe to escape the trap of its own making.[13] Two types of solidarity instruments are under discussion: one aims at stabilizing economies in emergency situations, and another at accelerating convergence. Both types of funds might, if successful, be mutually supportive.

The most common stabilization proposals relate to EU-level unemployment benefit schemes. In the recession, several countries were forced to reduce, rather than improve, income support to the unemployed when they were most needed but most difficult to fund. All the different European schemes proposed would help countries in situations of rapidly rising unemployment to maintain income support to the unemployed.[14]

One of the most-discussed proposals for accelerating social convergence is an EU-wide child guarantee that would combine setting standards for how children should be treated with financial support. The European Commission referred to 'a child guarantee supported by EU funds'[15] in its reflection paper on the Social Dimension of Europe, in the context of the consultation on the future of Europe. The late Tony Atkinson[16] proposed a child allowance scheme, developed together with a group of social scientists. Other proposals to accelerate social convergence include a European food stamp scheme and a basic minimum income system.

There are also proposals to combine support in emergency situations, and labour market and welfare reform. A Spanish economist proposes EU financial support to national systems of individual accounts to be used by workers (unemployed) for training and income support; and France Stratégie, a Spinelli Fund, to provide training and education loans; with the EU to provide funding in crisis periods.[17]

I am convinced that a Europe that wants to achieve equal opportunities for its people will at some stage develop social schemes that directly support individuals in need, in particular in situations when member states are not able to do so. This would show that the European Union cares about ordinary people, while accelerating recovery and convergence across Europe.

4.4 CONCLUSIONS

Europe needs a stronger social union. Not only because we face serious labour market and social challenges – the rise in inequality being the most common of these, and the suffering of major populations in the great recession the most visible – but also because European economic policies shape European social reality.

The Pillar of Social Rights is a signal that Europe's way of dealing with social issues has to change if European integration is to be supported by the majority of people. Europe needs a common understanding of the broad objectives, and how to reach them, corresponding to the level of integration achieved. The pillar principles give a broad picture of how Europeans should be treated in the labour market and when they face major life risks such as unemployment, lack of income or care responsibilities, or major life decisions such as how they should develop a professional career.

Implementation is crucial. The first test will be how member states and social partners respond to the recent Commission proposals on care leave, on ensuring that workers have decent labour contracts, and on access to social protection as well as to the proposed European labour authority. The European Semester will be the second test. Will we see the often-announced rebalancing between economic and social objectives, and will it effectively address social challenges in the different member states? In the longer term the question will arise whether the choice of the proclamation for adoption indicates a readiness to consider including these principles into the European Treaties, as was done with the Charter of Fundamental Rights.

NOTES

1. This chapter is written in a personal capacity and does not constitute a position of the European Commission nor in any way prejudges one. Responsibility for the information and views expressed herein lies entirely with the author.

2. The Commission launched in March 2016 an extensive consultation on a preliminary outline of a Pillar of Social Rights, and presented in April 2017 a proposal for the pillar together with a number of other documents including an overview Communication (an analysis of each principle, a social scoreboard with indicators and several specific policy proposals; see European Commission 2017d).

3. 'As a matter of fact, then, the EPSR Proclamation is devoid of binding legal force and first "requires" the adoption of dedicated measures to be legally enforceable. However, the clarification regarding the enforceability of the Proclamation may suggest a double interpretation. On one side, it may suggest an engagement of member states and EU institutions to go beyond the simple declaration of good intention. On the other, it represents a clear constraint to the scope and significance of the inter-institutional Proclamation which runs the risk of remaining a simple "starting-point", without real consequences' (Vesan and Corti 2017). The authors and others note that a proclamation can still produce legal effects when it is referred to by the Court of Justice of the European Union (CJEU), as was the case with the Proclamation of the Charter of Fundamental Rights before its incorporation into the Treaties.

4. See, for example, European Parliament (2017): 78 per cent of Europeans expected EU action on unemployment, and 70 per cent on health and social security.

5. The Labour Minister of Luxembourg Nicolas Schmitt expressed this feeling of a neglect of social impacts in an interview in advance of the Gothenburg Summit: 'When Europe continues with an ideology that focuses solely on the common market, on competitiveness there is cause for concern. When Europe largely forgets about all of those who lose out through the operation of the common market and consider that competitiveness will benefit everyone – which is absolutely false – there is cause for concern . . . In this context, the contention that social issues fall within the domain of the state is dangerous because such arguments can be used by nationalists of any colour' (Bloëdt 2017).

6. For an extensive discussion of drivers and policy implications of precarious jobs, see Schmid (2018).

7. Severe material deprivation rate is defined as the enforced inability to pay for at least four items out of nine (covered in the respective EU survey) considered by most people to be desirable or even necessary to lead an adequate life (for example: paying rent, mortgage or utility bill; keeping the home warm; or eating meat or other proteins regularly).

8. Juncker came to the issue in Athens, speaking to the Hellenic Federation of Enterprises: 'Even before taking office, I made it clear that mistakes – on all sides – had been made, and I wanted to change the way things are done. I wanted to replace the "Troika" with a more democratic and a more accountable structure. I argued that the European and national parliaments should play a bigger role. And I wanted a stronger social dimension for the European Union, and for any future programme'. The first social impact assessment can be found in European Commission (2015), and analysis under the framework of the International Labour Office in Koukiadaki and Grimshaw (2016).

9. For example, a declaration issued on 15 November 2017 by the PES (Party of European Socialists) ministers called for the adoption of a 'Social Action Plan' for each of the 20 principles of the Pillar of Social Rights. Similar demands are made by the European Trade Union Federation (ETUC) and civil society organizations.

10. Moreover the preamble refers to the fact that the Charter of Fundamental Rights was first proclaimed by the European Council in 2000. Given that the Charter was later integrated into the Lisbon Treaty, and has been binding since its entry into force in 2009, one may wonder what this reference might imply.

11. The Commission proposal for a directive on leaves and rights of carers (European

Commission 2017a) is negotiated in the Council Working Group on Social Affairs. The second consultation on the initiative on access to social protection was still ongoing in January 2018 (European Commission 2017c).

12. The S80/S20 ratio is calculated as the ratio of the mean income received by the 20 per cent of the population with the highest income to that received by the 20 per cent of the population with the lowest income. For example, a ratio of 4 means that the income of the wealthiest 20 per cent of the population is four times higher (on average) than the income of the 20 per cent least wealthy (http://www.statistiques.public.lu/en/methodol ogy/definitions/S/rappinterquint/index.html).

13. See Habermas (2013) and Offe (2016).

14. For an overview on the different schemes, see Dullien (2015) and Andor (2016); for a discussion of unemployment insurance and social and fiscal stability in federations, see Fischer (2017).

15. European Commission (2017e).

16. See proposal number 12 in Atkinson (2015).

17. See Jimeno (2017) and Aussilloux et al. (2017).

REFERENCES

Andor, L. (2016), Transition to Transfers: Options for EMU Level Unemployment Insurance. https://www.socialeurope.eu/transition-to-transfers.

Atkinson, A.B. (2015), *Inequality: What Can be Done?*, Cambridge, MA: Harvard University Press.

Aussilloux, V., B. Le Hir and H. Leclerc (2017), The Spinelli Fund: A European Compact for Skills. La Note d'Analyse 63, Paris: France Stratégie.

Bloëdt, A. (2017), An Interview with Nicolas Schmit, Luxembourg Minister of Labour, Employment and Social Economy. *Progressive Post*, 8 November. https://progressivepost.eu/must-introduce-social-considerations-various-economic-polic y-mechanisms-social-issues-not-isolated-economy/.

Council of the European Union (2017), Proposal for an Interinstitutional Proclamation on the European Pillar of Social Rights. Note 13129/17, Brussels.

Dullien, S. (2015), European Unemployment Insurance. In S. Durlauf and L.E. Blume (eds), *The New Palgrave Dictionary of Economics*, Palgrave Macmillan/Springer. Online Edition. https://link.springer.com/referenceworkentry/10.1057/978-1-349-95121-5_3006-1.

European Commission (2015), Assessment of the Social Impact of the New Stability Support Programme for Greece. SWD (2015) 162 final, Brussels.

European Commission (2017a), Communication from the Commission to the European Parliament, the Council, the Economic and Social Committee and the Committee of the Region, Establishing a European Pillar of Social Rights. COM/2017/0250 final. And Proposal for an Interinstitutional Proclamation on the European Pillar of Social Rights. COM/2017/0251 final.

European Commission (2017b), Proposal for a Directive of the European Parliament and of the Council on work–life balance for parents and carers. COM/2017/0253 final – 2017/085 (COD), Brussels.

European Commission (2017c), Proposal for a Directive of the European Parliament and of the Council on transparent and predictable working conditions in the European Union. COM(2017) 797 final, 2017/0355 (COD), Brussels.

European Commission (2017d), Second Phase Consultation of Social Partners under Article 154 TFEU on a possible action addressing the challenges of access to social protection for people in all forms of employment in the framework of the European Pillar of Social Rights. COM(2017) 7773 final, Brussels.

European Commission (2017e), Reflection Paper on the Social Dimension of Europe. COM (2017) 206, Brussels.

European Commission (2017f), *Social Scoreboard 2017*. Luxembourg: Publications Office of the European Union.

European Parliament (2017), Two Years until the 2019 European Elections. Special Eurobarometer of the European Parliament, Public Opinion Monitoring Unit Directorate-General for Communication, European Parliament, European Union.

Fischer, G. (2017), The US Unemployment Insurance, a Federal–State-Partnership: Relevance for Reflections at the European Level. IZA Policy Paper 129, Bonn: IZA-Institute of Labour Economics.

Five Presidents' Report (2015), Five Presidents' Report: Completing Europe's Economic and Monetary Union. Report by Jean-Claude Juncker in close coopera-tion with Donald Tusk, Jeroen Dijsselbloem, Mario Draghi and Martin Schulz, published by the European Commission, 5 June. https://ec.europa.eu/commission/ sites/beta-political/files/5-presidents-report_en.pdf.

Habermas, J. (2013), *Im Sog der Technokratie*. Kleine politische Schriften XII. Berlin: Suhrkamp.

Jimeno, J. (2017), Unemployment and the Role of Supranational Policies. IZA World of Labor, Bonn: IZA World of Labor.

Juncker, J.C. (2014), A New Start for Europe. Opening Statement in the European Parliament Plenary Session, Strasbourg, 15 July.

Koukiadaki A. and D. Grimshaw (2016), Evaluating the Effects of the Structural Labour Market Reforms on Collective Bargaining in Greece. Conditions of Work and Employment Series No. 85, Geneva: International Labour Office.

Offe, C. (2016), *Europa in der Falle*, Berlin: Suhrkamp.

Schmid, G. (2018), Towards an Employment Strategy of Inclusive Growth. In C. Deeming and P. Smyth (eds), *Reframing Global Social Policy: Social Investment for Sustainable and Inclusive Growth*, Bristol: Policy Press.

Vesan, P. and F. Corti (2017), EU Pillar of Social Rights: What Comes After Gothenburg? *Eu-Visions*. http://www.euvisions.eu/achievements-expectations-gothenburg/.

PART II

Technological change and innovation: heterogeneous growth opportunities across countries

5. Innovation in the CESEE region: the role of business environment, financing and reforms

Helena Schweiger[1]

At the start of the transition process, countries in the Central, Eastern and South-Eastern Europe (CESEE) region generally had unusually low levels of total factor productivity, reflecting inefficient allocation of resources under central planning. When production factors began to be redeployed more efficiently, total factor productivity initially grew rapidly.

However, by the time of the global financial crisis, productivity in the region had reached the levels seen in other emerging markets with similar income levels. This suggests that most of the easy options, correcting the distortions stemming from the legacy of central planning, have been exhausted. Further improvements in productivity will need to come from changes to the economies' economic structure and economic institutions, as well as policies supporting reforms and the development of human capital.

How can CESEE countries continue to grow? Looking from the bottom up, there are many ways in which firms can increase their productivity and thereby contribute to the improvement of aggregate productivity. Some, such as upgrading fixed assets and shedding excess labour, have already been exhausted to some degree. But there are still viable sources of growth left.

One of the most talked about is innovation. This chapter discusses the conditions for innovation by the private sector firms in the CESEE region. It starts by defining what counts as innovation and what it looks like in the region. It then looks more specifically at the differences in perceptions of the business environment between firms that innovate and those that do not, and at the financing conditions. After that, it defines the stages of innovation-based growth and assesses prerequisites for it, comparing CESEE with advanced economies. It concludes by outlining the reforms that could enhance productivity and technological progress at the firm level.

5.1   INNOVATION

What counts as innovation? Many people, including government officials and policy-makers, associate innovation with ground-breaking technology; in other words, innovations that advance the global technological frontier. However, while firms constantly work to improve their products and processes and introduce new ones, few are truly new at the global level. Data from the fifth round of the European Bank for Reconstruction and Development (EBRD) and World Bank (WB) Business Environment and Enterprise Performance Survey (BEEPS V) show that most newly introduced products and processes stem from the adoption of existing technologies that have been developed elsewhere, possibly with some customization in order to better serve the needs of the local market (see Figure 5.1). Such innovations do not advance the global technological frontier, but they still significantly improve the productivity of the firms that adopt them (EBRD 2014).

Likewise, many people tend to associate innovation with high-tech manufacturing sectors, such as pharmaceuticals, computers, electronic and optical products, aerospace, chemicals, machinery and equipment, and similar. But even low-tech firms, such as those in clothing or food products, can and do innovate in various ways.

The introduction of new products and processes often requires specific inputs, such as spending on research and development (R&D). R&D activities do not always lead to successful innovation. A company manufacturing paints, for example, may spend money on laboratory research investigating a new chemical compound for its paint, but not have any new paints on offer (at least for the time being). And conversely, the introduction of new products or processes may not always require R&D spending. It can also be facilitated by acquiring external knowledge. This can be done through the purchase or licensing of patented technologies, non-patented inventions and know-how derived from other businesses or organizations. BEEPS V data show that participating in global value chains (GVCs) or having a foreign owner can facilitate the acquisition of external knowledge.

As shown in Figure 5.2, CESEE countries are mostly in the 'make and buy' and 'buy' groups, with the exception of Albania, where few companies spend money on buying or producing knowledge. These differences in firms' innovation strategies reflect the level of economic development and how far the firms are from the technological frontier. Despite that, most government officials are keen to foster high-tech innovation in particular, regardless of the country's level of development (see Veugelers and Schweiger 2016).

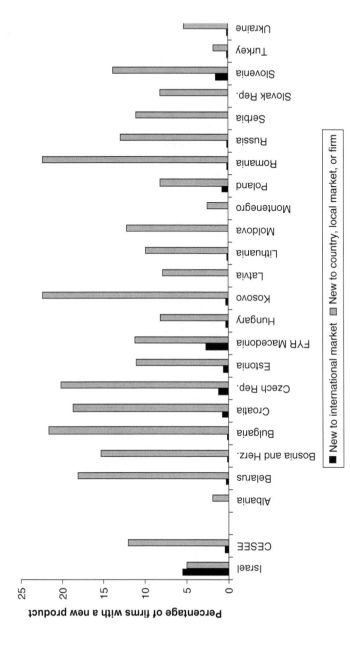

Notes: Based on cleaned data (see Box 1.1 in EBRD 2014 for details). CESEE average is an unweighted cross-country average. The data indicate the percentage of surveyed firms that have introduced new products in three years before the survey took place. BEEPS = Business Environment and Enterprise Performance Survey; MENA ES = Middle East and North Africa Enterprise Survey.

Source: BEEPS V, MENA ES and author's calculations.

Figure 5.1   Firms in the CESEE region focus on technology adoption

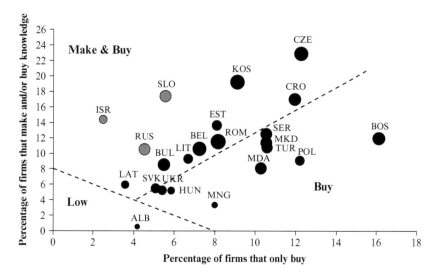

Notes: A 'make' strategy refers to in-house R&D, whereas a 'buy' strategy refers to outsourced R&D and the purchase or licensing of patents and know-how. The shaded bubbles denote countries where the percentage of firms that only ever follow a 'make' strategy is greater than the percentage of firms that only ever follow a 'buy' strategy. The size of the bubble corresponds to the percentage of firms that have engaged in product innovation (on the basis of cleaned data; see Box 1.1 in EBRD 2014 for details). BEEPS = Business Environment and Enterprise Performance Survey; MENA ES = Middle East and North Africa Enterprise Survey.

Source: BEEPS V, MENA ES and author's calculations.

Figure 5.2   Percentage of firms that make and/or buy knowledge

5.2   BUSINESS ENVIRONMENT

Firms' ability to innovate also depends on external factors. A poor business environment – widespread corruption, weak rule of law, burdensome red tape, and so on – can substantially increase the cost of introducing new products and processes and make returns to investment in new products and technologies more uncertain. These factors can undermine firms' incentives and ability to innovate.

The results of BEEPS V confirm this. As part of these surveys, each firm was asked whether various factors, such as access to land or labour regulations, were obstacles to doing business. Firms responded using a scale from 0 to 4, where 0 meant 'no obstacle' and 4 signified a 'very severe obstacle'. Based on these answers, firms that have introduced a new product or process in the last three years regard all aspects of their business

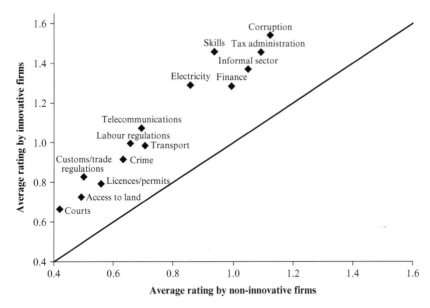

Notes: Values on the vertical axis correspond to the views of firms that have introduced a new product or process in the three years prior to the survey; values on the horizontal axis correspond to the views of other firms. Values are averages across firms on a scale of 0 to 4, where 0 means 'no obstacle', and 4 signifies a 'very severe obstacle'.
BEEPS = Business Environment and Enterprise Performance Survey.

Source: BEEPS V and author's calculations.

Figure 5.3   *Differences between innovative and non-innovative firms'*
                  perception of the business environment in CESEE

environment as a greater constraint on their operations than firms that have not engaged in product or process innovation.

This can be seen from the fact that all business environment constraints lie above the 45-degree line in Figure 5.3. The differences between the views of innovative and non-innovative CESEE firms are especially large when it comes to skills, electricity, corruption and telecommunications (with these diamonds lying furthest away from the 45-degree line). Inadequate skills, electricity and corruption, notably, are perceived to be among the main constraints for all firms, and they are even greater constraints for innovative firms. In contrast, telecommunications, labour regulations, and customs and trade regulations are not major concerns at the level of the economy as a whole, but they specifically affect innovative firms.

It is not surprising to see inadequate skills among the main constraints for all firms, and for innovative firms in particular. Most of the CESEE

countries have ageing populations, are faced with emigration of educated younger generations in particular, or both. Latest available World
Economic Forum global competitiveness indicators (WEF 2017) show that
the capacity to retain talent has decreased in several countries (especially
in Albania, Lithuania and Montenegro) in recent years. While some, such
as the Czech Republic, managed to increase this capacity, none of the
countries scores very well on their capacity to attract talent.

Innovative firms are also significantly affected by a number of other
aspects of the business environment. However, these tend to constrain
innovative and non-innovative firms alike, with only a slightly larger
impact on innovative firms. These include tax administration, practices of
informal sector competitors and access to finance.

5.3 FINANCING OF INNOVATION

While access to finance is not among the top three business environment
obstacles reported by innovative CESEE firms covered by BEEPS V, it is
nevertheless important to look at its role in helping firms to innovate. As
discussed earlier, innovation in CESEE often takes the form of adopting
existing products and processes from more developed countries and adapting them to local conditions. Funding constraints may limit the adoption
of technology, as external innovations are costly to integrate into a firm's
production structure. Firms therefore need sufficient financial resources to
properly adapt external technologies, products and processes to their local
circumstances.

Much of the CESEE region continues to be characterized by bank-based
financial systems, with only shallow public and private equity markets. Can
access to bank credit help firms to innovate in the absence of a meaningful
supply of risk capital? Broadly speaking, there are two schools of thought
on this issue.

One group stresses the uncertain nature of innovation, particularly
R&D. This makes banks less suitable as financiers for four reasons. First,
the assets associated with innovation are often intangible, firm-specific
and linked to human capital, which makes them difficult to collateralize.
Second, innovative firms typically generate volatile cash flows, at least initially. This does not fit well with the inflexible repayment schedule of most
loans. Third, banks may simply lack the skills needed to assess early-stage
technologies. Lastly, banks may fear that funding new technologies will
erode the value of collateral underlying existing loans (which will mostly
represent old technologies). For all these reasons, banks may be either
unwilling or unable to fund innovative firms.

A second group takes a much more optimistic view of the situation. One of the core functions of banks is the establishment of long-term relationships with firms, during which loan officers gain a deeper understanding of borrowers. Thus, banks may be well placed to fund innovative firms, as such enduring relationships will allow them to understand the business plans and technology involved. Moreover, firm innovation entails more than just R&D. Imitative innovation is arguably less risky and more in line with the risk appetites of most banks. Lastly, even without financing innovative projects directly or explicitly, banks can still stimulate firm-level innovation. When banks provide firms with straightforward working capital or short-term loans, this can free up internal resources, which firms can then use to finance innovation. Evidence from a broad range of developed countries suggests that firms generally prefer internal funds to any form of external finance when funding innovation.

Analysis in the EBRD Transition Report 2014 shows that access to bank credit determines the pace at which firms can upgrade their production processes, as well as the products and services they offer. Figure 5.4 shows the percentage of firms that engage in product and process innovation by their access to credit status. In the first group are firms that do not have bank credit, but they state that they do not need it. The second group comprises firms that needed bank credit, but were unable to access it and

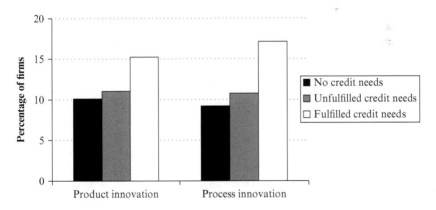

Notes: 'No credit needs' denotes firms with no need for bank credit. 'Unfulfilled credit needs' denotes firms with a need for bank credit that have either decided not to apply or were rejected when they applied. 'Fulfilled credit needs' denotes firms with a need for credit that have received a loan from a bank.

Source: EBRD (2014).

Figure 5.4 Access to credit and firm-level innovation

are thus credit-constrained. They either decided not to apply for a loan for fear of rejection, or were refused one when they applied. Firms in the third group had a need for credit and received a loan from a bank.

Looking at the likelihood of innovative activity, there is a striking difference between the firms with loans and the firms that are credit-constrained. Of the firms with an unmet need for credit, about 11 per cent have engaged in product and process innovation during the three years prior to the survey interview. When we look at the firms that have been granted loans, these percentages are significantly higher, at 15.3 and 16.6 per cent, respectively. In other words, firms with loans are around 40 per cent more likely to innovate than those without access to credit.

Roughly a quarter of all firms that were interviewed for the BEEPS V indicated that they needed bank credit but were unable to access it. Of course, not all the businesses will have been creditworthy, and banks may have been right not to lend to them. However, factors external to firms (and thus to their creditworthiness) are equally important for access to credit. The analysis in EBRD (2014) indicates that probability of a firm managing to access bank credit continues to be strongly influenced by the number and type of banks that happen to be in its immediate vicinity.

Despite rapid technological progress and financial innovation, small business banking remains by and large a local affair. If such geographical credit rationing is widely practised, all but the largest firms will depend on the ability and willingness of local banks to lend to them. This also means that local variation in the number and type of bank branches may explain why firms in certain areas are more credit-constrained than similar firms elsewhere. Improving access to bank credit may allow most CESEE firms to more effectively exploit the global pool of available technologies, increasing the productivity of these firms and helping these countries to catch up with more advanced economies.

Private equity (PE) and venture capital (VC) funds, on the other hand, are likely to be a better financing instrument for firms undertaking R&D, which takes many years to develop and has unpredictable returns, as well as for start-ups and younger firms. These funds provide equity to a diverse number of firms, together with know-how and incentives to help them realise their potential.

There is now growing evidence from both Europe and the United States that companies backed by PE or VC carry out more patented innovations and have their patents cited more often (an indication of the quality of these innovations) (see Cornelli et al. 2013; Lerner et al. 2011; Popov and Roosenboom 2012). The CESEE region has so far seen only modest levels of PE and VC financing, which has tended to remain focused on the United States and Western Europe.

The lack of developed stock markets, the scarcity of opportunities for initial public offerings and mergers and acquisitions, and the immature credit markets all serve to discourage PE and VC funds, for which viable exit strategies are crucial to realize financial returns. The region also scores less favourably in terms of its human and social environment, indicating that it does not have sufficient human capital to attract PE and VC investors. In addition, there is room for improvement both in terms of the ease of doing business and corporate R&D spending (in order to boost entrepreneurial opportunities), and in terms of investor protection and corporate governance rules.

5.4 ASSESSMENT OF PREREQUISITES FOR INNOVATION-BASED GROWTH

Previous sections have shown that the CESEE countries are at various stages of the catching-up process. This section looks at which country-specific factors are important as drivers of innovation, depending on a country's position relative to the global technological frontier, and provides an assessment for the CESEE region.

The first set of prerequisites for innovation-based growth relates to the general business environment; in other words, conditions that affect the operations and decisions of all firms in the economy, including firms that innovate. These are the quality of institutions, macroeconomic stability and the functioning of product, labour and financial markets.

The second set of prerequisites for innovation-based growth are those that affect innovative firms in particular. Accounting for differences in the levels of development, the conditions influencing innovative capacity can be divided into those affecting access to technology, those affecting firms' capacity to adopt and fully understand existing technologies, and those affecting the ability to create knowledge. Access to technology depends on a country's economic openness, the availability and use of information and communication (ICT) infrastructure and the extent to which openness to foreign direct investment (FDI) and trade facilitates the transfer of technology.

Absorptive capacity is underpinned by the quality of secondary and undergraduate education and the effectiveness of on-the-job training. The quality of the firms' management practices is likely to matter as well, and improving them is associated with improved productivity (Bloom and Van Reenen 2010; Bloom et al. 2012). Firms in CESEE countries have on average worse management practices than firms in advanced countries, though that of course does not mean that there are no well-managed CESEE firms: there are, but there are just fewer of them. Research by Bartz-Zuccala et al. (2018) suggests that productivity in lower-income economies is affected to a larger extent by management practices than by innovation, while the opposite holds in higher-income economies.

What matters for creative capacity, on the other hand, is the quality of postgraduate education; the availability of highly qualified scientists and engineers; the quality of the public research infrastructure; effective cooperation between public research and industry; the protection of intellectual property and the availability of risk financing.[2]

The assessment of prerequisites for innovation-based growth discussed above (the quality of institutions; the functioning of product, finance and labour markets; access to technology; absorptive capacity; and creative capacity) for CESEE countries as well as a number of advanced economies (which are operating closer to the technological frontier) is based on the World Economic Forum (WEF) global competitiveness indicators (WEF 2017).[3] Figure 5.5 shows the results. CESEE countries perform relatively well compared with advanced economies when it comes to the broad business environment conditions such as the functioning of markets, and the first ingredient for effective technology take-up, access to technology, but the gap in terms of quality of institutions remains sizeable.

The largest gap between the CESEE countries and the advanced economies relates to the capacity to create knowledge. CESEE countries score relatively well on the availability of scientists and engineers, thanks to the emphasis placed on science and technology in the days of centrally planned economies. However, they lag behind on venture capital availability and university–industry research collaboration in R&D. The gap in terms of their access to technology and absorptive capacity is smaller, but still substantial, driven primarily by the lower availability of latest technologies.

Within CESEE, countries differ substantially in terms of the conditions for innovation. As expected, countries in the 'make and buy' group tend to score higher than the 'buy' and 'low innovation' countries on all conditions. In turn, the 'buy' countries score higher than the 'low innovation' countries on all aspects.

Regardless of these differences, the fact that more highly developed CESEE countries score better on all conditions for innovation suggests the need to look at the factors for innovation-based growth as a 'system'. Further development on innovation requires progress on all indicators. A good illustration of this 'systemic' performance is Estonia, the best-performing country in the CESEE region on almost all considered indicators. Relative to the other CESEE countries, the superior scoring of

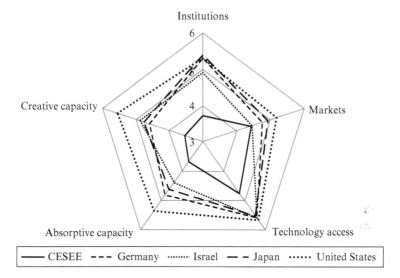

Institutions

Creative capacity

Markets

Absorptive capacity

Technology access

—— CESEE --- Germany ········ Israel — — Japan ······ United States

Note: The scores for each indicator range from 1 to 7, where 1 corresponds to the worst possible outcome and 7 corresponds to the best possible outcome. Scores for 'macroeconomic stability' are not shown. Data are not available for Belarus, Former Yugoslav Republic (FYR) of Macedonia and Kosovo. Figures for CESEE are unweighted cross-country averages.

Source: Author's calculations based on World Economic Forum (2017).

Figure 5.5   Assessment of framework conditions in CESEE countries and comparators

Estonia is most notable in its availability and use of ICT and venture capital availability (albeit it is still low compared with that in advanced economies). The latter improved after Microsoft bought Estonian-developed Skype in 2011 for US$8.5 billion; Skype's founding developers launched a venture capital fund and ex-Skypers ploughed money into new start-ups in Tallinn, further attracting United States investments.

5.5   REFORMS

Countries at different stages of development vary in their capacity to create and use knowledge, so one size does not fit all for innovation (or other) policies. Yet, innovation policies across the CESEE countries are surprisingly similar, characterized by an excessive focus on the creation of technology and insufficient attention to the absorption of technology (see

Veugelers and Schweiger 2016). EBRD (2017) outlines reforms that could enhance productivity and technological progress at the firm level.

First, governments can help firms and industries to improve their performance by supporting greater trade integration with the rest of the world. Competition, rather than governments, should determine market leaders at the domestic level. Greater integration into GVCs should be a priority for policy-makers looking to improve their economies' productivity growth. This also includes improving the quality of domestic infrastructure and logistics, to make host economies attractive targets for GVCs.

Second, flexible labour and capital markets and better competition policies are required to facilitate the efficient reallocation of resources. Creating a business environment that hastens the exit of less productive firms and fosters the growth of more productive ones is essential in order to speed up the reallocation process. This may require rethinking of bankruptcy laws and competition legislation, increasing the transparency of tax systems, and improvements to the rule of law.

Third, economic institutions and policies that support the growth of firms and industries need to evolve as a country develops. Smaller and more innovative firms will play a larger role in creating jobs and raising overall productivity as a country gets richer. Policies should prioritize better access to capital and technology for these firms. This may require some rebalancing of financial systems, improving the availability of specialist sources of finance such as venture capital and private equity.

5.6   CONCLUSION

Sustaining growth in CESEE economies will not be easy. There is no silver bullet, no 'one size fits all' solution. What is required is a transition to a new set of political and economic institutions that provide incentives to develop new products and services and improve the CESEE countries' creative capacity. Such institutional changes may be hard to accomplish, for example, because they run counter to the interests of incumbents that are benefiting from the status quo. However, the experiences of countries that have successfully achieved this transition, such as South Korea, provide grounds for optimism.

NOTES

1.   This chapter is largely based on EBRD (2014, 2017).

2. For a more detailed description and explanation of the various prerequisites and their measurement, see Veugelers (2011) and Veugelers and Schweiger (2016).
3. The sixth set of conditions is related to the macroeconomic environment, for which the scores are not reported. The scores reflect the establishment of various regulations (such as laws protecting intellectual property, or requirements that need to be fulfilled in order to start a new company) and their implementation, as well as expert assessments of the quality of economic institutions and firms' capacity to access and absorb technology.

REFERENCES

Bartz-Zuccala, W., P. Mohnen and H. Schweiger (2018), 'The role of innovation and management practices in determining firm productivity in developing economies', mimeo.

Bloom, N. and J. Van Reenen (2010), 'Why do management practices differ across firms and countries?', *Journal of Economic Perspectives*, **24** (1), 203–24.

Bloom, N., H. Schweiger and J. Van Reenen (2012), 'The land that lean manufacturing forgot? Management practices in transition countries', *Economics of Transition*, **20** (4), 593–635.

Cornelli, F., Z. Kominek and A. Ljungqvist (2013), 'Monitoring managers: does it matter?', *Journal of Finance*, **68** (2), 431–81.

EBRD (2014), *Transition Report 2014: Innovation in Transition*, London.

EBRD (2017), *Transition Report 2017: Sustaining Growth*, London.

Lerner, J., M. Sorensen and P. Strömberg (2011), 'Private equity and long-run investment: the case of innovation', *Journal of Finance*, **66** (2), 445–77.

Popov, A. and P. Roosenboom (2012), 'Venture capital and patented innovation: evidence from Europe', *Economic Policy*, **28** (71), 447–82.

Veugelers, R. (2011), 'Assessing the potential for knowledge-based development in the transition countries of Central and Eastern Europe, the Caucasus and Central Asia', *Society and Economy*, **33** (3), 475–501.

Veugelers, R. and H. Schweiger (2016), 'Innovation policies in transition countries: one size fits all?', *Economic Change and Restructuring*, **49** (2), 241–67.

World Economic Forum (WEF) (2017), *The Global Competitiveness Report 2017–2018*, Geneva.

6. Squaring the circle: the EU and the challenge of delivering better policies for a globalized world

Daria Taglioni[1]

Delivering economic growth and welfare to citizens requires countries to compete successfully and sustainably in the global economy. Competing successfully and sustainably on global markets, in turn, requires becoming hyper-competitive in specific tasks and niches. Policy-makers and business leaders are generally well aware of that, and they seek advice on how to address these needs in national growth plans and reform agendas. However, the why, the what, and how countries can be competitive in the global economy in the twenty-first century are far from being fully understood.

And yet, governments face challenges and need solutions that can be implemented now, not in a decade or so. Faced with a phenomenon that is multidimensional, and in absence of a definitive narrative of the opportunities and challenges from globalization, it is sometimes tempting in the public discourse to use simple paradigms to suggest solutions, even if economic analysis has demonstrated their limits. Some identify a role model to follow, to emulate policies that worked elsewhere. 'Can my country do what Singapore, Ireland, Germany, Japan or China did?' is a recurring question we hear from public officials, the private sector, and the media alike. Other times, governments propose and implement measures targeting specific sectors, products and groups of workers, failing to address the underlying systemic problems due to political cycles that are much shorter than sometimes decades-long structural economic cycles. In addition, the incentives for pursuing holistic, patient and incremental policy reform are scarce. Governments often focus on seeking entry points into manufacturing, despite empirical evidence suggesting that the services economy is an equally (or possibly more) important income and employment generator.

Clearly, questions relating to the challenges of globalization are also frequent, as inequality within countries has heightened (Helpman 2016). Globalization has led to more flexible markets, but flexible markets in turn have led to an increased pace of change and to heightened uncertainty. In the European Union (EU), this climate has triggered a political backlash against the deep nature of EU integration. Economic reasons for the backlash include the fact that many EU countries face limited fiscal space, and that the European cross-border market for equity risk-sharing remains underdeveloped. This means that even small downturns can lead to large economic, social and political costs. Adding to this, there are reasons of identity and tradition at play, including the fear that national governments have been pushed to the sidelines of global decision-making, and that the hybrid environment of national and supranational sovereignty of the EU is not working in the interest of its citizens.

What if the deep regional integration impressed by the EU construction is a key asset in making globalization work for its citizens, rather than a source of challenges? The view of this chapter is that the EU, if adequately reformed, offers the necessary large scale to successfully deliver better policies for a globalized world, well beyond what individual EU countries can achieve. Three mega-trends suggest that policy-making at the national level is increasingly unable to influence important domestic aspects and offer a rationale for having EU-level regulations that reach 'beyond the border' of nation states and that cover 'borderless' dimensions. First, global trade today is less about producing products in one country and shipping to another, and more about global value chains and which tasks a country specializes in. This changes the way countries can compete successfully on global markets. Second, most learning and economic growth nowadays happens through internationalization and exposure to other firms' and countries' technology. In this environment, traditional policies can have diminished or even perverse effects on domestic jobs and firms' competitiveness. The deep and pervasive provisions of the EU help the type of firm cross-border integration which is needed to deliver high profit margins and high-paying jobs. Finally, the information economy is increasingly dominated by powerful platforms, in which the EU plays a minor role. Digital platforms generate wealth and create employment, but they are also disrupting the way many markets work. These new economic actors can affect public goods delivery in fundamental ways. A common market of 446 million people is a powerful tool to ensure that digital platforms support employment, high-quality public-goods delivery, safety and the generation of positive and broad social impacts. How digital platforms will be regulated and how international activity will take place on them is key, as trade and economic activity will increasingly gravitate towards them. Countries are going to have different regulatory preferences based on their value systems, and a process involving international conversations on rules and treaties will be needed, since digital platforms tend to be global and likely to invest most aspects of society. The scale offered by the EU and the system of values, which is relatively homogeneous across the continent, delivers clout and negotiating power to EU countries far beyond what even its largest members could achieve alone.

Section 6.1 of this chapter discusses the key stylized facts that characterize the global economy in the twenty-first century. Section 6.2 discusses evidence on some of the limits of well-known traditional policy tools sometimes invoked in the public discourse. Section 6.3 discusses the policy implications of these mega-trends for the EU countries and makes the case that the EU, if reformed, offers the regional scale needed to deal with the complexity of the world we live in. Section 6.4 concludes.

6.1 ELEMENTS FOR BETTER NARRATIVES ON COMPETITIVENESS IN A GLOBALIZED WORLD

Borders between economic sectors have become increasing blurred through globalization and the fragmentation of production. Today, economists focus on specialized tasks along global value chains, seeking answers on how to best integrate local firms and workers into the dynamic world economy. Traditional takes on how countries compete are no longer valid. Competing successfully in the twenty-first century requires adapting to four key realities. First, traditional distinctions, such as manufacturing versus services, are increasingly a statistical artifact. Services are a key input into high value-added manufacturing. Heavily regulating them represents a tax on manufacturing. Second, when assessing competitiveness, the relevant unit of observation is not the product, the sector or the country. It is the firm which takes 'make or buy' decisions and defines selling strategies. Third, technology development has become global, causing learning and technology upgrading to happen through internationalization and exposure to the clusters of frontier technology dispersed across the globe. The next paragraphs look at these stylized facts in more detail.

Services are a Key Input into High Value-Added Manufacturing

High value-added tasks contain larger amounts of services and technology. Services can provide lots of good jobs, especially for countries currently only seeing limited gains from their involvement in manufacturing. A World Bank Group study (Sáez et al. 2014) demonstrates that the servicification process of manufacturing helps countries reach higher levels of domestic value-added. Based on results from a panel of 68 countries covered by the Trade in Value Added (TiVA) database, the study finds that servicification is critical in downstream production, that is, in the stages of production close to the final consumer. Interestingly, countries with higher levels of internet connectivity and positions at the beginning of the value chain undergo a greater servicification process over time.

Given the growing size of services, its role as a key input into high-value manufacturing, and its overall importance for productivity growth, restrictions on services delivery, within and across borders, are particularly concerning. Services regulations tend to be a more restrictive part of trade and industrial policy in many countries worldwide, including the EU, and they are often captured by import-competing industries. According to the Services Trade Restrictiveness Index of the Organisation for Economic Co-operation and Development (OECD), cross-border restrictions are particularly pronounced in air transport, legal services and accounting services, while distribution, sound recording and logistics tend to be the most liberalized. Sáez et al. (2014) find that lowering regulatory entry barriers for services, and in particular lowering equity restrictions and other regulation on foreign direct investment (FDI) related to foreign key personnel, greatly enhances domestic value-added growth in those downstream sectors which are more servicified.

The policy implication of this is that countries should consider reducing services restrictions, even if their focus is on manufacturing. Policies in the services sector are more instrumental in increasing the competitiveness and productivity of the downstream manufacturing sector than manufacturing policies (KPMG 2015; Lodefalk 2015). The EU services agenda addresses precisely these issues, introducing provisions to help businesses and consumers providing or using services in and from the EU. Provisions facilitating the establishment of business, provisions for enhancing cross-border services and those for simplifying procedures and formalities, as well as measures in support of customers, strengthen the rights of consumers and businesses, induce a higher quality of services and enhance information and transparency. These in turn contribute to create competitive strength in manufacturing.

Firms Interconnect in Ways that Are More Dynamic and Multifaceted than Ever

A large and ever-growing body of research shines a light on how firms make decisions on buying versus making, and on where and what to sell. Traditional theories of international trade often take a simplified view of the production process, assuming that firms use labour, capital and one technology type. Recent trade models (Feenstra and Hanson 1996; Matsuyama 2007; Grossman and Rossi-Hansberg 2008; Verhoogen 2008) study the complexities of modern production processes and make the case that production requires a rich set of activities, including manufacturing tasks, marketing, distribution, foreign trade finance activities and exporting services.

Exposure to foreign trade, investment and production sharing is a critical source of learning and knowledge transfer. Other things being equal, it has been established that importing, exporting and engaging in international production networks helps firms become globally competitive. Importers are larger and more productive than non-importers (Amiti and Konings 2007; Seker 2012). Openness to trade provides incentives to upgrade and exposure to new ideas. Imports enable firms to exploit complementarities between domestic and foreign capabilities (Goldberg et al. 2010; Halpern et al. 2015) and can increase access to technology and its embedded know-how (MacGarvie 2006; Koren and Csillag 2011). Exporting generates economies of scale that increase firms' propensity to undergo the cost of innovating and enables firms to learn about more sophisticated consumers and more competitive markets. For example, one explanation for the success of Chinese manufacturing exports is that these firms invested in capability-building to improve their product appeal in rich markets (Sutton 2007; Brandt et al. 2008; Schott 2008). Learning for firms and workers even originates from the very activity of exporting (De Loecker 2013), even in the case of non-skill-intensive exports. Firms that are simultaneously importers and exporters benefit, in addition, from important complementarities between the two (Kasahara and Lapham 2013). FDI can provide important additional learning opportunities, since the cost of transferring technology is reduced within integrated companies (Guadalupe et al. 2012), and foreign-owned companies tend to be better managed. And innovation tends to flow faster and more easily within global value chains (GVCs).

This discussion is particularly relevant for the European continent where connectivity through trade, investment and production sharing is high and has greatly increased in the past two decades. European GVCs are the key reason for the high productivity gains observed since the mid-1990s in Central and Eastern Europe. A major lesson is that open economic policies that maintain connectivity with firms at the global or European frontier are critical for growth. The sharp fall in demand with the global financial crisis plunged most countries into recession, resulting in calls to limit dependence on foreign markets to reduce economic volatility. But this is precisely the wrong conclusion to draw. Maintaining links with more productive firms through open policies towards foreign trade and investment is essential for domestic productivity growth, particularly in countries, regions or industries where firms are less productive. EU policies tend to facilitate learning and technology diffusion, by reducing the costs and uncertainty of trading, by smoothing price volatility and by helping to synchronize the business cycle across member countries.

Importantly, there are competition effects at play, as a result of which firms (and by extension countries) with weaker connections may experience losses. For example, Mexican suppliers to United States (US) companies reduced their investment in innovation due to interdependence in global production chains arising from increased GVC integration by their buyers with third parties in China. Other buyers (for example, German buyers) of the same Chinese suppliers also experienced adverse effects as their production costs in China rose as a consequence of the increased demand from the US (Arkolakis and Muendler 2011). This points to advantages of being part of integration agreements with the deepest connections. And the EU single market is the regional agreement with the deepest connectivity at the global level.

Technology Development Has a Strong Cross-Border Dimension

Technology is a way to be competitive on the tradable side of the economy, and is crucial in small open economies. Global production networks and cost-efficient cloud computing services enable supplier firms anywhere to upgrade technologically, and to produce global brands that can compete with long-established incumbents on the global markets. This is possible thanks to the learning and capital accumulated by firms that start as suppliers and sub-suppliers of global brands, through years of experience in international procurement practices and sourcing (Antràs et al. 2014). In short, it has never been easier to use world-class technology and services inputs to connect with other firms, suppliers and buyers, globally, and to learn from each other, share technologies and production systems and, through this process, to upgrade and become globally competitive.

The global diffusion of technology is a two-step process, according to neo-Schumpeterian models of technology diffusion (Aghion and Howitt 2006; Saia et al. 2015) and models of technology diffusion in multiple stages (Van der Wiel et al. 2008; Iacovone and Crespi 2010; Bartelsman et al. 2013). Frontier technology is created by the most productive firms worldwide ('global-frontier firms'), in clusters of leading-edge goods and services, and flows to the rest of the world in a two-step process: first from the global frontier to the most productive firms in a country ('national-frontier firms'), and then to all other firms in that economy. Importing from, and exporting to, global-frontier firms is one of the fastest routes for non-frontier firms to advance technologically and become more productive (Lopez-Garcia and Taglioni 2018). This is also shown to be empirically true for firms in Europe (Chiacchio et al. 2018):

- Step 1: National-frontier firms learn from global-technology-frontier firms and from complementary in-house innovation. They tend to have close linkages with global-frontier firms as either competitors or suppliers, or both (think of Samsung, which is both a supplier and a competitor to Apple Inc.). Global- and national-frontier firms tend to be at the medium to higher value-added segments of value chains and their learning focuses primarily on organizational capital, that is, improvement of managerial practices, organization of the supply chain, access to advanced research, and financing.
- Step 2: Domestically, technology and learning trickles down to other firms, predominantly through the domestic networks of national-frontier firms. The direct contact of mid- to low-productivity firms with global-frontier firms is intermittent, and typically involves goods and services with low value-added and low technology content.

Thanks to work by Furusawa et al. (2015), we also know why regional integration matters more than global connectivity. Distance seems to be a serious facet of technology transfer outcomes. Most firms are more likely to source more complex, specialized ('relation-specific') products from nearby firms. Simpler, more substitutable intermediates are often sourced from greater distances and – contrary to what has long been held as orthodox – the trade data do show significant 'churning' of suppliers, meaning that, both near and far, there is significant change in suppliers for most firms year on year.

Trade and Economic Activity Will Increasingly Gravitate towards Digital Platforms

Most people think that Amazon or Alibaba are e-commerce companies. That is wrong. They are digital platforms that function as the architects of increasing complex ecosystems of designers, entrepreneurs, marketers, payments, financing and credit outlets, logistics providers, online and offline retailers, supply chains and manufacturing. All of these actors interact in the ecosystem network, in rapid response, and driven by data and algorithms.[2] Such digitally enabled, data-driven innovative ecosystems will increasingly be where value will be created.

With only 27 major digital platforms and a market capitalization estimated at US$161 billion, Europe is under-represented in this new important area of the global economy (Van Alstyne et al. 2016). North American platforms and Asian companies dominate, with 63 platforms (and US$2.8 trillion market capital) and 42 platforms (US$670 billion), respectively.

There are two reasons why the lag of Europe in digital platforms is concerning: first, it will turn into a major competitive disadvantage for any industry that makes use of digital technologies; and second, it means that the global frontier of knowledge will shift away from Europe and towards countries that have invested in digital platforms. Owners of digital platforms will have a head start in developing the value-added businesses of the future, thanks to the skills they are developing in key technologies and applications, including cloud computing, artificial intelligence and machine learning, development of standards and interfaces to access the platforms, mobile internet and mobile payment systems in what is rapidly becoming a cashless consumer economy. Increasingly value is created by creativity and innovation, and not by tangible investments. Creativity and innovation thrive and are accelerated in the powerful digital ecosystems. Countries that invest in digital platforms will hence also have greater ability to succeed in creativity and innovation-based activities. Knowledge clusters tend to be located where digital platforms are created. New technologies, new processes and new products require a fair amount of decodification and recodification according to innovative criteria. As such, they tend to arise from clusters where the pool of specialized skills and support functions is at the same time deep and broad. With everything becoming digital, there will be a natural tendency to locate innovative activities where pools of digital specialists are. The activity of decodification and codification of new processes also implies that such clusters are natural standard-setting bodies. The role of first-mover knowledge clusters can, therefore, be self-reinforcing, making the lag of Europe in the area of knowledge platforms possibly difficult to bridge.

In this environment, having a huge and largely homogeneous domestic market is an advantage. As such, the EU single market is a key asset in allowing Europe to catch up in platform innovation. It is also a better-suited legislative level than the national level for regulating these new powerful industries. Why do we need regulation? Digital technologies are rapidly becoming the foundation of entire economies, but they operate in a still inexistent regulatory environment. Digital technologies have the potential to bring huge benefits in terms of inclusive patterns of growth, innovation and entrepreneurial opportunities. Digital platforms can be an opportunity, especially for smaller firms and individuals, to offset the productivity, size and geography handicap and leapfrog. But the downside risks of a publicly available, unregulated digital network are larger than has been generally understood, with the list including a long and growing list of small and big problems.

Hence, regulating these technologies will be necessary to warrant trade and investment, and international agreement will be necessary on the uses and abuses of the internet and data. Regulations are likely to be balkanized, reflecting different value systems across countries and world regions. At the same time, with size and density of the network being important determinants of success, the effectiveness of national regulations by individual EU countries may be limited. The EU, on account of its size, can instead help in creating sufficient incentives for digital innovation to develop in Europe, and for regulating it. It can help to align platform practices with EU public objectives, to ensure that employment, public goods delivery, safety and broad social impacts are well aligned with the European social model, which is broadly homogeneous across the continent.

Taken together, these four major developments suggest that traditional tools for enhancing countries' external competitiveness and defending domestic jobs may either have limited scope for success or create winners and losers, even domestically. The environment described above requires a range of deep and pervasive provisions for learning and growth to happen. This is what the EU common regulatory framework offers, as will be discussed in the next section.

6.2 WHY DEEP SUPRANATIONAL INTEGRATION MAY BE A NECESSITY RATHER THAN A MATTER OF CHOICE

The basic tenets of comparative advantage have not changed, and trade policy still looms large. But the effects of cross-border policies have changed, in a world where the nature of trade has changed, and where trade involving the exchange of customized inputs, incomplete contracts, and costs associated with the search for suitable foreign input suppliers are increasingly dominant. Using better quantitative data to untangle international production and heterogeneity on impacts at the firm level shows us that input–output structures of production mitigate the impact of policy on trade. Exchange rate devaluation, tariffs surcharges and other policies aimed at creating an artificial advantage for domestic production create winners and losers, not only internationally, but also within the economies that impose them. Evidence from three different episodes and policy instruments are discussed in this section for illustration: the impact of the 2009 devaluation of the Polish zloty on Polish firms' competitiveness; the effects of rules of origin in the North American Free Trade Agreement

(NAFTA) and of other defensive trade policy measures on the firms they were supposed to help; and, finally, estimates of the trade cost for the exit of the United Kingdom (UK) from the EU, as a quantitative indication of the benefits from sharing a EU common regulatory framework.

Traditional Policy Tools and Contemporary Effects

The real exchange rate has often been considered a key determinant of export performance. For example, the 40 per cent devaluation of the Polish zloty against the euro in 2009 is believed by some to have helped Poland maintain its export competitiveness and dampen the effect of the global financial crisis (Toroj 2012). Yet, according to a later study, the benefits were limited to a small number of firms: Albinowski et al. (2016) find that the effect of real exchange rate devaluation on exports was positive for the smaller and less productive firms. These firms had low shares of imported intermediate goods, which explains why they benefited from the devaluation of the zloty, without facing more costly imports. Meanwhile, more productive firms, which are highly connected to international production networks, gained no benefit from the exchange rate devaluation. These findings, associated with those described earlier on the importance of international linkages for learning and upgrading technologically, suggest that trade-related shocks can be best addressed through policies of stabilization rather than exchange rate interventions.

Tariffs and defensive trade policy measures are tools traditionally used to manage countries' international competitiveness. Better understanding upstream value-chain linkages provides greater clarity on the effect of tariffs on final goods. For instance, consider Country A, which produces significant value-added upstream that it exports as an intermediate good to Country B, which uses those intermediates in producing a final product. When Country B exports that final product back to Country A, if Country A has a high tariff on that good, that tariff is likely to be reducing the gains for its own upstream producers of the intermediate. Work by Blanchard et al. (2016) on this topic empirically illustrates the case for lower bilateral tariffs and less temporary trade barriers (anti-dumping, countervailing duties, and so on). Conconi et al. (2017) show that trade policy – and, in particular, preferential tariffs and rules of origins (RoO) in free trade agreements – can crucially distort firms' sourcing decisions. Focusing on NAFTA, they construct a unique dataset that allows for the mapping of input–output linkages in its RoO. Using a difference-in-differences approach, they find that preferential tariff liberalization and RoO on final goods drastically reduced imports of intermediate goods from third countries. Hence, careful analysis of RoOs in trade agreements shows that, while these are intended to support domestic industries, they can also create distortionary effects that lead to less efficient inputs and less competitive firms.

Quantifying the Economic Value of EU Membership

Turning to the costs of leaving the EU, it is estimated that EU membership increased UK goods and services trade by 42 per cent, and value-added trade by 14 per cent on average. The benefits were particularly strong for the UK services industries, and for the part of the economy most embedded in global and regional value chains. Because of EU membership, UK services trade more than doubled, and the country's backward and forward participation in GVCs increased by more than 30 per cent each (Mulabdic et al. 2017). Exiting the EU is estimated to cost the UK up to 28 per cent in terms of value-added trade. As trade flows adjust slowly to changes in trade costs, these effects will not be sudden, but rather materialize over time. The loss of a common framework for disciplines such as sanitary and phytosanitary measures (SPS), technical barriers to trade (TBT), movement of capital, the General Agreement on Trade in Services (GATS), Trade-Related Aspects of Intellectual Property Rights TRIPS), competition policy, intellectual property rights (IPR) and investment is found to be most significantly harmful.

The costs of the UK leaving the EU, and the disproportionately high costs for the most productive and internationally connected firms and industries, make a clear case for having a common regulatory framework to cope with the challenges of a modern global economy. EU regulations create a fair internal market where no company or country can gain competitive advantage by abolishing regulations, but they can all sell their products and services throughout the Union and benefit from policies designed to both reduce trade and production costs and open markets. The greater competitive environment fosters quality and product differentiation, leading to high profit margins for EU firms domestically as well as globally. Common frameworks and rules for key issues such as intellectual property (IP) protection, standards, technical specifications, competition policy and similar deep provisions avoid excessive market fragmentation, low profits, short company life spans, and underinvestment in research and development (R&D) and in other long-horizon assets. Finally, EU members automatically benefit from trade deals that the EU strikes as a single large entity with other countries.

As the trade landscape becomes increasingly global, it is imperative for countries to have robust frameworks in place for the future when shocks to the system may jeopardize gains. Barrot and Sauvagnat (2016) show

how, in our much more connected world, when one firm is hit by a natural disaster, the implications ripple through the supplier network. On average, a supplier to that firm will see sales growth drop by two percentage points. These losses can be even more significant when that supplier produces complementary (specialized) goods for that buyer, or carries out critical R&D and holds important patents. Common rules at the EU level are likely to be less subject to capture than national regulations.

6.3 WHAT POLICIES ARE NEEDED FOR GLOBALIZATION TO BENEFIT ALL?

There is little doubt that the future is one of continued global interconnectedness and digital technologies. These trends have the opportunity to facilitate smaller firms and individuals in the world economy, to open markets to isolated workers and firms, and to bring more services at affordable costs to citizens around the world. Their success greatly depends on having the right policies and institutions in place. It is particularly important, however, to discuss policies for maximizing value-added growth separately from policies aimed at reducing or preventing inequality.

Policies for reducing or preventing inequality are also important, and their importance grows in a more complex environment subject to frequent disruptions, such as the dominant one in the twenty-first century. While it is demonstrated that trade spurs growth and tends to be associated with greater productivity, competitiveness and more income, the relationship between trade and inequality is less straightforward. In this respect, the Stolper–Samuelson Theorem argues that changes in goods prices, for example through increased trade, necessarily create a conflict between households owning different factors. If this benefits low-skilled labour, inequality would decline; while if this benefits highly skilled labour and capital, inequality would increase. If trade causes prices to fall, someone will experience a decline in real income. This explains why the increase in trade between industrialized and developing countries has led to an increase in relative demand for low-skilled workers in developing countries, and has reduced it in industrialized countries, raising inequality between high-skilled and low-skilled workers. Helpman (2016) finds that 'trade played an appreciable role increasing wage inequality, but its cumulative effect has been modest', suggesting that systematic large-scale increases in inequality can be avoided by adapting and adjusting to the new competitive environment through facilitating reallocations of factors of production within an economy.

Given these findings, and the fact that international openness is a major booster of income growth, the related increases in inequality can best be addressed not through protectionism but rather through fostering stabilization and solidarity policies in the context of continued commitment to deep regional integration. While some EU policies already mitigate inequality, the current efforts of deepening the EU may offer the opportunity to achieve more ambitious results on this front. In particular, the EU should focus more on people besides firms, on combining instruments of market discipline with cross-border risk-sharing, and continuing to develop tools to support investment in infrastructure and innovation for adjusting and taking advantage of the twenty-first-century economy. At the EU level this means focusing on the regional dimension, continued deep integration agreements with frontier knowledge clusters, policies focusing not on jobs but on workers and human capital enhancement and knowledge, and investment in infrastructure and complementary policies.

Keep Focusing on the EU Regional Dimension

Given the small population and domestic markets of many EU countries, trade costs and geographic deficits, regional value chains serving regional markets enable less productive firms to achieve minimum scale requirements and to develop the capabilities to become competitive on a global scale. Policies that allow them to achieve this are those that allow productivity and value-added to grow. Estimating the role of policy in generating growth in value-added over a sample of 61 countries and 34 industries from 1995 to 2011, Kummritz et al. (2017) identify policies that allow for better connectivity and trade as major growth drivers. It takes policies to enhance hard (transport and logistics) and soft (digital, firm-to-firm and people-to-people) connectivity, particularly at the regional level. However, policies for trade and connectivity can only work if they take place under market discipline. For this reason rigorous frameworks on competition policy, IP protection, standards, and agreed technical, sanitary and other specifications also matter, as they build a business climate and institutions in which market initiatives can thrive. Fostering financial development, the quality of domestic services, innovation and skills are finally key complements to the above for competing successfully in high-value industries and tasks. And increasingly, long-term growth depends on sustainable models in terms of environmental, social and governance (ESG) impacts.

For European nations this means to keep reducing barriers to intra-regional trade and to greater integration, particularly in areas affecting higher value-added activities and the knowledge economy. Continued deep integration agreements with frontier knowledge clusters are necessary to be competitive in the new information and communications technology (ICT)-dominated environment. Countries and companies will need to be part of global production and knowledge networks, upgrade infrastructure and connectivity systems, and ensure regulatory certainty.

Focus on People besides Firms

Regulations need to ensure that the link between productivity and distribution, and between economic and social impacts, works. This requires ensuring social cohesion with policies that focus on individuals rather than jobs (retrain, educate, support mobility and income, maybe associated with well-targeted and non-distortive vertical interventions) as well as a package of policies for openness with social, governance and infrastructural support at the regional level (the EU single market is possibly the best example of successful opening and avoidance of the middle-income trap for most members). This also applies to industrialized countries, and includes supporting workers who have suffered wage cuts and/or job loss due to technical progress and globalization.

Human capital enhancement and reducing barriers to knowledge also matter. Countries will need to develop the needed talent through technical skills acquisition and, crucially, also soft skills. This includes a focus on language skills, managerial training and the kind of cross-domain skills that link background in technology, engineering and the sciences with an ability to process this information creatively and adaptively. In particular, governments will need access to strong data analytics paired with policy knowledge; this requires a mix of international awareness as well as an ability to apply international practices locally, financial sophistication and risk management, systems thinking, and the ability to engage with and learn from a wide variety of societal actors. They will also need to reduce barriers to foreign skilled personnel and individual services. This includes the need to develop mutual recognition arrangements for professional services that help to facilitate the inflow of global talent, as well as strong IPR to attract technology-intensive foreign investors.

Investment in Infrastructure and Complementary Policies

Infrastructure investment can help to prevent the wedge that the digital revolution creates between the networked (countries, individuals, firms) and the non-networked. Infrastructure (physical, digital and institutional) connecting global hubs with peripheral countries and global cities with both smaller centres and rural areas opens opportunities and ensures that the development potential of the digital technologies reaches a large fraction of the world's population. Without infrastructure-building, the matching of technologies, services and talents at the global level unleashed by the interplay between digital innovation and globalization would lead to distributional effects, including shifts in global income towards the networked (countries, individuals, firms) and a task remuneration structure that further tilts away from production functions to services, innovation and core R&D functions.

Contract Enforcement and Governance

Cutting-edge digitally powered goods and services are likely to be outsourced based on sophisticated contractual arrangements. This means that areas such as contract enforcement and the rule of law are again important foundational areas.

6.4 CONCLUSION

In conclusion, the timing is critical for the EU not only to maintain, but to upgrade its drivers of growth and keep up with the increased pace of change in the global economy. For European firms to innovate, compete, export and generate sufficient wealth to deliver high-paying jobs and keep funding the existing social safety nets, their home countries may need to convincingly keep adhering to a common regulatory framework of the deep provisions that matter in the digitally powered global economy of the twenty-first century. National policies and the 'balkanization' of the EU may instead push European firms away from the technological global frontier. Misguided incentives at the national level may create unfair competition and uncertainty in the common market, overcapacity, market fragmentation, poor technology choices, generate economic conflict between countries, and ultimately reduce productivity and economic growth for all.

NOTES

1. The findings, interpretations and conclusions expressed in this chapter are entirely those of the author. They do not necessarily represent the views of the International Bank for Reconstruction and Development/World Bank and its affiliated organizations, or those of the Executive Directors of the World Bank or the governments they represent.
2. Platform innovation describes the process of developing new products and services by leveraging globally available technologies. They solve information problems and provide new ways of linking users or consumers to the producers of the relevant goods and services. In doing so, they create brand new markets, employment and growth opportunities. The digital basis of these business models produces sizeable network effects which can lead to the 'hyperscale', where network effects lead the most successful platform to substitute and disrupt traditional market segments and to dominate the market (Parker

et al. 2016). Notable examples exist in industries as different as personal mobility (Uber, Google), accommodation (Airbnb), media (Facebook), and consumer photography (Instagram). Digital platforms can be an opportunity for smaller firms and individuals to offset the productivity and geography handicap and leapfrog.

REFERENCES

Aghion, P. and P. Howitt (2006), 'Appropriate growth policy: a unifying frame-work', *Journal of the European Economic Association* **4** (2/3): 260–314.

Albinowski, M., J. Hagemejer, S. Lovo and G. Varela (2016), 'The role of exchange rate and non-exchange rate related factors in polish firms' export performance', Policy Research Working Paper Series 7899, World Bank.

Amiti, M. and J. Konings (2007), 'Trade liberalization, intermediate inputs, and productivity: evidence from Indonesia', *American Economic Review* **97** (5): 1611–38.

Antràs, P., C.T. Fort and F. Tintelnot (2014), 'The margins of global sourcing: theory and evidence from US firms', Working paper, https://economie.esg.uqam.ca/wp-content/uploads/sites/54/2017/09/Fort_Teresa_-_Octobre_2015.pdf.

Arkolakis, C. and M. Muendler (2011), 'The extensive margin of exporting products: a firm-level analysis', NBER Working Paper No. 16641.

Barrot, J.-N. and J. Sauvagnat (2016), 'Input specificity and the propagation of idiosyncratic shocks in production networks', *Quarterly Journal of Economics* **131** (3): 1543–92.

Bartelsman, E., J. Haltiwanger and St. Scarpetta (2013), 'Cross-country differences in productivity: the role of allocation and selection', *American Economic Review* **103** (1): 305–34.

Blanchard, E., C.P. Brown and R. Johnson (2016), 'Global supply chains and trade policy', NBER Working Paper 21883, January.

Brandt, L., J. Van Biesebroeck and Y. Zhang (2008), 'Creative accounting or creative destruction? Firm-level productivity growth in Chinese manufacturing', *Journal of Development Economics* **97** (2): 339–51.

Chiacchio, F., K. Gradeva and P. Lopez-Garcia (2018), 'The post-crisis TFP growth slowdown in CEE countries: exploring the role of global value chains', ECB Working Paper 2143.

Conconi, P., R. Venturini, L. Puccio and M. García-Santana (2017), 'From final goods to inputs: the protectionist effects of rules of origin', CEPR Discussion Papers 11084.

De Loecker, J. (2013), 'Detecting learning by exporting', *American Economic Journal: Microeconomics* **5** (3): 1–21.

Feenstra, R.C. and G.H. Hanson (1996), 'Globalization, outsourcing and wage inequality', *American Economic Review* **86** (2): 240–45.

Furusawa, T., K. Ito, T. Inui and H. Tang (2015), 'Offshoring, relationship-specificity, and domestic production networks', Discussion Papers 15122, Research Institute of Economy, Trade and Industry (RIETI).

Goldberg, P.K., A.K. Khandelwal, N. Pavcnik and P. Topalova (2010), 'Imported intermediate inputs and domestic product growth: evidence from India', *Quarterly Journal of Economics* **125** (4): 1727–67.

Grossman, G.M. and E. Rossi-Hansberg (2008), 'Task trade between similar countries', *Econometrica* **80** (2): 593–629.

Guadalupe, M., O. Kuzmina and C. Thomas (2012), 'Innovation and foreign ownership', *American Economic Review* **102** (7): 3594–627.

Halpern, L., M. Koren and A. Szeidl (2015), 'Imported inputs and productivity', *American Economic Review* **105** (12): 3660–703.

Helpman, E. (2016), 'Globalization and wage inequality', NBER Working Paper Series 22944.

Iacovone, L. and G.A. Crespi (2010), 'Catching up with the technological frontier: micro-level evidence on growth and convergence', *Industrial and Corporate Change* **19** (6): 2073–96.

Kasahara, K. and B. Lapham (2013), 'Productivity and the decision to import or export: theory and evidence', *Journal of International Economics* **89** (2).

Koren, M. and M. Csillag (2011), 'Machines and machinists: capital–skill complementarity from an international trade perspective', mimeo, Central European University.

KPMG (2015), 'KPMG Global Manufacturing Outlook 2015: Preparing for battle – Manufacturers get ready for transformation', https://home.kpmg.com/bh/en/home/insights/2015/05/preparing-for-battle.html.

Kummritz V., D. Taglioni and D.E. Winkler (2017), 'Economic upgrading through global value chain participation: which policies increase the value added gains?', Policy Research Working Paper Series 8007, World Bank.

Lodefalk, M. (2015), 'Tear down the trade policy silos! Or, how the servicification of manufacturing makes divides in trade policymaking irrelevant', https://www.researchgate.net/publication/279246190_Tear_down_the_trade_policy_silos_Or_how_the_servicification_of_manufacturing_makes_divides_in_trade_policymaking_irrelevant.

Lopez-Garcia, P. and D. Taglioni (2018), 'Knowledge transfers from international openness in trade and investment: the European case', in David Gould (ed.), *Critical Connections: Why ECA's Regional and Global Network of Interconnections Matter for Inclusive Growth and Stability*, Washington, DC: World Bank.

MacGarvie, M. (2006), 'Do firms learn from international trade?', *Review of Economic Statistics* **88** (1): 46–60.

Matsuyama, K. (2007), 'Aggregate implications of credit market imperfections', NBER Working Paper 13209.

Mulabdic, A., A. Osnago and M. Ruta (2017), 'Trading off a "soft" and "hard" Brexit', VOX CEPR Policy Portal, https://voxeu.org/article/trading-soft-and-hard-brexit.

Parker, G.G., M.W. Van Alstyne and S.P. Choudary (2016), *Platform Revolution: How Networked Markets Are Transforming the Economy and How to Make Them Work for You*, New York: W.W. Norton & Company.

Sáez, S., D. Taglioni, E. Van der Marel, C.H. Hollweg and V. Zavacka (2014), 'Valuing services in trade: a toolkit for competitiveness diagnostics', Washington, DC: World Bank Publications.

Saia, A., D. Andrews and S. Albrizio (2015), 'Productivity spillovers from the global frontier and public policy: industry-level evidence', OECD Economics Department Working Papers, No. 1238, Paris: OECD Publishing.

Schott, P.K. (2008), 'The relative sophistication of Chinese exports', NBER Working Paper 12173.

Seker, M. (2012), 'Importing, exporting, and innovation in developing countries', *Review of International Economics* **20** (2): 299–314.

Sutton, J. (2007), 'Quality, trade, and the moving window: the globalization process', *Economic Journal* **117** (524): 469–98.

Toroj, A. (2012), 'Poland and Slovakia during the crisis: would the euro (non-) adoption matter?', Polish Ministry of Finance Working Paper No. 13-2012.

Van Alstyne, M.W., G.G. Parker and S.P. Choudary (2016), 'Pipelines, platforms, and the new rules of strategy', *Harvard Business Review* **94** (4): 54–62.

Van der Wiel, H., H. Creusen, G. van Leeuwen and E. van der Pijll (2008), 'Cross your border and look around', DEGIT Conference Papers c013_005, DEGIT, Dynamics, Economic Growth, and International Trade.

Verhoogen, E.A. (2008), 'Trade, quality upgrading and wage inequality in the Mexican manufacturing sector', *Quarterly Journal of Economics* **123** (2): 489–530.

7. Non-tariff measures for better or worse

Mahdi Ghodsi, Julia Gruebler, Oliver Reiter and Robert Stehrer

The importance of tariffs as trade policy tools is decreasing, as tariff rates have declined considerably since the 1990s. This is particularly true for intra-industry trade between developed countries. At the same time, the number of different types of non-tariff measures being applied is increasing.

Since the onset of negotiations of the Comprehensive Economic and Trade Agreement (CETA) in 2009 between Canada and the European Union (EU), and even more so with the start of negotiations of the Transatlantic Trade and Investment Partnership (TTIP) in 2013 between the United States (US) and the EU, the growing importance of non-tariff measures has also been reflected in public debates on the effects of trade agreements.

In light of the recently experienced trade slowdown, economists who believe that increased international trade is contributing to higher living standards argue for a reduction or harmonization of non-tariff measures to stimulate trade, which has been stagnating since 2011 (e.g., Baldwin and Evenett 2009; Cadot et al. 2015; Francois et al. 2015). Those who believe that trade has a negative impact on economic prosperity argue not to conclude (in the case of TTIP) or ratify (in the case of CETA) further trade agreements.

Both sides, however, usually presume that non-tariff measures are reducing trade, which – as we shall argue – is not necessarily the case. Only recently, trade economists have started to acknowledge that non-tariff measures need not be non-tariff barriers. For some types of non-tariff measures, such as quotas and prohibitions, the effect on bilateral trade is indisputably negative. Yet, other types of non-tariff measures, for example sanitary and phytosanitary measures, bear the potential of quality upgrading which could boost trade. Likewise, some technical barriers to trade such as labelling requirements provide additional information to consumers, potentially shaping consumption patterns and increasing trust, which might be trade-promoting. The 2012 *World Trade Report* of the World Trade Organization (WTO), which was dedicated to non-tariff measures, concluded that these measures could increase international trade, whenever the positive effect on the demand side is bigger than the negative impact on the supply side.

This chapter aims at shedding light on questions such as: Which types of non-tariff measures are reported to the WTO, and how did they evolve over time? How did non-tariff measures affect trade between the mid-1990s and today, and how did effects differ across types of non-tariff measures, countries and products?

7.1 MAKING USE OF A NEW DATASET ON NON-TARIFF MEASURES

Despite the growing importance of non-tariff measures in international trade, data on non-tariff measures usable for econometric analysis are still scarce. Many researchers set up their own datasets on non-tariff measures to answer their research questions for specific products, types of non-tariff measures and countries (e.g., Li and Beghin 2014; Peterson et al. 2013). One of the first types of non-tariff measures, for which a comprehensive database for a wide range of countries and products traceable over time was collected, was antidumping. The databases compiled by Chad Bown (2007) on antidumping measures, and later additionally for other temporary trade restrictiveness indicators, are provided by the World Bank (Bown 2016). Recently, joint efforts were made by the World Bank, the United Nations Conference on Trade and Development (UNCTAD), International Trade Centre (ITC), the WTO and regional development banks, to collect data for more types of non-tariff measures and a broader set of countries, with special focus on filling the data gaps for developing countries. One of these data collection efforts resulted in the cross-sectional CEPII dataset on non-tariff measures, generally known as 'NTM-MAP' (Gourdon 2014), used to evaluate the impact of non-tariff measures (e.g., Cadot and Gourdon 2016).

Another promising data source allowing also for a panel structure of data on non-tariff measures is the Integrated Trade Intelligence Portal (I-TIP[1]) of the WTO. It is intended to serve as a platform providing all information compiled by the WTO on trade policy measures ranging from regional trade agreements over WTO accession commitments to tariffs and non-tariff measures. We focus on the subsection 'I-TIP Goods', which provides all information on non-tariff measures notified to the WTO that apply to merchandise trade. For simplicity, we will henceforth refer to this subsection as the I-TIP database.

Types of Non-Tariff Measures under Examination: From Standards to Prohibitions

In our analysis, we consider seven different forms of non-tariff measures and specific trade concerns raised against two types of non-tariff measures. Public debates on non-tariff measures and consumers' concerns usually address sanitary and phytosanitary measures, which primarily target the agri-food sector, and technical barriers to trade, which aim largely at the manufacturing sector. The literature on the impact of these measures is quickly growing, mainly with a focus on one specific product and/or region (e.g., Peterson et al. 2013; Gelan and Omore 2014; Arita et al. 2015; Dal Bianco et al. 2016). As can be seen in Figure 7.1, these two types of non-tariff measures are notified most frequently to the WTO, but – as we shall argue later – they are not necessarily the most trade-restrictive ones.

Sanitary and phytosanitary measures aim at protecting human, animal and plant life and can take different forms. If products or characteristics thereof pose a threat to human, animal or plant health, countries can impose temporary prohibitions or restrictions, but they can also take the form of standards. A concrete example is a bilateral sanitary and

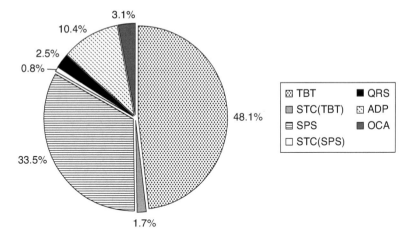

Note: TBT = technical barriers to trade, STC = specific trade concerns, SPS = sanitary and phytosanitary measures, QRS = quantitative restrictions, ADP = antidumping, OCA = other counteracting measures.

Source: WTO I-TIP, wiiw calculations, based on total number of notifications to the WTO up to March 2016.

Figure 7.1   Notifications on non-tariff measures by type

phytosanitary measure of the EU, blocking the import of dried beans from Nigeria due to pesticide residues at levels exceeding the reference dose as stated by the European Food Safety Authority.[2] However, sanitary and phytosanitary measures need not address a single product or specific exporting country, exemplified by the EU taking measures to prevent the spread of transmissible diseases, such as spongiform encephalopathies.[3] More than 30 per cent of all notifications on non-tariff measures in our dataset concern sanitary and phytosanitary measures.

Technical barriers to trade can take similar forms to sanitary and phytosanitary measures (prohibition, labelling requirements, and so on), but serve a different purpose. An example is an energy labelling requirement for storage cabinets, including those used for refrigeration. The stated aim of the EU is to pull the market towards more environmentally friendly products by providing more information to end-users.[4] While sanitary and phytosanitary measures mainly target the agri-food sector, technical barriers to trade typically affect the manufacturing sector, especially machinery and electrical equipment. Technical barriers to trade form the biggest group of notifications on non-tariff measures in our dataset, with a share of more than 45 per cent.

We also consider specific trade concerns raised at the WTO committees dealing with sanitary and phytosanitary measures and technical barriers to trade. Member countries of the WTO can raise questions regarding other WTO members' proposed non-tariff measures or their implementation of non-tariff measures. Adding up specific trade concerns against sanitary and phytosanitary measures and technical barriers to trade, this group represents 2.5 per cent of all notifications in our data.

A third group comprises so-called counteracting measures, also known as contingent protection measures. Their purpose is to counteract temporarily the negative impact on the importing economy from increased imports. Within this group, antidumping is the most prominent trade policy tool, accounting for about 10 per cent of all notifications. It is used to combat predatory dumping that causes damage to the domestic industry of the importing country. In a case of price dumping and a proof of damage to the domestic industry (see, e.g., Bown and Meagher 2010; Spearot and Ahn 2016), the importing country can impose antidumping duties, thereby increasing the import price and lowering imports.

Another practice that is considered 'unfair' by WTO norms is to subsidize exports. In this case, the counteracting measures are called countervailing duties. Safeguard measures are temporary non-discriminatory policies that apply to a specific product, but to all exporters of this product, in order to facilitate the importing economy to adjust to a strong increase of imports. Special safeguards apply to agricultural products on a bilateral basis in response to a rise in imports or a fall in import prices. Throughout the chapter, notifications of these three types of contingent protection are often summarized as 'other counteracting measures' due to their small number. Around 1.5 per cent of all notifications are attributable to special safeguards, while safeguard measures and countervailing duties account for shares of 0.9 per cent and 0.8 per cent, respectively. In addition to the relatively new types of non-tariff measures described above, the WTO I-TIP database also covers traditional non-tariff measures such as licencing, quotas and prohibitions, which we refer to collectively as quantitative restrictions, representing merely 2.5 per cent of the notifications.

Exploiting Information on Notifications to the WTO: Over Time, Space and Industries

The complemented I-TIP database on notifications on non-tariff measures to the WTO translated to a panel data format is the core dataset of our analysis. Substantial effort has been undertaken to match missing product codes at the six-digit level of the Harmonized System (HS) to each notification.

Figure 7.2 shows the growing number of non-tariff measures over time, particularly of measures regarding technical barriers to trade, and sanitary and phytosanitary measures. The last years saw a strong increase of notifications concerning technical barriers to trade and sanitary and phytosanitary measures, culminating a record high of 1640 new notifica-

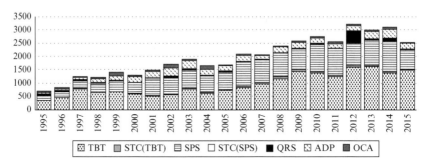

Notes: TBT = technical barriers to trade, STC = specific trade concerns, SPS = sanitary and phytosanitary measures, QRS = quantitative restrictions, ADP = antidumping, OCA = other counteracting measures. STC summarizes specific trade concerns to the SPS and to the TBT committee. Figure for the year 2016 not shown as it comprises the first quarter (January–March) only.

Source: WTO I-TIP, wiiw calculations.

Figure 7.2   Number of notifications on non-tariff measures per year

tions on technical barriers to trade in 2013 and 1137 new notifications on sanitary and phytosanitary measures in 2014. Contrasting these figures with the number of specific trade concerns raised at the WTO, we could argue that there were reservations against 2.5 per cent and 3.5 per cent of all notifications on sanitary and phytosanitary measures and technical barriers to trade, respectively.

With more than 10 per cent of all notifications, antidumping represents the third-largest group of non-tariff measures. We note two peaks, in 2002 and again in 2014. Other counteracting measures account for around 3 per cent of all notifications. Since 2010 their figures have been driven by countervailing duties, for which an upward trend is observable, with a maximum of 49 notifications in 2014. A clear downward trend is, however, visible for specific safeguards, which were heavily used in the late 1990s but have gradually dwindled since then. Quantitative restrictions amount to an even smaller share of around 2.5 per cent. They, however, usually target a greater number of exporters than do counteracting measures, which changes relative standing of quantitative restrictions when we translate the initial dataset of notifications into a bilateral format used for estimation.

As the I-TIP data are a collection of notifications to the WTO, information on non-tariff measures imposing countries is limited to WTO members. Our investigation covers the period 1995–2014. During that time the WTO grew from 127 members (126 countries plus the European Union) to 160 members. However, the I-TIP database covers only 140 members.

The top five WTO members imposing non-tariff measures are (in descending order) the United States, China, the European Union, Brazil and Canada, with more than 1800 notifications each. These 140 territories imposing non-tariff measures target 176 trading partners. The country most frequently targeted by non-tariff measures is China, followed by the United States, South Korea, the European Union and Taiwan.

In Figure 7.3, we visualize this pattern for notifications on non-tariff measures in force in 2014. Using the income group classification of the World Bank (2015), we group countries in our data into low, lower middle, upper middle and high-income countries. For notifications on non-tariff measures issued by or addressing the European Union as a whole, we assigned the high-income group to the EU.

Considering only the bilateral notifications to WTO indicate that richer countries tend to belong to the heaviest users of bilateral non-tariff measures, but simultaneously are also most frequently targeted by bilateral non-tariff measures. One argument is that developed countries can afford and therefore ask for higher standards for products they consume. On the other hand, the dominance of high-income countries in our data is also influenced by differences in reporting, with respect to both accuracy as well

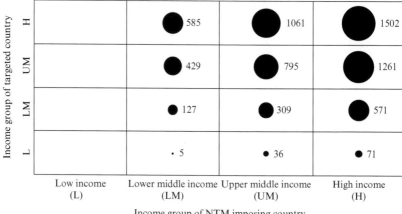

Notes: Not including non-tariff measures imposed against all trading partners; including specific trade concerns. When non-tariff measures were issued by or targeting the European Union as a whole, we counted the EU as one single high-income region.

Source: WTO I-TIP; wiiw calculations.

Figure 7.3   Non-tariff measures in force in 2014, by income group

as completeness of notifications. Some countries report every non-tariff measure applicable, whereas others report only non-tariff measures which depart from international standards.

Having this new dataset at hand, an obvious question to be asked is: Which products are primarily subject to non-tariff measures, and to which types of non-tariff measures? Splitting notifications on non-tariff measures according to product sections of the Harmonized System (Version 2002), it is evident that the three product groups facing the highest number of non-tariff measures belong to the agri-food sector, with live animals ranked first, followed by vegetable products, beverages and prepared foodstuffs. Remembering that the primary purpose of sanitary and phytosanitary measures is to protect human, animal and plant life, it is not surprising that this type dominates notifications on non-tariff measures addressing agri-food good.

Products of chemical industries as well as the HS group formed by machinery and electrical equipment still face more than 5000 notifications each. They are also subject to sanitary and phytosanitary measures, yet, technical barriers to trade form the primary type of non-tariff measures. Most of the quantitative restrictions and a significant number of antidumping in our data could be assigned to these two product categories and base metals.

7.2 ESTIMATING THE TRADE EFFECT OF NON-TARIFF MEASURES ON TRADE

In this section, we summarize results of an analysis[5] which followed a gravity approach to evaluate the impact of non-tariff measures on imports using the complemented I-TIP database. To start our analysis, we set up a panel dataset of bilateral import flows between WTO members i and their trading partners j for all products h at the HS six-digit product level during the period 1995–2014. We then estimate the effect of non-tariff measures on import quantities using the Poisson maximum likelihood estimator proposed by Santos Silva and Tenreyro (2006). Trade policy instruments included in the regression analysis are tariffs t_{ijht-1} in the form of ad valorem tariff rates and non-tariff measures NTM_{ijht-1}^n:

$$ln(m_{ijht}) = \beta_{0h} + \beta_{1h}\ln(1 + t_{ijht-1}) + \sum_{n=1}^{N-1}\beta_{2h}^n NTM_{ijht-1}^n$$

$$+ \sum_{i=1}^{I}\beta_{2ih}^{n'}\omega_i NTM_{ijht-1}^{n'} + \beta_{3h}c_{ijt-1} + \omega_{ijh} + \omega_{ht} + \mu_{ijht,}$$

$$\forall h; \forall n, n' \in \{ADP, CVD, SG, SSG, SPS,$$

$$TBT, QRS; STC_{SPS}, STC_{TBT}\} \text{ where } n' \neq n \quad (7.1)$$

The variables for non-tariff measures show the number of NTMs of type n imposed by country i on the imports of product h from country j in year $t-1$ in place[6] and notified to the WTO. As we are interested in importer-specific effects of non-tariff measures, we further interact the variables for non-tariff measures with importer dummies ω_i. $\beta_{2ih}^{n'}$ quantifies the importer-specific impact of one type of non-tariff measures n' under consideration, while β_{2h}^n controls for the effect of all other types of non-tariff measures in place. The procedure is repeated for all seven types of non-tariff measures and two sorts of specific trade concerns, such that our results are a collection of all importer-specific coefficients $\beta_{2ih}^{n'}$ for all policy instruments.

We opted for lagging the trade policy variables by one period for two reasons. The first rationale is that we expect demand, in particular for intermediate products, not to react immediately after policy changes are introduced. The second reason concerns the very nature of contingent protection. Antidumping or counteracting measures as well as (special) safeguards only apply when imports are already strongly increasing. If we did not consider any lag, our coefficients could pick up the prior import-increasing effect, for example price dumping by the exporting country, rather than the effect of the non-tariff measures imposed as a reaction to the import influx by the importing country.

In addition to trade policy variables, we control for country-pair characteristics that are changing over time, such as the market potential, that is, the sum of trading partners' gross domestic products (GDPs), differences between trading partners with respect to real GDP per capita, and endowments in labour, capital stock and agricultural land relative to GDP. Other control variables include dummy variables indicating whether the importer and the exporter are members of the WTO, or whether they are both members of a preferential trade agreement (PTA).

The constant β_{0h} represents product fixed effects. Time fixed effects ω_{th} aim at taking up economic shocks influencing all trading partners. Country-pair fixed effects ω_{ijh} should account for time-invariant country-pair characteristics such as their geographical distance or colonial history. Finally, μ_{ijht} constitutes the error term, which is clustered by country-pairs to give results that are robust against heteroscedasticity.

Throughout we exclude intra-EU trade flows. Although we do observe the quantity of non-tariff measures imposed by country, we do not observe the degree of heterogeneity – or, in the case of the EU, homogeneity – of the measures. The dataset does not provide information, for example, on which packaging requirement or which limit of pesticide residues is more costly to implement. It only tells us that regulations on packaging and pesticides were notified to the WTO. Given the principle of mutual recognition and the fact that non-tariff measures for EU member states are typically set at the EU level, the inclusion of bilateral non-tariff measures for EU members would lead to a downward bias of our results.

Trade Effects by Type of Non-Tariff Measures

For the majority of importer–product pairs (55 per cent) only one type of non-tariff measure applied. Another 28 per cent of observations were targeted by two types of non-tariff measures; 12 per cent by three types. Yet there are also importer–product pairs for which we find that four (3.8 per cent), five (1.5 per cent), six (0.3 per cent) or even seven (0.03 per cent) categories of non-tariff measures were used.

A first overview of aggregate estimation results gives an understanding of the importance of non-tariff measures for trade flows on a global scale. By definition, the minimum value for our trade effects is −100 per cent. On the positive side, trade-promoting effects of non-tariff measures can theoretically exceed 100 per cent.

Table 7.1 shows summary statistics over all observations – that is, importer–product combinations – per type of non-tariff measure. On the left, we consider all computed trade effects; whereas on the right, we consider binding trade effects, that is, effects significantly different from zero at the 10 per cent level. Roughly 60 per cent of our estimates show negative effects of non-tariff measures on imports, comparable to findings in recent literature (e.g., Beghin et al. 2015; Bratt 2017). This share increases to around 67 per cent when only binding trade effects are considered. The share of negative binding trade effects is highest for antidumping measures (72 per cent), countervailing duties (75 per cent) and quantitative restrictions (75 per cent).

Trade effects by importer: Europe and Africa deserve closer attention
For the geographical display, we consider two ways of aggregation applying the country classification of the World Bank. The first is to take the simple average over trade effects per importing (that is, imposing non-tariff measures) country, as shown in the upper panel of Table 7.2. In the lower panel we show the results, when we impose import weights using the import values per HS six-digit product per importing country. The average figures per region correspond to the simple average over all countries of the region, meaning that within a region every country has equal weight.

Both options have their merits. Applying import weights to the trade effects might better reflect the economic importance of a product within an economy than does the simple average figure over all products. On the other hand, if non-tariff measures are trade-impeding, using import weights automatically biases the effect of non-tariff measures towards too-small effects. We therefore opt for showing both.

The greatest trade-reducing effects are reported for sanitary and phytosanitary measures and quantitative restrictions of sub-Saharan Africa. The most trade-supportive effects are found for the region of South Asia for sanitary and phytosanitary measures and technical barriers to trade against which trading partners raised concerns at the WTO. Furthermore, standards and restrictions adopted by Europe and Central Asia seem to be more import-impeding than North American policies.

Another way of aggregating our country- and product-specific trade effects is to group them by income groups according to the country classification of the World Bank, as shown in Table 7.3. Simple average figures suggest that the trade-impeding effects of sanitary and phytosanitary measures decrease with higher income levels. Conversely, technical barriers to trade seem to be more trade-restrictive for richer countries. Quantitative restrictions bring imports to low-income countries practically to a halt, while these countries do not (effectively) apply any contingent protective policies.

Table 7.1 Simple average over trade effects of non-tariff measures

NTM	All estimates			Significant impact of non-tariff measures (p < 0.1)		
	Mean	Median	Observations	Mean	Median	Observations
SPS	-4.95	-2.23	74,744	-14.22	-19.19	35,814
TBT	-7.17	-4.43	201,229	-16.82	-19.92	99,382
QRS	-14.03	-12.78	39,230	-32.41	-64.67	20,767
ADP	2.99	-48.76	23,287	1.86	-70.9	18,326
CVD	-12.2	-51.89	2,239	-19.6	-81.82	1,569
SG	64.88	9.83	1,817	103.19	52.17	937
SSG	19.98	-10.47	436	17.01	-45.2	212
STC$_{(SPS)}$	51	-12.86	8,363	68.91	-52.15	5,007
STC$_{(TBT)}$	18	-24.13	46,412	19.58	-57.43	29,940
Observations			397,757			211,954

Notes: NTM = non-tariff measures, SPS = sanitary and phytosanitary measures, TBT = technical barriers to trade, QRS = quantitative restrictions, ADP = antidumping, CVD = countervailing duties, SG = safeguard measures, SSG = special safeguards, STC = specific trade concerns.

Considered are only importer–product pairs for which at least one type of non-tariff measures applied. As one importer–product pair can be affected by multiple types of non-tariff measures, the total number of effects by type of non-tariff measures exceeds the number of effects by importer–product pairs.

Source: wiiw calculations.

Table 7.2 Binding trade effects by region and types of non-tariff measures

	Region	SPS	TBT	QRS	ADP	CVD	SG	SSG	STC(SPS)	STC(TBT)
Simple average	Europe & Central Asia	−2.55	−13.38	−4.3	0	−0.3	0.56	0	2.81	2.8
	North America	−0.63	−2.89	−0.19	1.88	−0.29	−0.37	0.17	0.39	2.87
	Latin America & Caribbean	−3.93	−17.57	−1.1	1.24	0.08	2.81	−0.16	0	12.65
	East Asia & Pacific	−4.65	−10.57	−0.23	−0.03	−0.03	0.02	0.15	0.68	2.1
	South Asia	33.12	0.36	−0.25	0.77	0.11	2.99		11.06	56.57
	Middle East & North Africa	−5.81	−5.81	−5.63	−0.39	−0.64	3.7	−0.06	0.24	0.17
	Sub-Saharan Africa	−22.5	−13.55	−45.28	0.18	0	0.04			−0.55
Import-weighted average	Europe & Central Asia	−0.4	−9.17	−5.37	0.48	0.01	0.4	0.03	2.04	1.11
	North America	−0.7	−0.87	0.14	1.16	−0.6	−0.09	0.17	0.5	1.87
	Latin America & Caribbean	1.69	−2.86	−2.57	1.18	0.84	1.49	0.48	0.43	5.25
	East Asia & Pacific	−1.07	−1.57	3.32	3.39	−0.67	0.15	0.07	−0.12	2.09
	South Asia	50.02	1.63	−18.74	2.07	0.21	0.21	.	11.62	25.94
	Middle East & North Africa	−1.47	−4.66	−3.82	−0.07	3.93	3.39	−0.01	0.06	2.99
	Sub-Saharan Africa	−10.77	8.94	−18.26	0.43	0.12	0.08			−0.22

Notes: SPS = sanitary and phytosanitary measures, TBT = technical barriers to trade, QRS = quantitative restrictions, ADP = antidumping, CVD = countervailing duties, SG = safeguard measures, SSG = special safeguards, STC = specific trade concerns. Figures refer to binding trade effects (statistically different from zero at 10%).

Source: wiiw calculations.

Table 7.3 Binding trade effects by income group and types of non-tariff measures

	Income Group	SPS	TBT	QRS	ADP	CVD	SG	SSG	STC$_{(SPS)}$	STC$_{(TBT)}$
Simple average	Low income	−10.48	−3.45	−99.99						
	Lower middle income	−12.68	−7.16	1.81	0.18	0.11	1.72	0.17	1.46	11.31
	Upper middle income	−5.07	−11.08	−1.87	1.34	−0.01	2.67	−0.09	0.55	10.76
	High income	−1.39	−16.89	−3.43	−0.06	−0.29	0.25	0.01	2.01	2.23
Import-weighted	Low income	5.83	23.53	−99.66						
	Lower middle income	−4.51	−0.86	9.59	1.06	0.21	0.96	0.67	0.67	6.85
	Upper middle income	−1.09	−1.3	−1.26	3.69	0.44	1.49	−0.11	0.73	4.08
	High income	0.98	−9.04	−3.48	0.1	0.07	0.46	0.04	1.52	1.52

Notes: SPS = sanitary and phytosanitary measures, TBT = technical barriers to trade, QRS = quantitative restrictions, ADP = antidumping, CVD = countervailing duties, SG = safeguard measures, SSG = special safeguards, STC = specific trade concerns. Figures refer to binding trade effects (statistically different from zero at 10%).

Source: wiiw calculations.

Trade effects by product types

The effects of non-tariff measures might vary not only by characteristics of the countries imposing non-tariff measures but also by the type of product targeted by the policy. Every year during the period 1995–2014, imports of intermediates represented more than 52 per cent of global imports, and the importance of global value chains as exemplified by intermediate goods trade is increasing over time. Table 7.4 therefore summarizes our estimates according to the use of the product as: (1) an intermediate product entering the production of another product; or (2) a good ready for final consumption; or (3) a component contributing to gross fixed capital formation (GFCF). Concordance tables from HS Rev. 1996 to the Broad End-use Category (BEC) classification are used to form these three categories of products.

We expected the fastest reaction to price increases for the demand of households, while reactions of firms' demand for intermediates might be slower due to established international production networks. For large investments in assets based on longer-term planning, import demand might be less price-elastic, such that the reduction in import quantities might be slower than the policy-induced increase of the import price of these goods (see, e.g., Ghodsi et al. 2016).

However, simple averages across all calculated trade effects emphasize the trade-impeding effects of standards and regulations embedded in sanitary and phytosanitary measures and technical barriers to trade particularly for intermediates, while quantitative restrictions show similar effects across product types. In import-weighted terms, effects of sanitary and phytosanitary measures, technical barriers to trade and quantitative restrictions on imports of intermediate products and final consumption goods are scaled down considerably, while the negative trade effect for fixed capital becomes even more pronounced.

The HS product classification is organized in 99 chapters, which are grouped into 21 sections. Figure 7.4 presents simple average trade effects for each HS section. Luxury products, minerals, as well as arms and ammunition, represent HS sections showing the greatest import-reducing effects of non-tariff measures, greatly attributable to quantitative restrictions and technical barriers to trade. These are followed by animal and vegetable fats, as well as live animals, while vegetable products are found halfway down the product list.

However, our regression output allows taking a much closer look at (groups of) products of specific interest, suggesting a great diversity of trade effects across products. For example, consider meat products (HS 02), which belong to the product groups that are affected by a great variety of different types of non-tariff measures and are imported by a vast number of countries worldwide. Meat products in turn represent a

Table 7.4 *Binding trade effects by product use and types of non-tariff measures*

Product use		SPS	TBT	QRS	ADP	CVD	SG	SSG	STC$_{(SPS)}$	STC$_{(TBT)}$
Simple average	Intermediates	−3.11	−16.43	−2.99	0.35	−0.19	0.31	0	0.9	1.9
	Final Consumption	−2.96	−7.34	−3.16	−0.31	−0.02	0.62	0.04	2.66	3.21
	GFCF	−0.27	−7.75	−3.29	2.01	−0.08	0.06		−0.02	6.8
Import-weighted	Intermediates	−0.19	−2.87	−0.04	4.12	−0.02	0.11	−0.01	0.52	1.89
	Final Consumption	−0.41	−1.51	−0.97	0.05	0.4	0.28	0.15	3.62	4.2
	GFCF	−0.65	−6.55	−6.64	1.28	−0.04	0.01		0	0.62

Notes: SPS = sanitary and phytosanitary measures, TBT = technical barriers to trade, QRS = quantitative restrictions, ADP = antidumping, CVD = countervailing duties, SG = safeguard measures, SSG = special safeguards, STC = specific trade concerns. Figures refer to binding trade effects (statistically different from zero at 10%).

Source: wiiw calculations.

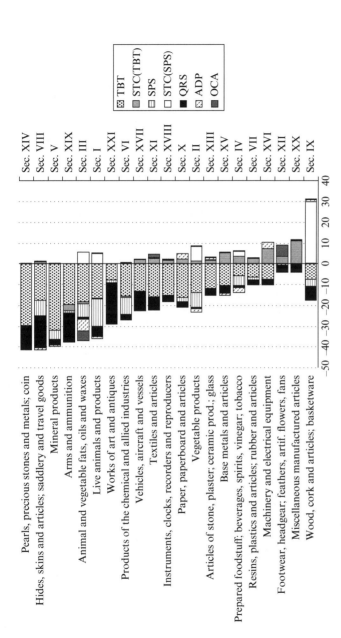

Notes: Considering only importer–product pairs for which at least one type of non-tariff measure applied. Simple average is computed across all trade effects that are significantly different from zero at the 10% level, grouped by HS section. HS = Harmonized System, TBT = technical barriers to trade, STC = specific trade concerns, SPS = sanitary and phytosanitary measures, QRS = quantitative restrictions, ADP = antidumping, OCA = other counteracting measures.

Source: wiiw calculations.

Figure 7.4   *Binding trade effects of non-tariff measures by HS section*

group of ten HS four-digit products. One of them is poultry (HS 0207), which can be further decomposed to 19 HS six-digit poultry products, for example to discuss the chlorinated chicken case (Gruebler 2017).

7.3   CONCLUSION: THERE IS NO 'ONE SIZE FITS ALL' POLICY RECOMMENDATION

We used the amended data provided by the Integrated Trade Intelligence Portal (I-TIP) of the WTO to estimate respective trade effects with respect to non-tariff measures for more than 100 importers and more than 5000 products over the period 1995–2014. About 60 per cent of all trade effects suggest trade-impeding effects of non-tariff measures, which are particularly pronounced for quantitative restrictions and technical barriers to trade.

Geographically, the greatest import-restricting effects were found for sub-Saharan Africa. We also note that standards and restrictions implemented in Europe and Central Asia affect imports more than do North American non-tariff measures. At the product level, we find non-tariff measures to be most trade-restrictive for luxury products, minerals, as well as arms and ammunition, followed by products of the agri-food sector. Although one might consider it appropriate to aggregate notifications on non-tariff measures and corresponding estimates of trade effects along country and product characteristics, we want to emphasize the diversity of non-tariff measures and their effects at the disaggregated product level.

NOTES

1. WTO I-TIP database online: https://www.wto.org/english/res_e/statis_e/itip_e.htm.
2. WTO Document: G/SPS/N/EU/131, 29 June 2015.
3. WTO Document: G/SPS/N/EU/67, 4 March 2014.
4. WTO Document: G/TBT/N/EU/178, 28 January 2014.
5. An extended version of this chapter was published as Ghodsi et al. (2017). The report and data on estimated trade effects are available online free of charge at: www.wiiw.ac.at.
6. The I-TIP database provides the date of withdrawal for antidumping and countervailing duties measures, and end dates for some quantitative restrictions, safeguard measures and special safeguards. For other types of non-tariff measures this information is not available. For our analysis, we assume that they have not been withdrawn since.

REFERENCES

Arita, S., L. Mitchell and J. Beckman (2015), 'Estimating the effects of selected sanitary and phytosanitary measures and technical barriers to trade on

US–EU agricultural trade', Economic Research Report No. 199, USDA, November.

Baldwin, R. and S. Evenett (eds) (2009), 'The collapse of global trade, murky protectionism, and the crisis: recommendations for the G20, a VoxEU.org publication', London: CEPR.

Beghin, J., A.-C. Disdier and S. Marette (2015), 'Trade restrictiveness indices in presence of externalities: an application to non-tariff measures', *Canadian Journal of Economics*, **48** (4), 1513–36.

Bown, C.P. (2007), 'Global Antidumping Database Version 3.0', World Bank Policy Research Working Paper No. 3737, October.

Bown, C.P. (2016), 'Global Antidumping Database', World Bank, June. http://econ.worldbank.org/ttbd/gad/.

Bown, C.P. and N. Meagher (2010), 'Mexico – olive oil: remedy without a cause?', *World Trade Review*, **9** (1), 85–116.

Bratt, M. (2017), 'Estimating the bilateral impact of nontariff measures on trade', *Review of International Economic*, **25** (5), 1105–29.

Cadot, O. and J. Gourdon (2016), 'Non-tariff measures, preferential trade agreements, and prices: new evidence', *Review of World Economics*, **152**, 227–49.

Cadot, O., E. Munadi and L.Y. Ing (2015), 'Streamlining non-tariff measures in ASEAN: the way forward', *Asian Economic Papers*, **14** (1), 35–70.

Dal Bianco, A., V. Boatto, F. Caracciolo and F. Santeramo (2016), 'Tariffs and non-tariff frictions in the world wine trade', *European Review of Agricultural Economics*, **43** (1), 31–57.

Francois, J., M. Manchin, H. Norberg, O. Pindyuk and P. Tomberger (2015), 'Reducing transatlantic barriers to trade and investment: an economic assessment', Economics Working Papers No. 1503, Johannes Kepler University Linz, May.

Gelan, A. and A. Omore (2014), 'Beyond tariffs: the role of non-tariff barriers in dairy trade in the East African Community Free Trade Area', *Development Policy Review*, **32** (5), 523–43.

Ghodsi, M., J. Gruebler, O. Reiter and R. Stehrer (2017), 'The evolution of non-tariff measures and their diverse effects on trade', wiiw Research Report No. 419, Vienna, May.

Ghodsi, M., J. Gruebler and R. Stehrer (2016), 'Import demand elasticities revisited', wiiw Working Paper No. 132, Vienna, November.

Gourdon, J. (2014), 'CEPII NTM-MAP: a tool for assessing the economic impact of non-tariff measures', CEPII Working Paper No. 2014-24, December.

Gruebler, J. (2017), 'Trade effects of non-tariff measures: the "chlorinated chicken" case', *wiiw Monthly Report* No. 4/2017, Vienna, April.

Li, Y. and J. Beghin (2014), 'Protectionism indices for non-tariff measures: an application to maximum residue levels', *Food Policy*, **45**, 57–68.

Peterson, E., J. Grant, D. Roberts and V. Karov (2013), 'Evaluating the trade restrictiveness of phytosanitary measures on US fresh fruit and vegetable imports', *American Journal of Agricultural Economics*, **95** (4), 842–58.

Santos Silva, J.M.C. and S. Tenreyro (2006), 'The log of gravity', *Review of Economics and Statistics*, **88** (4), 641–58.

Spearot, A. and D. Ahn (2016), 'US-Carbon Steel (India): multi-product firms and cumulation of products', *World Trade Review*, **15** (2), 351–73.

WTO (2012), *World Trade Report 2012: Trade and Public Policies: A Closer Look at Non-Tariff Measures in the 21st Century*, Geneva: World Trade Organization.

APPENDIX

Table 7A.1 Regional classification of countries

East Asia and Pacific

#	Code	Country
1	AU	Australia
2	BN	Brunei Darussalam
3	KH	Cambodia
4	CN	China
5	HK	China, Hong Kong SAR
6	MO	China, Macao SAR
7	FJ	Fiji
8	ID	Indonesia
9	JP	Japan
10	MY	Malaysia
11	MN	Mongolia
12	MM	Myanmar
13	NZ	New Zealand
14	PH	Philippines
15	KR	Republic of Korea
16	SG	Singapore
17	TW	Taiwan
18	TH	Thailand
19	VN	Viet Nam

Europe and Central Asia

20	AL	Albania
21	AM	Armenia
22	AT	Austria
23	AZ	Azerbaijan
24	BY	Belarus
25	BE	Belgium
26	BA	Bosnia & Herzegovina
27	BG	Bulgaria
28	HR	Croatia
29	CY	Cyprus
30	CZ	Czech Republic
31	DK	Denmark
32	EE	Estonia
33	FI	Finland
34	FR	France
35	GE	Georgia
36	DE	Germany
37	EL	Greece
38	HU	Hungary
39	IS	Iceland
40	IE	Ireland
41	IT	Italy
42	KZ	Kazakhstan
43	KG	Kyrgyzstan
44	LV	Latvia
45	LT	Lithuania
46	LU	Luxembourg
47	ME	Montenegro
48	NL	Netherlands
49	NO	Norway
50	PL	Poland
51	PT	Portugal
52	MD	Republic of Moldova
53	RO	Romania
54	RU	Russian Federation
55	RS	Serbia
56	SK	Slovakia
57	SI	Slovenia
58	ES	Spain
59	SE	Sweden
60	CH	Switzerland
61	MK	TFYR of Macedonia
62	TR	Turkey
63	UA	Ukraine
64	UK	United Kingdom

Latin America and Caribbean

No.	Code	Country
65	AG	Antigua and Barbuda
66	AR	Argentina
67	AW	Aruba
68	BS	Bahamas
69	BB	Barbados
70	BZ	Belize
71	BO	Bolivia
72	BR	Brazil
73	CL	Chile
74	CO	Colombia
75	CR	Costa Rica
76	DM	Dominica
77	DO	Dominican Republic
78	EC	Ecuador
79	SV	El Salvador
80	GD	Grenada
81	GT	Guatemala
82	HN	Honduras
83	JM	Jamaica
84	MX	Mexico
85	MS	Montserrat
86	NI	Nicaragua
87	PA	Panama
88	PY	Paraguay
89	PE	Peru
90	KN	Saint Kitts and Nevis
91	LC	Saint Lucia
92	VC	St. Vincent and the Grenadines
93	SR	Suriname
94	TT	Trinidad and Tobago
95	TC	Turks and Caicos Islands
96	UY	Uruguay
97	VE	Venezuela

Middle East and North Africa

No.	Code	Country
98	DZ	Algeria
99	BH	Bahrain
100	DJ	Djibouti
101	EG	Egypt
102	IR	Iran
103	IL	Israel
104	JO	Jordan
105	KW	Kuwait
106	LB	Lebanon
107	MT	Malta
108	MA	Morocco
109	OM	Oman
110	QA	Qatar
111	SA	Saudi Arabia
112	PS	State of Palestine
113	SY	Syrian Arab Republic
114	TN	Tunisia
115	AE	United Arab Emirates
116	YE	Yemen

North America

No.	Code	Country
117	BM	Bermuda
118	CA	Canada
119	US	United States

South Asia

No.	Code	Country
120	BD	Bangladesh
121	BT	Bhutan
122	IN	India
123	MV	Maldives
124	NP	Nepal
125	PK	Pakistan
126	LK	Sri Lanka

Table 7A.1 (continued)

Sub-Saharan Africa

127	BJ	Benin	140	GM	Gambia	154	NG	Nigeria
128	BW	Botswana	141	GH	Ghana	155	RW	Rwanda
129	BF	Burkina Faso	142	GN	Guinea	156	ST	Sao Tome & Principe
130	BI	Burundi	143	GW	Guinea-Bissau	157	SN	Senegal
131	CV	Cabo Verde	144	KE	Kenya	158	SC	Seychelles
132	CM	Cameroon	145	LS	Lesotho	159	SL	Sierra Leone
133	CF	Central African Republic	146	MG	Madagascar	160	ZA	South Africa
134	TD	Chad	147	MW	Malawi	161	SD	Sudan (Former)
135	KM	Comoros	148	ML	Mali	162	SZ	Swaziland
136	CG	Congo	149	MR	Mauritania	163	TG	Togo
137	CI	Côte d'Ivoire	150	MU	Mauritius	164	TZ	Tanzania
138	ET	Ethiopia	151	MZ	Mozambique	165	UG	Uganda
139	GA	Gabon	152	NA	Namibia	166	ZM	Zambia
			153	NE	Niger	167	ZW	Zimbabwe

Note: World Bank list of economies (July 2015), Montserrat not classified by the World Bank. Information on West Bank and Gaza used for Palestine.

Table 7A.2 Income classification of countries

Low income			Lower-middle income					
1	BJ	Benin	24	AM	Armenia	44	MR	Mauritania
2	BF	Burkina Faso	25	BD	Bangladesh	45	MA	Morocco
3	BI	Burundi	26	BT	Bhutan	46	MM	Myanmar
4	KH	Cambodia	27	BO	Bolivia	47	NI	Nicaragua
5	CF	Central African Republic	28	CV	Cabo Verde	48	NG	Nigeria
			29	CM	Cameroon	49	PK	Pakistan
6	TD	Chad	30	CG	Congo	50	PH	Philippines
7	KM	Comoros	31	CI	Côte d'Ivoire	51	MD	Republic of Moldova
8	ET	Ethiopia	32	DJ	Djibouti	52	ST	Sao Tome and Principe
9	GM	Gambia	33	EG	Egypt	53	SN	Senegal
10	GN	Guinea	34	SV	El Salvador	54	LK	Sri Lanka
11	GW	Guinea-Bissau	35	GE	Georgia	55	PS	State of Palestine
12	MG	Madagascar	36	GH	Ghana	56	SD	Sudan (Former)
13	MW	Malawi	37	GT	Guatemala	57	SZ	Swaziland
14	ML	Mali	38	HN	Honduras	58	SY	Syrian Arab Republic
15	MZ	Mozambique	39	IN	India	59	UA	Ukraine
16	NP	Nepal	40	ID	Indonesia	60	VN	Viet Nam
17	NE	Niger	41	KE	Kenya	61	YE	Yemen
18	RW	Rwanda	42	KG	Kyrgyzstan	62	ZM	Zambia
19	SL	Sierra Leone	43	LS	Lesotho			
20	TG	Togo						
21	TZ	Tanzania						
22	UG	Uganda						
23	ZW	Zimbabwe						

Table 7A.2 (continued)

Upper-middle income			High income		
63	AL	Albania	107	AG	Antigua and Barbuda
64	DZ	Algeria	108	AR	Argentina
65	AZ	Azerbaijan	109	AW	Aruba
66	BY	Belarus	110	AU	Australia
67	BZ	Belize	111	AT	Austria
68	BA	Bosnia and Herzegovina	112	BS	Bahamas
69	BW	Botswana	113	BH	Bahrain
70	BR	Brazil	114	BB	Barbados
71	BG	Bulgaria	115	BE	Belgium
72	CN	China	116	BM	Bermuda
73	CO	Colombia	117	BN	Brunei Darussalam
74	CR	Costa Rica	118	CA	Canada
75	DM	Dominica	119	CL	Chile
76	DO	Dominican Republic	120	HK	China, Hong Kong SAR
77	EC	Ecuador	121	MO	China, Macao SAR
78	FJ	Fiji	122	HR	Croatia
79	GA	Gabon	123	CY	Cyprus
80	GD	Grenada	124	CZ	Czech Republic
81	IR	Iran	125	DK	Denmark
82	JM	Jamaica	126	EE	Estonia
83	JO	Jordan	127	FI	Finland
84	KZ	Kazakhstan			
85	LB	Lebanon			
86	MY	Malaysia			
87	MV	Maldives			
88	MU	Mauritius			
89	MX	Mexico			
90	MN	Mongolia			
91	ME	Montenegro			
92	MS	Montserrat			
93	NA	Namibia			
94	PA	Panama			
95	PY	Paraguay			
96	PE	Peru			
97	RO	Romania			
98	LC	Saint Lucia			
99	RS	Serbia			
100	ZA	South Africa			
101	VC	St. Vincent and the Grenadines			
102	SR	Suriname			
103	MK	TFYR of Macedonia			
104	TH	Thailand			
105	TN	Tunisia			
106	TR	Turkey			

High income (ctd.)

128	FR	France	142	NL	Netherlands	156	SI	Slovenia
129	DE	Germany	143	NZ	New Zealand	157	ES	Spain
130	EL	Greece	144	NO	Norway	158	SE	Sweden
131	HU	Hungary	145	OM	Oman	159	CH	Switzerland
132	IS	Iceland	146	PL	Poland	160	TW	Taiwan
133	IE	Ireland	147	PT	Portugal	161	TT	Trinidad and Tobago
134	IL	Israel	148	QA	Qatar	162	TC	Turks and Caicos Islands
135	IT	Italy	149	KR	Republic of Korea			
136	JP	Japan	150	RU	Russian Federation	163	AE	United Arab Emirates
137	KW	Kuwait	151	KN	Saint Kitts and Nevis			
138	LV	Latvia	152	SA	Saudi Arabia	164	UK	United Kingdom
139	LT	Lithuania	153	SC	Seychelles	165	US	United States
140	LU	Luxembourg	154	SG	Singapore	166	UY	Uruguay
141	MT	Malta	155	SK	Slovakia	167	VE	Venezuela

Note: World Bank list of economies (July 2015), Montserrat classified according to information provided by the United Nations. Information on West Bank and Gaza used for Palestine.

PART III

The winner takes it all? Distributional effects of reforms

8. Structural reforms and income distribution: an empirical analysis

Orsetta Causa

Structural reforms are regularly assessed based on their ability to boost gross domestic product (GDP) per capita. This emphasis relies on the assumption that higher GDP per capita is systematically associated with rising living standards for the vast majority of citizens. This view is increasingly being challenged. The worrying evolution of income inequality in many countries suggests that distributional considerations need to be more systematically taken into account in policy-making. In a nutshell, what are the policy options for making pro-growth policies inclusive?

New research by Causa et al. (2016) sheds some light on this question by adopting a more granular approach to the evaluation of pro-growth policies. First, the analysis delivers the effect of reforms on household incomes at the bottom, the middle and the top of the distribution. This helps to better understand the distributional implications from pro-growth reforms. In particular, it allows for distinguishing reforms that boost incomes across the whole distribution, but relatively more among the rich than among the poor, from those that boost incomes in the middle class and among the rich but have no effect upon or depress incomes among the poor. Second, the analysis considers the channels of macroeconomic growth by decomposing the policy effect into growth in employment and growth in labour productivity. This provides a better understanding of the mechanisms through which policies benefit household incomes at different points of the income distribution.

8.1 USING GENERAL MEANS TO UNCOVER THE GRANULARITY OF INCOME DISTRIBUTION

Income distributions are generally characterized using income standards, that is, functions that gauge the distribution by a single income level indicating the general affluence of the distribution or some part of it (Foster and Szekely 2008). The mean and the median are examples of income standards that are widely used as stylized measures of a country's overall level of material conditions. More narrowly, the mean income of some specific part of the population, such as the bottom 40 per cent or 20 per cent, called partial means, are also used, in particular for the measurement of poverty.

The analytical framework outlined in Causa et al. (2015) and Hermansen et al. (2016) aims to uncover the granularity of the income distribution, moving progressively from the bottom to the top, by the use of general means as income standards. Unlike partial means, general means take into account the entire income distribution, but emphasize lower or higher incomes depending on the value taken by a specific parameter, α, often referred to as the order of the general mean. Taking the entire income distribution into account avoids the need to set arbitrary thresholds that give full weight to some parts of the distribution and no weight to the remaining parts, as is the case in poverty measurement for example. General means adopt a more flexible stance by putting different weights on different parts of the income distribution. Such flexibility allows for explicitly considering a continuum of social preferences, depending on, for instance, the differential weight attributed to the living conditions of the poor relative to those of the middle class.

For an income distribution $x = (x_1, \ldots, x_N)$, the general mean of order α, $\mu(x, \alpha)$, is defined as:

$$\mu(x,\alpha) = \left(\frac{1}{N}\sum_{i=1}^{N} x_i^{\alpha}\right)^{\frac{1}{\alpha}} if\ \alpha \neq 0$$

$$= \prod_{i=1}^{N} x_i^{\frac{1}{N}} if\ \alpha = 0$$

A useful property of the general means is their monotonicity with respect to the parameter α, that is, α' > α implies $\mu(x,\alpha') > \mu(x,\alpha)$. General means increase as α rises and decrease as α declines: a lower α gives more emphasis to lower values in an income distribution, while conversely a higher α gives more emphasis to higher values in an income distribution. The arithmetic mean thus becomes a special case (α = 1) of the general mean, which forms a natural benchmark and dividing line between bottom- and top-sensitive general means. Thus, variations in the parameter α allow for computing income levels focusing on any segment of the income distribution, from the bottom to the top. In fact, the more α approaches -∞, the more $\mu(x,\alpha)$ converges towards the lowest income in the distribution. This case echoes the Rawlsian perspective, as the income distribution is summarized by the affluence of its poorest member. Conversely, when α approaches +∞, $\mu(x,\alpha)$ converges towards the income of its richest member.

Using real household income data from the Income Distribution

Database compiled by the Organisation for Economic Co-operation and Development (OECD), Figure 8.1 displays general means curves for market income and disposable income for selected countries. Each panel presents the value of general means associated with a continuum of α. For example, for both market and disposable income, all bottom-sensitive general means ($\alpha < 1$) are similar in Germany and the United States, whereas all top-sensitive general means ($\alpha > 1$) are higher in the United States. As a result, the difference in inequality (as well as in average income) between Germany and the United States comes almost entirely from differences in the upper part of the distribution. Thus, general means make it possible to assess the 'location' of inequality, that is, to identify the portions of the income distribution that drive inequality.

General means also allow shedding light on the impact of redistribution through taxes and transfers. This can be achieved by comparing market and disposable income-based general means. For instance, in Denmark, Germany and the United States, redistribution reduces disposable income compared to market income in the upper part of the distribution, while increasing it in the lower part. By contrast, in Chile, the Czech Republic and Spain, taxes and transfers tend to leave disposable income compared to market income virtually unchanged in the lower half of the distribution while slightly reducing it in the upper half.

Finally, the granular general means-based approach can be used to analyse income developments at any point of the distribution. Growth in the general mean of order α, $g(x_{t+1}, x_t, \alpha)$, is given by:

$$g(x_{t+1}, x_t, \alpha) = \frac{\mu(x_{t+1}, \alpha) - \mu(x_t, \alpha)}{\mu(x_t, \alpha)}$$

Figure 8.2 shows general means-based growth curves on the basis of real household market and disposable income data for selected OECD countries over the period covered by the analysis. The vertical axis represents $g(x_{t+1}, x_t, \alpha)$ and the horizontal axis the values of α. When $\alpha = 1$, the curve's height measures growth in average income. For $\alpha > 1$, faster growth in the general mean than in average income points to an increase in inequality. Conversely, for $\alpha < 1$, faster growth in the general mean than in average income points to a decrease in inequality. More generally, an S-profile indicates an increase in inequality (for example, Italy, the United States and France) and an inverted S-profile a decrease (for example, Czech Republic, Turkey and Poland). The relative flatness of the curve provides a qualitative assessment of the magnitude of associated changes in inequality along with their underlying sources. For instance, not only did inequality in disposable income increase more strongly in Italy than in Canada, but it

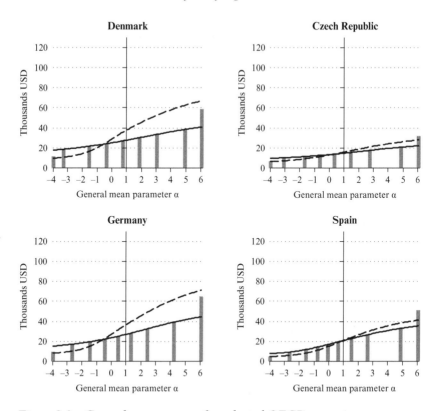

Figure 8.1   General means curves for selected OECD countries

happens that the poor in Italy lost ground even in absolute terms, while in Canada all incomes have grown, albeit in an unequal way.

As an extension, general means growth curves allow assessment of the impact of taxes and transfers on income distribution developments. For instance, in Canada, Denmark and Finland, the rise in market income inequality has been almost completely offset by redistribution: growth in real disposable income has been very similar across the distribution, while that of real market income has been stronger in the upper compared to the lower half of the income distribution. Finally, this granular approach allows the uncovering of the very specific and differentiated impact of redistribution on specific income groups. Such is the case in the United Kingdom, where mean disposable income of the middle class grew faster than mean market income, while such incomes grew at the same rate at the low and the high end of the distribution. This indicates that redistribution has tended

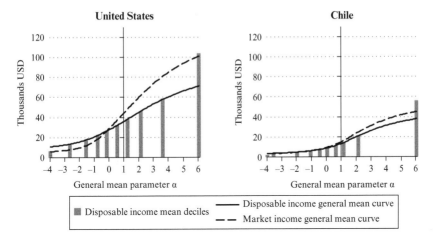

Notes: Household incomes across the distribution are measured by the full range of income standards, that is, from top- to bottom-sensitive income standards (see text for details). Disposable incomes cover the full population, while market incomes are restricted to the working-age population (age 18–65). Data refer to 2011 for Denmark, Germany and Chile; 2012 for the Czech Republic, Spain and United States.
Household incomes are expressed in US dollars, constant prices and constant purchasing power parities (PPPs; OECD base year 2010) with PPPs for the private consumption of households. Grey bars represent the mean income for each decile as reported in the OECD Income Distribution Database.

Sources: Organisation for Economic Co-operation and Development (OECD) Income Distribution Database; Hermansen et al. (2016).

to benefit the middle class. General means growth curves can thus provide a nuanced and extensive analysis of income distribution developments.

To summarize, using general means as income standards delivers, within a single analytical framework, a comprehensive assessment of countries' income distributions. General means can also be used in a straightforward way to build synthetic measures of inequality of a general form, that is, Atkinson inequality measures (Atkinson 1970). This analytical framework can thus be used to track changes in income levels for different income groups as well as to see whether the resulting changes in inequality have been widespread or concentrated in narrower segments of the distribution. It is thus particularly well suited for policy analysis and for tracking the incidence of growth on inequality: the possibility to diagnose, on the basis of a simple measure, whether inequality increases occurred across the whole distribution of income or within a narrower part of the distribution allows a finer understanding of distributional developments; and, as a result, better fine-tuning and design of appropriate policy responses.

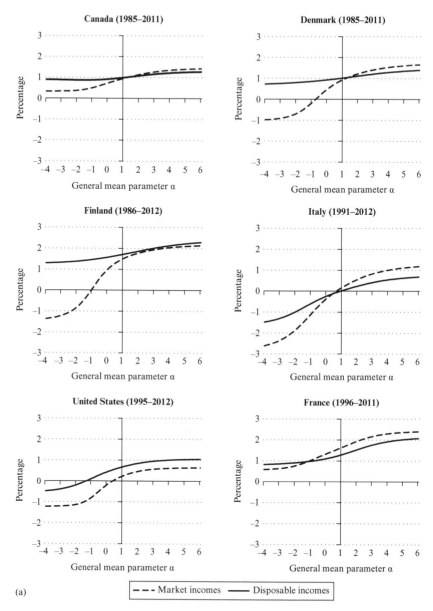

(a)

Notes: Household incomes across the distribution are measured by the full range of income standards, that is, from top- to bottom-sensitive income standards (see text for details). The data show average annual growth rates and refer to the period between the first and the last observations included in the analysis. Disposable incomes cover the full population, while market incomes are restricted to the working-age population (age 18–65).

Income data are expressed in US dollars, constant prices and constant purchasing power parities (PPPs; OECD base year 2010) with PPPs for the private consumption of households.

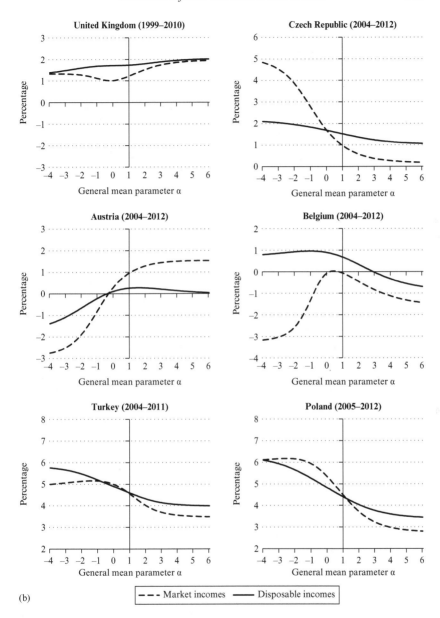

(b)

Sources: Organisation for Economic Co-operation and Development (OECD) Income Distribution Database; Hermansen et al. (2016).

Figure 8.2   General means-based growth curves for selected OECD countries

8.2 THE DISTRIBUTIONAL EFFECTS OF GROWTH AND ITS SOURCES: BASELINE ESTIMATES

As a baseline step, the analysis starts by revisiting the link between growth and household incomes across the distribution (Box 8.1). This sets the stage for the analysis of the link between growth-enhancing reforms and household incomes across the distribution; that is, the distributional effects of growth-enhancing reforms. Growth is likely to have differential effects on different income groups, and this is captured through the general means approach.

The sample covers OECD countries for the period going from the mid-1980s to around 2012, but with varying time coverage across countries.[1] The main findings can be summarized as follows. First, there is no evidence that GDP growth triggered the rise in inequality, once controlling for other factors. On average across OECD countries, GDP growth has lifted household disposable incomes across the distribution. This assessment derives from visualizing the GDP growth incidence curve (Figure 8.3, Panel A). This curve is broadly flat at the unitary GDP per capita elasticity of household disposable income. However, associated cross-country estimates inevitably encompass cross-country differences in the distributional incidence of growth. Even from a purely descriptive perspective, OECD countries experienced heterogeneous developments in this respect (Hermansen et al. 2016).

Second, the finding that GDP growth has benefited household disposable incomes at large results from the differential effects of the sources of growth, namely labour productivity and labour utilization, on income distribution. Labour productivity growth has benefited relatively more rich households and households in the upper middle class (corresponding to values of α roughly above 1), while associated growth dividends were somewhat lower among poor households (for example, $\alpha = -4$) (Figure 8.3, Panel B). This implies that productivity growth has been slightly disequalizing.

Labour utilization growth has disproportionally benefited poor households and households in the middle class (corresponding to values of α roughly around 0), while associated growth dividends were insignificant for rich households (for example, $\alpha > 4$) (Figure 8.3, Panel C). This implies that labour utilization has allowed lifting the material conditions of the poor people and that it has been equalizing.

The conclusion from this baseline analysis is that the composition of growth is a key determinant of its incidence across the distribution. Insofar as growth is ultimately driven by productivity, and insofar as this is associated with rising income inequality, ensuring that growth is associated with strong job creation is crucial to make it more inclusive. These baseline findings are combined into a macro–micro approach to deliver a complete distributional assessment of labour productivity and labour utilization-enhancing reforms.

BOX 8.1   BASELINE SPECIFICATION OF THE DISTRIBUTIONAL INCIDENCE OF GROWTH AND ITS SUBCOMPONENTS[a]

The fundamental determinants of GDP, that is, human and physical capital, labour-augmenting efficiency and population growth, are well established in growth theory and the production function framework, but there exists no such framework in the case of household incomes with an explicit consideration of its distribution. In the absence of a theoretical foundation, a natural starting point is to assume that in the long run the level of household income at each point of the distribution is mainly driven by the level of GDP per capita, which transmits to households with a lag (see Causa et al. 2015):

$$\Delta \ln\mu_\alpha(x_{it}) = \beta_{0,\alpha} - \beta_{1,\alpha}\ln\mu_\alpha(x_{it-1}) + \beta_{2,\alpha}\Delta \ln GDP_{it} + \beta_{3,\alpha}\ln GDP_{it-1} + \beta_{4,\alpha}NX_{it} + \gamma_t + \eta_i + \varepsilon_{it}$$

where periods t and $t-1$ correspond to observations two years apart, $\Delta \ln\mu_\alpha(x_{it})$ is the growth in household income across the distribution (the order of the general mean α allows for uncovering different portions of the distribution, from bottom to top), $\Delta \ln GDP_{it}$ is the growth in GDP per capita, NX_{it} is the ratio of net exports to GDP included to control for persistent gaps between household incomes and domestic output,[b] γ_t denotes time controls (a linear time trend), and η_i denotes country fixed effects. Due to the presence of the lagged dependent variable to account for convergence, the specification is estimated as a system using the generalized method of moments (system GMM).[c] This allows derivation of a consistent estimate of the long-run elasticity of household incomes with respect to GDP per capita, given by $\varepsilon_{\mu\alpha,GDP} = \beta_{3,\alpha}/\beta_{1,\alpha}$.

The impact of GDP is subsequently decomposed along its two main subcomponents, labour productivity (*LP*) and labour utilization (*LU*), expanding the previous specification as follows:

$$\Delta \ln\mu_\alpha(x_{it}) = \theta_{0,\alpha} - \theta_{1,\alpha}\ln\mu_\alpha(x_{it-1}) + \theta_{2,\alpha}\Delta \ln LP_{it} + \theta_{3,\alpha}\ln LP_{it-1} + \theta_{4,\alpha}\Delta \ln LU_{it} + \theta_{5,\alpha}\ln LU_{it-1} + \theta_{6,\alpha}NX_{it} + \gamma_t + \eta_i + \varepsilon_{it}$$

Labour productivity and labour utilization are (as GDP) treated as endogenous variables and the equation is also estimated through system GMM. This allows derivation of consistent estimates of the long-run elasticity of household incomes across the distribution with respect to labour productivity, $\varepsilon_{\mu\alpha,LU} = \theta_{3,\alpha}/\theta_{1,\alpha}$. and with respect to labour utilization, $\varepsilon_{\mu\alpha,LU} = \theta_{5,\alpha}/\theta_{1,\alpha}$.

Notes:

a   See Hermansen et al. (2016) for a full presentation of the baseline specification and econometric approach.

b   The underlying rationale is that mean household income elasticity to domestic production is more likely to deviate from 1 in more open economies under persistent external imbalances whereby households tend to consume more (deficit) or less (surplus) than their income. In addition, previous work has shown that the difference between growth in real GDP and in real mean household income is, to a large extent, driven by differences in growth of output relative to consumer prices (Causa et al. 2015). In turn, the evidence would suggest that this is, to a good extent, driven by terms-of-trade effects. Results in this chapter are qualitatively unchanged if the openness variable is replaced by the current account, the terms-of-trade, or the price of consumption relative to output.

c   See Blundell and Bond (1998).

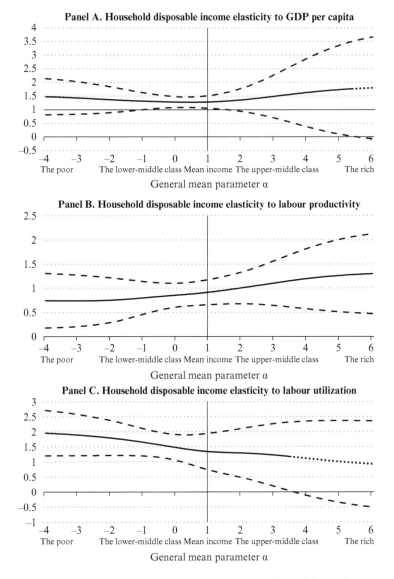

Panel A. Household disposable income elasticity to GDP per capita

Panel B. Household disposable income elasticity to labour productivity

Panel C. Household disposable income elasticity to labour utilization

Notes: Elasticities estimated by system GMM. See Hermansen et al. (2016) for details.
Dashed lines represent the 90% confidence interval bands.

Source: Hermansen et al. (2016).

*Figure 8.3   The distributional effects of growth and its sources: baseline
                    estimates*

8.3   THE DISTRIBUTIONAL EFFECTS OF STRUCTURAL REFORMS: A COMBINED MACRO–MICRO APPROACH

The assessment of the effects of growth-enhancing reforms on income inequality is based on a combined macro–micro approach which encompasses growth and household incomes across the distribution (see Box 8.2). In this vein, the total effect of a given policy reform on household incomes can be decomposed and interpreted as follows (Figure 8.4).

Macro effects are reform-driven changes in labour productivity and/or labour utilization which benefit household incomes across the distribution. This encompasses distribution-neutral effects calibrated on the basis of recent empirical analysis of the effects of structural reforms on growth and its components – that is, from Gal and Theising (2015) and from Égert (2017) – with distribution-sensitive effects derived from the policy-augmented baseline estimation, that is, reform-driven changes in labour productivity and labour utilization. See Causa et al. (2016) for details about the way external estimates obtained in the above-cited papers are combined with internal estimates obtained in this chapter with a view to ensuring econometric consistency.

Micro effects are reform-driven changes in household incomes which are not channelled through macroeconomic effects but add to reform-driven growth effects. The micro effects are based on new estimates of the effects of structural reforms on household incomes across the distribution. These estimates build on the baseline estimation framework. As a result, these micro reform effects on household incomes are conditional on growth effects. By contrast, they do not control for potential confounding effects from other reforms as well as for interaction effects with other reforms, because the approach retained in this chapter only allows policies to be considered in isolation (that is, one at a time). This limitation should be kept in mind when interpreting the results, the risk being that estimated effects of a given policy change result from some simultaneous change in another policy area rather than the direct effect of the policy per se. However, the treatment of endogeneity in the estimation aims at lowering the effects of such confounding factors.

8.4   THE DISTRIBUTIONAL EFFECTS OF STRUCTURAL REFORMS: MAIN FINDINGS

The main findings on the effects of pro-growth reforms on the distribution on household disposable income can be summarized as follows, on the

BOX 8.2   ASSESSING THE IMPACT OF STRUCTURAL
REFORMS ON INCOME DISTRIBUTION: A
COMBINED MACRO–MICRO FRAMEWORK

The baseline model presented above can be augmented and combined with results on the quantification of the macroeconomic effects of structural reforms to deliver a complete assessment of the impact of structural reforms on household incomes across the distribution.

First, augmenting this baseline model with structural policy indicators (Z) allows identification of the micro effects of growth-enhancing policy reforms on the long-term level of household incomes across the distribution,[a] conditional on and beyond their impact channelled through growth and its subcomponents, that is, the macro effects:

$$\Delta\ln\mu_\alpha(x_{it}) = \theta_{0,\alpha} - \theta_{1,\alpha}\ln\mu_\alpha(x_{it-1}) + \theta_{2,\alpha}\Delta\ln LP_{it} + \theta_{3,\alpha}\ln LP_{it-1} + \theta_{4,\alpha}\Delta\ln LU_{it} +$$
$$\theta_{5,\alpha}\ln LU_{it-1} + \theta_{6,\alpha}NX_{it} + \theta_{7,\alpha}Z_{it-1} + \gamma_t + \eta_i + \varepsilon_{it} \qquad (8.1)$$

Second, growth-enhancing policy reforms are deemed to deliver growth effects, that is, changes in labour productivity (LP) and labour utilization (LU). Such changes in labour productivity and labour utilization benefit differentially household incomes across the distribution; that is, growth effects also encompass distributional effects, as demonstrated in the baseline model. As a result, reform-driven macroeconomic effects generate macro effects on the long-term level of household incomes across the distribution. Such macro effects, available in the literature and in particular from ongoing work conducted by the OECD (Gal and Theising 2015; Égert 2017), can be combined in a fully fledged macro–micro approach.

The combination of all these effects can be written as follows:

$$E_{\mu\alpha z} = \pi_{LP\alpha z}\cdot\varepsilon_{LPz} + \pi_{LU\alpha z}\cdot\varepsilon_{LUz} + D_{\mu\alpha z} \qquad (8.2)$$

where $E\mu\alpha_z$ denotes the long-run elasticity of household income in a given income group (governed by α) with respect to a change in the policy variable Z. This corresponds to the total reform effect and combines mutually exclusive macro and micro effects:

- The first term captures the macro effect channelled through labour productivity. This is in turn the product of two effects: (1) the distribution-sensitive return to household income from labour productivity growth ($\pi_{LP}\alpha_z$), which is conditional on policies Z; and (2) distribution-neutral macroeconomic growth effects of a policy reform on labour productivity (ε_{LPz}).
- The second term captures the macro effect channelled through labour utilization, analogous to labour productivity.
- The third term ($D\mu\alpha_z$) captures micro distributional reform effects, that is, distribution-sensitive changes in household income that are not driven by changes in labour productivity and labour utilization. Those are estimated directly from (8.1) using system GMM estimation techniques, and assuming policy variables are strictly exogenous.

Reform-driven macroeconomic effects ($\varepsilon_{LP,z}$ and $\varepsilon_{LU,z}$) have been estimated in the context of a recent updated assessment of the quantitative impact of policies and institutions on labour utilization and productivity (Gal and Theising 2015; Égert 2017). Distributional effects are estimated on the basis of the policy-augmented version of the baseline model (equation 8.1). These layers of empirical work are combined in a single framework in order to deliver a comprehensive assessment of the impact of structural policies on growth and the income distribution

Note:

[a] Due to the limited degrees of freedom in the income distribution data used (for instance, short time horizon, break in the series, and so on), using system GMM for the micro effects precludes the estimation of multivariate reform scenarios (as well as the introduction of non-linear effects or interactions between policies). However, the lack of control for potential confounding factors is deemed to be attenuated by an appropriate treatment of endogeneity allowed by SYS-GMM.

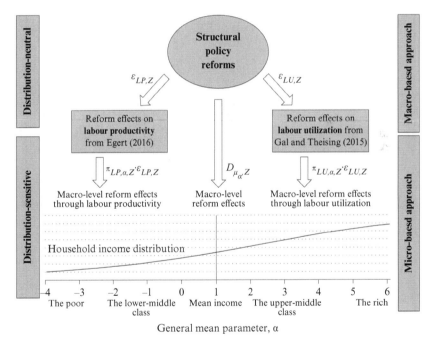

Source: Causa et al. (2016).

Figure 8.4 A combined macro–micro framework

basis of OECD cross-country evidence since the mid-1980s (Causa et al. 2016).[2] Most pro-growth reforms have little impact on income inequality when the latter is assessed through measures that emphasize the middle class. By contrast, a higher number of pro-growth reforms have an impact on income inequality and thus may raise trade-offs and synergies between growth and equity objectives when inequality is assessed through measures that emphasize the poor. This corresponds to higher degrees of inequality aversion.

Social protection and labour market reforms are the sources of most of the trade-offs between growth and equity objectives. In particular, reductions in the generosity of unemployment benefits and social assistance are found to leave poor households behind even when such reforms generate aggregate employment gains (Figure 8.5). Raising employment while making it more inclusive requires well-targeted active labour market policies (ALMPs) with a view to enhancing employability among the low-skilled, the long-term unemployed and discouraged jobseekers.

Increasing public spending on education, in particular on childcare and

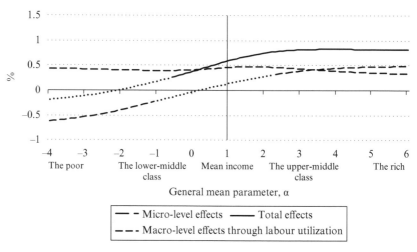

Notes: A reduction in unemployment benefit (UB) average gross replacement rates by 1 percentage point is estimated to increase household disposable income by 0.3–0.8 per cent from the lower-middle class to the most affluent households. This total effect can be decomposed along a micro-level effect and macro-level effect through labour utilization. See Box 8.2 for details of the empirical approach and the definition of the effects. Non-significant estimates (at the 10 per cent level) are indicated by dots on general mean curves.

Source: Causa et al. (2016).

Figure 8.5   *Effects of a reduction in unemployment benefit average across replacement rates on household disposable incomes*

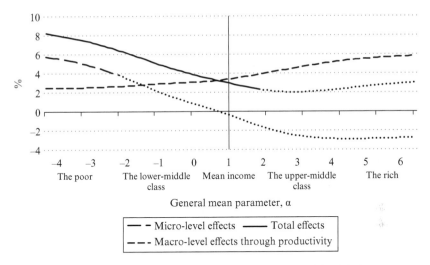

Notes: An increase in government spending on education (in per cent of GDP) by 1 percentage point is estimated to increase household disposable incomes by 2–8 per cent on average from the poor to the middle class. This total effect can be decomposed along a micro-level effect and macro-level effect through labour productivity. See Box 8.2 for details of the empirical approach and the definition of the effects.
Non-significant estimates (at the 10 per cent level) are indicated by dots on general mean curves.

Source: Causa et al. (2016).

Figure 8.6 *Effects of an increase in government spending on household disposable incomes*

early childhood education, boosts growth and at the same time reduces income inequality, for instance by enhancing the labour market inclusion of women (Figure 8.6).

Spurring productivity by easing barriers to firm entry and competition in product markets produces strong macroeconomic gains without raising trade-offs between efficiency and equity objectives, since the associated income gains are fairly equally shared across households (Figure 8.7). This reflects two distributionally offsetting effects: higher labour productivity, which tends to benefit the most affluent households disproportionately; and higher employment, which tends to benefit the less affluent households disproportionately.

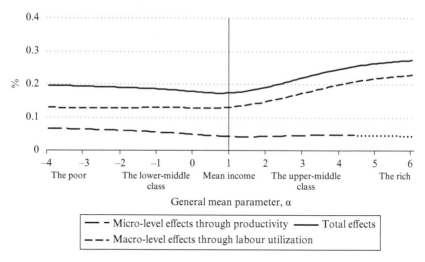

Figure 8.7   Effects of a reduction in regulation in network industries on household disposable incomes

Notes: A reduction in regulation in network industries (ETCR aggregate, index 0–6) by 1 per cent is estimated to increase household disposable incomes by around 0.2 per cent on average across the distribution. This total effect can be decomposed along macro-level effects through labour productivity and labour utilization. The micro-level effect is insignificant for all income groups and thus not reported and not included in the total effect. See Box 8.2 for details of the empirical approach and the definition of the effects.
Non-significant estimates (at the 10 per cent level) are indicated by dots on general mean curves.
ETCR = regulation in energy, transport and communications.

Source: Causa et al. (2016).

8.5   CONCLUSION

Making reforms for inclusive growth is about exploiting synergies, and designing policy packages to mitigate trade-offs. It is thus all about details. At the current juncture there is a crucial need for more growth, but also to make it more inclusive. This is not out of reach, as countries exhibit great scope for packaging structural reforms to target both growth and equity objectives.

NOTES

1.   See Hermansen et al. (2016) for details on the data coverage.

2. Based on Atkinson inequality measures with varying levels of inequality aversion, see Causa et al (2016).

REFERENCES

Atkinson, A.B. (1970), 'On the measurement of inequality', *Journal of Economic Theory*, **2** (3), 244–63.

Blundell, R.W. and S.R. Bond (1998), 'Initial conditions and moment restrictions in dynamic panel data models', *Journal of Econometrics*, **87** (1), 115–43.

Causa, O., M. Hermansen and N. Ruiz (2016), 'The distributional impact of structural reforms', OECD Economics Department Working Paper No. 1342, Paris: OECD Publishing, http://dx.doi.org/10.1787/5jln041nkpwc-en.

Causa, O., A. de Serres and N. Ruiz (2015), 'Can pro-growth policies lift all boats? An analysis based on household disposable income', *OECD Journal: Economic Studies*, **2015** (1), 227–68. http://dx.doi.org/10.1787/eco_studies-2015-5jrqhbb1t5jb.

Égert, B. (2017), 'Regulation, institutions and productivity: new macroeconomic evidence from OECD countries', OECD Economics Department Working Paper No. 1393, Paris: OECD Publishing, http://dx.doi.org/10.1787/579ceba4-en.

Foster, J.E. and M. Szekely (2008), 'Is economic growth good for the poor? Tracking low incomes using general means', *International Economic Review*, **49** (4), 1143–72.

Gal, P. and A. Theising (2015), 'The macroeconomic impact of structural policies on labour market outcomes in OECD countries: a reassessment', OECD Economics Department Working Paper No. 1271, Paris: OECD Publishing, http://dx.doi.org/10.1787/5jrqc6t8ktjf-en.

Hermansen, M., N. Ruiz and O. Causa (2016), 'The distribution of the growth dividends', OECD Economics Department Working Paper No. 1343, Paris: OECD Publishing, http://dx.doi.org/10.1787/7c8c6cc1-en.

9. Labour market hierarchies and the unemployment–wage nexus in CESEE and in the EU

Paul Ramskogler

Economics is a contested field; a 'dismal science' as it is sometimes called. Nonetheless, a certain number of – more or less undisputed – key assumptions tend to prevail over longer horizons; this is the closest economics ever gets to having axioms. Whenever one of these key propositions is contested, the field is shaken with irritation.

One of these key propositions is the assumption that there is a – more or less stable – relationship between the rate of unemployment, wage growth and thus ultimately the inflation rate. This relationship is commonly called the Phillips curve, which has come to form one of the key building blocks of economics, being not only a cornerstone of forecasting procedures but also one of the key instruments in the intellectual tool kit of policy-makers, most notably central bankers. The idea is simple and straightforward. If inflation (expectation) is too low, monetary policy becomes more expansionary in order to stimulate growth. This will reduce the unemployment rate and push up wage growth and thereby inflation. If inflation is too high, the process is reversed. This inverse relation between the unemployment rate and inflation is represented by the Phillips curve. If this relation breaks down, central bankers risk missing the mark.

However, it is exactly the Phillips curve relationship that has now increasingly been called into question. This is quite a significant development. The last instance when the Phillips curve came under scrutiny – the stagflationary period of the late 1970s – yielded a fundamental overhaul of the mainstream of economics and heralded the demise of old-style Keynesianism and its replacement by the monetarist revolution. To be sure, the Phillips curve concept – obviously – did not perish in those days. To the contrary, it reappeared in a new guise, but having experienced some key adaptions that were to fundamentally change the way policies would be conducted henceforth. In particular, this led to the introduction of the expectations-augmented Phillips curve, whose most notable feature was that the Phillips curve relation was thought to be only valid in the short run but not in the long run (where it was considered to be 'vertical'). This might sound like sophistry, but the implications are huge. The most important corollary is that the Phillips curve 'cannot be exploited'; that is, it is not possible to accept a higher level of equilibrium inflation simply to permanently lower the unemployment rate, as the latter is determined structurally outside the realm of the nominal sphere. It will thus be most efficient simply to maintain a stable inflation rate – eventually in the form of an inflation target – in the way described above. This adaption of the Phillips curve became the crucial hinge in modelling and hypothesizing the link between real and nominal developments. It thus became a centrepiece of the New Keynesian model, which has come to be the most prominent macroeconomic model class. In the three-equation exposition of the New Keynesian model, the Phillips curve is one of the three equations on which the model is built, and it continues to dominate monetary policy discussions worldwide. However, the viability of the revival of the short-run Phillips curve has come to be somewhat doubtful.

More and more policy institutions have begun to modify this traditional relationship (OECD 2014, 2017; ECB 2017; IMF 2017). In particular, it appears as if the Phillips curve has flattened substantially since the global financial crisis, implying that the impact of the unemployment rate on inflation has declined considerably. If this is the case, any given increase in inflation will require a substantially stronger reduction of the unemployment rate than before. In this chapter, I analyse this question with a particular focus on the Central, Eastern and South-Eastern Europe (CESEE) region. Concretely, I argue that the Phillips curve, of course, still exists but that it has to be understood in close relation with the structure of the respective labour market. My key result is that labour market dualities matter, and that the more people are located in subordinate segments of the labour market, the flatter the Phillips curve will be.

9.1   THE EVOLVING RELATIONSHIP BETWEEN UNEMPLOYMENT AND WAGE GROWTH

To be sure, a ripe discussion that tries to pin down reasons for the flattening of the Phillips curve is ongoing. The European Central Bank (ECB) (2017) for instance has demonstrated that a broader approach to the measurement of the unemployment rate – including, for instance, variables such as underemployed workers – can somewhat increase the correlation between unemployment and wage growth. Further, the Organisation for Economic Co-operation and Development (OECD)

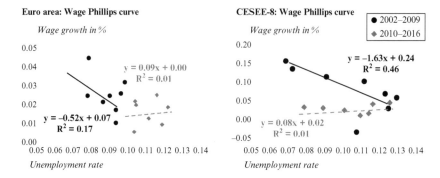

Notes: y = −0.5x +0.1 gives the increase for wages triggered by any given reduction of the unemployment rate; R^2 = the 'goodness of fit' meaning the suitability of any given explanatory variable to forecast the development of the explained variable; thus a value of e.g. y = −0.5x + 0.1 with a R^2 of 0.17 implies that a decrease in the unemployment rate of 1 per cent will lead to an increase of wages of 0.5 per cent which will explain 17 per cent of the overall development of wages (while the rest is determined by other, unobserved, variables). CESEE-8 = the Czech Republic, Estonia, Hungary, Latvia, Lithuania, Poland, Slovakia and Slovenia.

Source: Eurostat.

Figure 9.1   The wage Phillips curve in the euro area and in CESEE-8

(2014, 2017) has underlined the possibility that the relation between the unemployment rate and wage growth might differ in periods of recessions and booms. Finally, the International Monetary Fund (IMF) (2017) has found that there is some impact of involuntary part-time employment on the growth of wages per employee. All of these institutions, however, produced econometric proof that the Phillips curve has indeed flattened since the crisis that started to emerge in 2008; that is, they found evidence hinting at a decline of the relationship between wage growth and the unemployment rate.

Let me nonetheless illustrate this finding. Figure 9.1 shows a very simple representation of the Phillips curve using cross-country averages both for the European Union (EU) as well as for CESEE. In Figure 9.1 – as in the rest of the chapter – I use 2010 (Q3 2010 when working with quarterly data) as the starting date of the crisis. The reason for this decision is that 2010 is the year the crisis turned into a true European crisis, which can be motivated by the fact that the yields on government benchmark bonds skyrocketed in that year (and in that quarter). This is just to give a first impression; I will check the finding more rigorously below, yet it helps me to make a point.

The straight black lines in the figure capture the situation as it was before the crisis. It is evident that as you move from right to left – that is, as the unemployment rate declines – you experience an increase in wage growth. This is true for both the EU at large but particularly so for CESEE-8 (that is, the Czech Republic, Estonia, Hungary, Latvia, Lithuania, Poland, Slovakia and Slovenia). However, if you look at the dashed grey line this correlation appears to have disappeared after the crisis.

Of course averaging, particularly in this case, often has the tendency to exaggerate things, but the basic point is clear. If the situation captured in Figure 9.1 is to be permanent, conventional approaches to policy-making will be in trouble. It is thus crucial to find out what is driving this development and whether there are alternative ways to overcome it. To make the link to the title of this book explicit, what areas can be targeted by structural reforms in order to alleviate the job of monetary policy-makers and restore the short-run validity of the Phillips curve?

9.2   THE DETERMINANTS OF WAGE GROWTH

In order to be able to answer this question I need to discuss the theoretical determinants of wages and wage growth more broadly. Wage developments – including, particularly, relative wages – have been singled out as one of the most important aspects of European stability (Hancké 2013). But what determines this crucial variable?

It will hardly come as a surprise to a professional observer of economics that there is not one single answer to this question. This, of course, is not the case because of a lack of explanations; it is rather because of their abundance. However, this does not need to be a drawback. Some recipes simply need many ingredients to reach their full flavour. Let me briefly discuss the most important approaches. Subsequently, I will try to find a synthetic estimation approach.

The Big Picture: The Phillips Curve

I have already talked at length about the arguably most prominent theory in connection with wage-setting: the Phillips curve. It started back in the 1960s as the mere observation of an empirical relationship (Phillips 1958) and, as already indicated, it has become one of the key building blocks of standard macroeconomic models.

The basic idea is that there is a negative relationship between wages and some measure of labour market slack, such as the unemployment rate. Hereby, the unemployment rate is considered to serve as some kind of proxy for the bargaining power of employees. As the unemployment rate increases, the bargaining power of employees declines and the upward pressure on wages is mitigated, which in the macroeconomic aggregate yields the negative relationship between unemployment and wage growth that has already been discussed. However, what is the reason for this effect?

From a microeconomic point of view, the unemployment rate can be interpreted as a proxy for the likelihood of an employer to quickly find a substitute for an employee in the case that any given employee is not happy with their wage and quits in order to take up another job. The unemployment rate, thus, captures competition within the labour force; in this case it captures competition between employees and the unemployed. At the bottom line, the Phillips curve thus conceptionalizes wage growth as a function of the unemployment rate. The unemployment rate, therefore, will be the first ingredient of our wage-setting function.

Stuck in the Middle: Bargaining Theories and the Wage-Setting Curve

While the Phillips curve captures a theory of wage growth, another line of theories is mainly concerned with the determination of the level of wages, putting a strong emphasis on the bargaining situation. These theories belong to a group of models that try to explain different market failures, such as non-clearing wage levels on labour markets. The common thread that runs through these models is the assumption of asymmetric information or fixed costs.

For instance, insider–outsider models (see, e.g., Lindbeck and Snower 1986, 2002) are theories in which hiring and firing is costly. This gives rise to rents that can be shared between employers and employees, which can be captured via the level of the reservation wage, which in turn is likely to be co-determined by productivity (Blanchard and Katz 1999).

At the same time, efficiency wage theories (see, e.g., Akerlof and Yellen 1990) assume that employers cannot fully supervise employees, making it possible for employees to shirk. The degree of shirking then again is a function of productivity. Whatever the exact hinge might be, the important takeaway here is that bargaining theories will model wage levels as a function of productivity in one or the other form. Taking differences – that is, looking at the change in productivity – then can help to explain wage growth. Productivity growth is thus the second ingredient of our wage equation.

Becoming Granular: Human Capital Theory

Further, productivity is the link to the next large group of theories that are usually summarized by the term 'human capital theory'. Many economists are not mainly interested in aggregate wage developments, but in the determination of and in the difference between the wages of individuals (Beblo et al. 2003). That is, they seek to investigate wage formation at the individual level and then investigate reasons for differences in the outcomes. This, for instance, can be used to quantify the degree of discrimination. One of the most important of these approaches – the so-called Oxaca–Blinder decomposition (Blinder 1973; Oxaca 1973) – models wages as a function of individual endowments. However, endowments are only used as a proxy for unobservable productivity at the individual level. Yet at the aggregate level – which is of major interest here – productivity is observable. As a result, the human capital concept can be considered to be the microeconomic sibling of bargaining theories, as productivity again figures prominently in the explanation of wages. Human capital theory is thus already covered in our equation.

Realizing Structure: Dual Labour Market Theory

To some extent this holds true for dual labour market theory as well. It began as a derivation of human capital theories in the late 1970s and early 1980s and was mainly focused on the explanation of wage differences in the form of discrimination due to race or gender (Reich et al. 1973; Harrisson and Sum 1979). However, in the 1990s the theory experienced a macroeconomic relaunch in policy reports capturing a more general feature of contemporary labour markets. In a nutshell, the basic idea of the approach is that there are two different segments of the labour market (see, e.g., Dickens and Lang 1985): there is a primary segment and a secondary segment, with employees in the secondary segment typically suffering from a wage penalty, which can be corroborated by empirical evidence (Hirsch 2016). Consequently, employees only work in the secondary segment because the primary segment of the labour market is rationed, which of course implies that they would be willing to quit their current jobs in order to accept a job offer in the primary sector.

However, this is – I would like to stress – a point at which we are back to the beginning of our digression on wage determinants. To be more explicit, recall that in the conceptualization of the Phillips curve there is a negative relationship between wage growth and the unemployment rate that is caused by competition within the labour force. Dual labour market theory now states that employees in the secondary segment of the market are potential competitors for employees in the primary segment. So if it is competition by the unemployed that has a negative effect on wages according to the Phillips curve theory, isn't it likely that competition of secondary employees has a similar effect on the wages of primary employees?

Let me illustrate the hypothesized effect using a football analogy. In football, a team usually consists of 11 key players who are the standard starting formation. There might be injuries and tactical changes, so the set of players that have regular and significant playing time might be somewhat higher, say 15, but those 15 players are the core of the team. Every now and then, contracts with individual players have to be renegotiated. Now imagine that you are a team manager. One of your key players asks for a settlement that you consider to be excessive. What are your options? Of course, the simplest option available is to settle the contract at a higher rate and move on. However, other players might mimic that behaviour, and before long you will likely have to go hat-in-hand to your financiers, who will probably arrive at the conclusion that you are not the best manager for the team after all.

So what are the alternatives? The second option, of course, is not to accept the higher wage claim and to replace the player with someone who you find on the job market. This, however, is costly. You will have to pay scouts, agent's fees and so on, and at the end of the day there is no guarantee that the player will be efficient in their new environment. They might not get along with their new teammates, their coach or the tactics of your team. There is a huge variety of possible outcomes and you encounter a significant increase in uncertainty.

However, there is a further alternative. You might send someone in from the substitute bench or pull up a player from the second or the youth team. These players are comparably cheap, will be docile and motivated as they are happy to get a chance, and what is more, there is no asymmetric information: you already know them. There is even a further benefit of that option. The existence of the mere possibility to do so, in itself, might be sufficient to keep the claims of your key players at bay. You simply need a sufficiently large set of potential substitutes, and without further ado, your key players will know that they are not irreplaceable, which will likely keep their claims in check. This is exactly the effect I am going to test below with regard to labour market dualities. The last ingredient for our wage-setting function thus will be a variable that proxies labour dualities.

9.3   THE MACROECONOMIC IMPACT OF DUALITIES: IN EUROPE AND CESEE

The Role of Labour Market Dualities

The scope of the determinants for wages is thus obviously wide. Consequently, there are quite a few potential candidates that might help to understand the flattening of the Phillips curve, amongst which the unemployment rate and productivity figure most prominently. Fortunately, these factors are not mutually exclusive, as has been shown neatly by Blanchard and Katz (1999) who demonstrated that the Phillips curve, bargaining and human capital theories can be captured with one estimable equation:

$$\Delta w_t = a + \beta_1 \Delta p_{t-1} + \beta_2 \Delta y_{t-1} + \beta_3 WS_{t-1} + \beta_3 u_{t-1}$$

where w are hourly wages. Given that usually the bargain is about real values, changes in prices p – that is, inflation – co-determine wages. Further, y is productivity and u is the unemployment rate, whereas t is an index capturing time and Δ indicates annual growth rates. WS is the wage share and it enters the equation as the 'leftover' of some algebraic manipulation that is undertaken to make the theories consistent. However, controlling for the effect of WS makes a lot of sense since it signals whether the process of wage-setting is stable or inflationary. Yet, while this equation captures three out of four of the aforementioned concepts, dual labour market theory is still not represented. How, thus, can I account for labour market dualities?

This is a difficult question, particularly because any answer to it will not be universally valid. For instance, part-time employees in Japan (Asano et al. 2011) constitute a different job class, complete with separate job title, poor prospects and a wage penalty. In a country such as the Netherlands, however, part-time employment is almost as common as full-time work and not nearly as discriminated against as in Japan. Further, the problem with using part-time employment as an indicator for labour market dualities is that its dynamic is usually driven by female labour force participation (see, e.g., Blau and Kahn 2016), yielding a situation in which this variable reflects gender aspects of a society rather than its overall degree of labour market stratification. As a result, I use temporary contracts as a proxy for labour market dualities. To some extent, temporary contracts reflect the structure of an economy as they are partly driven by the size of the agricultural or tourism sector. However, employees in jobs in these sectors can nonetheless be considered as potential competitors for jobs of a similar skill level, but with better prospects. Consequently, temporary contracts will arguably render the best available proxy for labour market dualities. As a result, the equation that will be the basis for the estimations below is of the following form:

$$\Delta w_t = a + \beta_1 \Delta p_{t-1} + \beta_2 \Delta y_{t-1} + \beta_3 WS_{t-1} + \beta_4 u_{t-1} + \beta_5 ter_{t-1}$$

where *ter* is the incidence of temporary contracts, calculated in percentage of the labour force. Additionally, I will calculate a composite variable – the stratification rate – that comprises temporary employees plus the unemployed, in percentage of the labour force.

Figure 9.2 shows the dynamics and relative importance of temporary employees. Recall that the labour force is the aggregate of all employees plus the unemployed. All employees can further be subdivided into permanent employees and temporary employees. Figure 9.2 shows the contributions of all those subgroups, permanent employees, temporary employees and the unemployed to changes in the total of the labour force.

There are three important features to be considered. First, the incidence of temporary employees is an extremely procyclical variable, while unemployment is countercyclical. However, second, temporary contracts are even more procyclical than the unemployment rate is countercyclical. This means that when the two variables are combined into the composite stratification rate the resulting variable becomes flatter at the edges. Third, it should be noted that whenever permanent employment contributes more to the growth of the labour force than temporary employment, we are confronted with a situation in which the incidence of temporary contracts actually decreases. This factor has been particularly strong in CESEE-8 during the very last years of the observation period.

A Glimpse at the Environment: Labour Market Dualities and Wage Growth in the EU

Before investigating the CESEE-8 region in more detail let me take a cursory look at the effects that labour market dualities have in the larger aggregate of the EU-25. I am estimating a simple panel using country fixed effects and time dummies (see Table 9.1; suppressed in the results tables due to reasons of space) for annual data for the EU-25. Here, I leave out Romania (RO), Bulgaria (BG) and Croatia (HR), as data for these countries are extremely fragmented. The data are taken from Eurostat's labour force survey for all data in relation with employment and hours worked, as well as from Eurostat's European System of Accounts (ESA) for data on productivity and wages. Finally, I use data from the harmonized index of consumer prices to control for price developments. In order to be able to

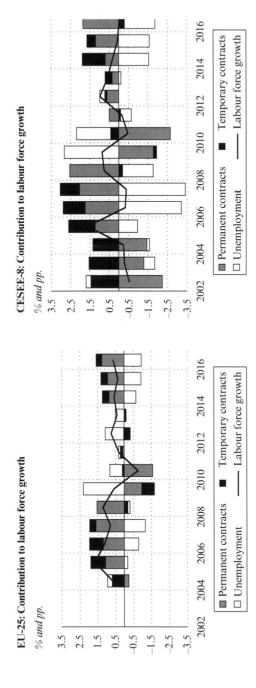

Notes: EU-25 = Austria, Belgium, Bulgaria, Cyprus, the Czech Republic, Denmark, Estonia, Germany, Finland, France, Greece, Hungary, Ireland, Italy, Malta, Latvia, Lithuania, Luxembourg, the Netherlands, Poland, Portugal, Romania, Slovakia, Slovenia, Spain, Sweden and the United Kingdom. CESEE-8 = the Czech Republic, Estonia, Hungary, Latvia, Lithuania, Poland, Slovakia and Slovenia.

Source: Eurostat.

Figure 9.2   Contribution to labour force growth in the EU-25; contribution to labour force growth in CESEE-8

Table 9.1   Determinants of annual wage growth in the EU-25

	(1)	(2)	(3)
L.Inflation	0.200	0.080	0.150
	(1.26)	(0.47)	(0.88)
L.Wage share	−0.244***	−0.370***	−0.263***
	(−3.32)	(−5.31)	(−3.68)
L.Productivity growth	0.285**	0.191	0.280**
	(2.50)	(1.64)	(2.42)
L.Relative income	−0.163***	−0.177***	−0.200***
	(−7.30)	(−7.33)	(−7.72)
L. Unemployment rate, before	−0.783***		−0.905***
	(−6.91)		(−7.29)
L. Unemployment rate, after	−0.607***		−0.690***
	(−7.53)		(−7.50)
L. Stratification rate, before		−0.721***	
		(−6.76)	
L. Stratification rate, after		−0.816***	
		(−7.71)	
L. Temporary rate, before			−0.308*
			(−1.67)
L. Temporary rate, after			−0.494**
			(−2.45)
Constant	0.959***	1.596***	1.136***
	(3.59)	(5.70)	(3.94)
N	374	364	364

t-statistics in parentheses. Includes Estonia, Hungary, Latvia, Lithuania, Poland, Slovenia and Slovakia. L. indicates first lags. * = $p < 0.10$; ** = $p < 0.05$; *** = $p < 0.01$. Note: p = the statistical significance of a given result.

Source: Author's calculation.

assess whether the effects of labour market slack before and after the crisis have changed, I interact these variables with dummy variables, thereby isolating their effects before and after the crisis.

Estimating the equation above shows that most of the control variables have the expected signs and are statistically significant. The latter is not the case for inflation but this is consistent with similar findings for European Economic and Monetary Union (EMU) (see, e.g., Rusinova et al. 2015). The wage share has a negative and statistically significant impact on wage growth, which signals the stability of the system, as any increase in the wage share will not become self-sustaining but rather reduce wage growth in the subsequent period. Productivity has the expected positive effect. Finally, relative income has a negative impact on wage growth, indicating that the catching-up process was ongoing during the period of observation.

As regards the unemployment rate, I can confirm the finding of a flatter Phillips curve that was the starting point of the discussion in this chapter. Indeed, the negative relation between the unemployment rate and hourly wage growth has declined when post- and pre-crisis periods are compared. This of course also implies that every given reduction in the unemployment rate yields a smaller hike of wage growth thereafter. However, looking at the effects of the temporary employment rate it is obvious that their effects have increased quite substantially. Even more, controlling for temporary employment also increases the explanatory power of the unemployment rate, again clearly hinting at the fact that there is some form of interaction going on between the two. This, finally, is corroborated by the stratification rate, which indicates that temporary contracts help to understand the complex interaction between labour market dualities and wage growth, particularly after the crisis.

The Impact of Labour Market Structures in CESEE

However, the major interest here lies in the determination of wages in CESEE-8. Repeating, thus, the exercise from above for the subsample of CESEE-8 yields the same results, as can be seen in models (1)–(3) from Table 9.2. There is no statistically significant effect of inflation, the wage share stabilizes the system, and productivity growth has positive – though in these models not statistically significant – effects. Further, even within this group of emerging economies, relative income verifies that a slow adjustment process is going on. The reduction of the effect of the unemployment rate in the post-crisis period is even more pronounced here than in the bigger sample. This is the case for the incidence of temporary contractors as well, given that the coefficient for this variable doubled following the crisis.

It should be noted that these effects are robust to a battery of robustness checks such as controlling for net migration, changes in the nominal or real effective exchange rate, and the incidence of labour market reforms. However, an essential and quite popular robustness test is not possible given the limited data at hand. Usually, wage-setting regressions tend to control for the effects of past wage growth on current wage growth. From a theoretical perspective this makes a lot of sense, because this accounts for longer-run dynamics of wage-setting processes. Further, it factors in the effects of longer lags of control variables via their effect on lagged wages.

However, doing this in the context of a fixed effects panel gives rise to the so-called Nickell bias in the coefficient estimates. Fortunately, it

Table 9.2 Determinants of annual wage growth in CESEE-8

	(1)	(2)	(3)	(4)	(5)	(6)
L. Wage growth per hour				0.540***	0.552***	0.523***
				(9.15)	(9.57)	(8.91)
L.Inflation	0.302	0.099	0.203	0.227**	0.203*	0.213*
	(1.10)	(0.35)	(0.73)	(2.02)	(1.78)	(1.89)
L. Wage share	−0.331**	−0.535***	−0.313**	−0.069	−0.117**	−0.077
	(−2.53)	(−4.51)	(−2.36)	(−1.42)	(−2.46)	(−1.55)
L.Productivity growth	0.130	0.119	0.115	0.213***	0.204***	0.234***
	(0.48)	(0.45)	(0.44)	(3.08)	(2.98)	(3.39)
L.Relative income	−0.100*	−0.179***	−0.264***	−0.043*	−0.067***	−0.088***
	(−1.70)	(−2-73)	(−3.25)	(−1.91)	(−2.74)	(−3.15)
L. Unemployment rate, before	−0.704***		−1.238***	−0.331***		−0.512***
	(−3.33)		(−4.46)	(−3.75)		(−4.40)
L. Unemployment rate, after	−0.391		−0.735**	−0.197		−0.336**
	(−1.29)		(−2.33)	(−1.33)		(−2.16)
L. Stratification rate, before		−0.989***			−0.395***	
		(−3.80)			(−3.67)	
L. Stratification rate, after		−1.098***			−0.477***	
		(−3.59)			(−3.83)	
L. Temporary rate, before			−0.666*			−0.205
			(−1.69)			(−1.28)
L. Temporary rate, after			−1.122**			−0.374**
			(−2.57)			(−2.24)
Constant	1.328**	2.145***	1.176**	−0.068	−0.116*	0.101
	(2.47)	(4.42)	(2.14)	(−1.03)	(−1.78)	(−1.51)
N	120	120	120	477	477	477

Notes: t-statistics in parentheses. Includes Estonia, Hungary, Latvia, Lithuania, Poland, Slovenia and Slovakia. L indicates first lags. $* = p < 0.10$; $** = p < 0.05$; $*** = p < 0.01$. p = the statistical significance of a given result.

has been demonstrated that this bias limits towards infinity as the time dimension of the sample is increased. Concretely, it has been shown that the bias becomes sufficiently small for $T = 30$ (Judson and Owen 1999). In my case this is unfortunately not possible in an environment of annual data. However, I can repeat the above exercise using quarterly data in order to check whether my results hold in this regard. As can be seen from models (4)–(6) in Table 9.2, this indeed is largely the case. The control variables have comparable effects using quarterly data and controlling for a lagged dependent variable. With regard to labour market slack, however, it is noteworthy that the economic significance of the coefficients declines somewhat. Nonetheless, my major results – a decline in the effect of the unemployment rate and a remarkable increase in the impact of temporary contracts on wages after the crisis – are still valid.

This implies that temporary contracts indeed had a very significant role in the post-crisis development of wages in the region. To be sure, wages have been picking up recently, but so has the ratio of permanent contracts against the background of a declining incidence of temporary contracts.

9.4   CONCLUSION

I have argued and demonstrated above that labour market dualities – concretely, the incidence of temporary contracts – have a significant impact on wage growth. This is novel to the contemporary understanding of wage-setting processes. Further, I have shown that this impact has substantially increased since the crisis, which helps to understand the flattening of the Phillips curve.

The major corollary of the discussion above is the following. The link between labour market slack and wage growth still exists. However, this link has become more complex through the impact of the crisis. Before the crisis, the major threat for employees was to become unemployed. Thus, the unemployment rate was sufficient to capture the degree of slack, and thereby the degree of competition between members of the labour force. This has substantially changed. Apparently, the crisis increased the fear of social decline from a privileged position on the labour market to a subordinate position. The sheer extent and universal character of the crisis arguably made even open-ended jobs seemingly more insecure than has hitherto been the case. This increased the heat of competition felt even by 'regular' employees, particularly also with regard to competition stemming from the lower strata of the labour market. A broader understanding of slack – such as the stratification rate developed above – is likely to improve our understanding of contemporary labour markets.

REFERENCES

Akerlof, G. and J. Yellen (1990), The fair wage–effort hypothesis and unemployment. *Quarterly Journal of Economics*, **105** (2), 255–83.

Asano, H., T. Ito and D. Kawagchi (2011), Why has the fraction of contingent worker increased? A case study of Japan. RIETI Discussion Paper Series.

Beblo, M., D. Beninger, A. Heinze and F. Laisney (2003), Measuring selectivity-corrected gender wage gaps in the EU. ZEW Discussion Paper No. 03-74.

Blanchard, O. and L. Katz (1999), Wage dynamics: reconciling theory and evidence. *American Economic Review: Papers and Proceedings*, **89** (2), 69–74.

Blau, F. and L. Kahn (2016), The gender wage gap: extent, trends, and explanations. NBER Working Paper, No. 21913.

Blinder, A. (1973), Wage discrimination: reduced form and structural estimates. *Journal of Human Resources*, **8** (4), 436–55.

Dickens, W. and K. Lang (1985), A test of dual labour market theory. *American Economic Review*, **75**, 792–805.

ECB (2017), Assessing labour market slack. *Economic Bulletin*, **3**, 31–5.

Hancké, B. (2013), *Unions, Central Banks and EMU – Labour Market Institutions and Monetary Integration in Europe*, Oxford: Oxford University Press.

Harrisson, B. and A. Sum (1979), The theory of dual segmented labour markets. *Journal of Economic Issues*, **13**, 687–706.

Hirsch, B. (2016), Dual labour markets at work: the impact of employers' use of temporary agency work on regular workers' job stability. *Industrial and Labour Relations Review*, **69**, 1191–215.

IMF (2017), *World Economic Outlook*, Washington, DC: IMF.

Judson, R. and A. Owen (1999), Estimating dynamic panel data models: a guide for macroeconomists. *Economic Letters*, **65**, 9–15.

Lindbeck, A. and D. Snower (1986), Wage setting, unemployment and insider–outsider relations. *American Economic Review – Papers and Proceedings*, **76** (2), 235–9.

Lindbeck, A. and D. Snower (2002), The insider–outsider theory: a survey. IZA Discussion Paper Series, 534, 1–51.

OECD (2014), Non-regular employment, job security and the labour market divide, *OECD Employment Outlook*, Paris: OECD.

OECD (2017), *OECD Employment Outlook*, Paris: OECD.

Oxaca, R. (1973), Male–female wage differentials in urban labour markets. *International Economic Review*, **14** (13), 693–709.

Phillips, W. (1958), The relation between unemployment and the rate of change of money wage rates in the United Kingdom, 1861–1957. *Economica*, **25** (100), 283–99.

Reich, M., D. Gordon and R. Edwards (1973), Dual labour markets – a theory of labour market segmentation. *American Economic Review*, **63**, 359–65.

Rusinova, D., V. Lipativ and F. Heinz (2015), How flexible are real wages in EU countries? A panel investigation. *Journal of Macroeconomics*, **43**, 140–54.

PART IV

Past and current reform strategies in Europe

10. Structural reforms in Slovakia: past and present (never-ending story . . .)

Jozef Makúch

Since its establishment as an independent state in 1993, Slovakia has travelled a long and bumpy path. We have had to cope with liberalization, deregulation and privatization. Our adaptation to a free and open market based on fair competition was based on learning by doing. The conditions for major reforms were created at the turn of millennium by a turnaround in domestic politics. Comprehensive and consistent reform steps guided us towards accession to the European Union (EU), and Slovakia became attractive for foreign direct investment (FDI), which accelerated the catch-up process. We faced very complex macroeconomic and institutional changes. Structural reforms in almost all areas and of all kinds were shaping Slovakia right up to its entry into the euro area.

Recent crises have revealed the importance and wisdom of fiscal rules. Therefore fiscal reform has continued, with the introduction of the Fiscal Responsibility Act (including a 'debt brake') and the Value for Money project. Further sustainable growth requires a sound labour market (a flexible and well-qualified labour force), increasing value-added investment, and an improving business environment. Hence there is no scope for reform fatigue.

10.1 SOME DETAILS OF THE REFORM PROCESS IN SLOVAKIA

In order to stabilize macroeconomic developments, it was necessary to restructure the financial sector (especially the banking industry) and to consolidate public finances. The steps taken to ensure the long-term sustainability of public finances and public sector efficiency included tax reform, fiscal decentralization, social reform and pension reform. Institutional reforms (legal and regulatory) were of the utmost importance for ensuring a functioning market economy. Acknowledging the country's achievements, the World Bank named Slovakia the world's leading economic reformer of 2004: introducing flexible working hours, easing the hiring of first-time workers, opening a private credit registry, cutting the time to start a business in half and, thanks to a new collateral law, reducing the time to recover debt by three-quarters (World Bank 2005).

We managed to increase economic freedom and to improve the business environment, making it attractive for domestic and foreign investment. Such policy measures resulted in higher economic growth and, in turn, faster convergence. With the reforms producing favourable results, Slovakia was integrated into international organizations and, most importantly, joined the EU.[1]

Thanks to reforms, Slovakia attracted FDI and reported a speeding-up of convergence towards the EU average. Reforms continued to boost the catch-up process until the onset of the Great Recession. For the period 2004–2008, when the rate of convergence with the EU-15[2] average was 2 per cent for Hungary, 3 per cent for the Czech Republic, and 6 per cent for Poland, Slovakia's convergence rate reached 14 per cent cumulatively. Slovakia's household consumption level per capita reached that of the Czech Republic in 2010, which represented a great success given that the gap between the countries had been 24 percentage points in 1995.

Our credit ratings improved substantially, and in 2004 Standard & Poor's assigned Slovakia the same investment grade as the Czech Republic. In 2009 Slovakia even went one grade higher (in sharp contrast to 1994, when it had been five grades lower). Between 2000 and 2008 Slovakia recorded the highest rates of economic growth in Europe. At the same time, its unemployment rate fell from 20 per cent to less than 10 per cent, its public deficit dropped from 12 per cent to around 2 per cent of gross domestic product (GDP), and its sovereign debt fell from more than 50 per cent to 28 per cent of GDP. At that time, our FDI inflows were the highest in the region.

Reform effects were widespread throughout the economy. They supported appreciation of the equilibrium exchange rate to such an extent that the Slovak economy coped with 20 per cent appreciation while it was a member of the European Exchange Rate Mechanism (ERM) II without its competitiveness being adversely affected (see Figure 10.1).

Potential output increased significantly on account of FDI-related productivity acceleration that pushed GDP growth to almost 11 per cent in 2007 (see Figure 10.2).

Important labour market reforms in Slovakia were concentrated in two periods: the first, around 2003, shortly prior to EU accession; and the second, in the aftermath of the Great Recession. During the first period, Slovakia adopted important measures to increase labour market flexibility, such as reducing redundancy costs, increasing overtime

Note: SKK/EUR = exchange rate of the Slovak koruna against the euro. SKK_EUR eq* = equilibrium exchange rate of the Slovak koruna against the euro.

Source: National Bank of Slovakia.

Figure 10.1 Nominal bilateral equilibrium exchange rate

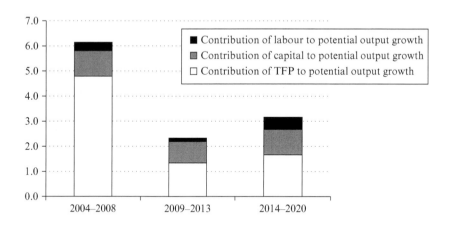

Note: TFP = total factor productivity.

Source: National Bank of Slovakia.

Figure 10.2 Potential output growth and its structure

limits, introducing renewable temporary contracts, and abolishing trade unions' power of veto over organizational changes. These changes cut costs related to job creation and thus supported employment growth. Furthermore, income replacement rates for the long-term unemployed were significantly reduced, thereby incentivizing the unemployed to seek employment, rather than to rely on government support. At the same time, pensioners were allowed to work full-time while retaining their pension income.

In the second period, Slovakia reduced the tax wedge for low-income employees and adopted measures to support female labour market participation, such as introducing job-sharing, building kindergarten facilities, and providing allowances to working parents. Furthermore, Slovakia supported employment opportunities for the long-term and young unemployed by providing retraining projects and employment subsidies, and by reducing the cost of hiring these people. Finally, a dual education project was started in 2015 in order to bring employers directly into the secondary education system and to support students' employment prospects.

What effects have these reforms had on the labour market? First, labour supply grew appreciably in both periods, and especially in the post-global financial crisis period. Although the working-age population has been falling in recent years, labour force and participation rates have continued to grow and thus to support the economy's productive capacity. Second, there has been a clear and sustained downward trend in the long-term unemployment rate, which is now at historically low levels.

On the basis of the estimated relationship between GDP and employment growth rates (Okun's law), there is evidence that actual employment growth has been stronger than estimated employment growth. For the period 2013–2017, the cumulative difference in headcount employment was around 70 000, which to some extent demonstrates the impact of the labour market policy measures implemented in recent years.

From the fiscal perspective, public finances have been set on a clear consolidation path since the great recession. Slovakia's fiscal position is far sounder and more sustainable compared with many other countries. The public deficit is shrinking and is projected to continue on that course. The medium-term objective, however, is still not met and is not projected to be met until several years hence. On the other hand, under the 'no policy change scenario', there is some scope for slight fiscal stimulus concentrated on capital spending, compensation and social transfers.

Demographic projections for the period until 2060 are not favourable. The combination of increasing life expectancy and a falling fertility rate should increase pension system costs and put increasing pressure on public finance sustainability. In order to mitigate old-age pension costs, a new pension system was introduced in 2003. It comprises three pillars: the state-run earnings-related scheme (first pillar); a largely compulsory defined contribution scheme (second pillar); and a voluntary defined contribution scheme (third pillar). While entailing several key changes, the new system continues to support the diversification of pension income resources and risks and the active accumulation of savings during working life.

A 2012 amendment to the Fiscal Responsibility Act introduced a 'debt brake' rule and an independent fiscal council (the Council for Budget Responsibility). The debt brake rule helps to improve fiscal discipline by imposing sanctions for the breaching of the specified public debt limit (which from 2018 to 2028 is to be reduced by 1 per cent of GDP per year, until the upper limit for public debt stands at 50 per cent of GDP). In addition, a balanced budget rule (under the 'Fiscal Compact') was implemented into Slovak law in 2014.

Fiscal reform continued in 2016 with the introduction of the Value for Money initiative, under which the efficiency of public finances is assessed in order to increase savings in public expenditure. The first round of assessments covered health care and transport infrastructure, which represent 40 per cent of all public expenditure. These spending reviews identified areas most in need of efficiency gains, and it is crucial that their findings are taken into account in the budget-drafting process.

Slovakia offers a clear example of the favourable results of well-implemented structural reforms. We must not, however, rest on our laurels; there is still much to do in many areas. Although our long-term unemployment is falling, it is still among the highest in the EU. At the same time, it is striking that Slovakia's spending on active labour market policies as a percentage of GDP is among the lowest. We are still behind other countries in surveys measuring the quality of the business environment and living standards, including surveys on corruption, the ease of doing business, and the quality of education and health care. In the health sector, steps must be taken to avoid the build-up of debt. The education system should provide knowledge and skills which match employers' requirements, while the research and development and information technology spheres should bring important innovations that further accelerate potential output. Hiring foreign workers is overcomplicated and employment protection has tightened again in recent years, all of which limits the economy's flexibility and its attractiveness to foreign investors.

10.2 CONCLUSION

Everybody knows that structural reforms are of utmost importance for sustainable growth, for better welfare and for eliminating macroeconomic imbalances. So why is there such reluctance to implement them? Mainly because of the short-term losses they give rise to within the political cycle.

Therefore international institutions, especially the International Monetary Fund, recommend taking the business cycle into account (good times are better for reforms) and implementing strong and focused demand-supporting policies (having regard to the Gini coefficient).

NOTES

1. See http://www.eu2016.sk/en/slovakia-and-the-eu/history-of-slovakias-eu-membership for a history of Slovakia's EU membership.
2. EU-15 = Austria, Belgium, Denmark, Finland, France, Germany, Greece, Ireland, Italy, Luxembourg, Netherlands, Portugal, Spain, Sweden, United Kingdom.

REFERENCE

World Bank (2005), *Doing Business in 2005 – Removing Obstacles to Growth*, Washington, DC: World Bank.

11. Crisis management and economic policy shifts in Hungary after 2010

Barnabás Virág

The global financial market turbulence of 2008 hit Hungary amid a triple internal crisis, and therefore it had particularly severe adverse effects. The cornerstones of the economic policy stabilization launched in 2010 were measures aimed at growth-friendly fiscal consolidation, raising employment and reducing the country's external vulnerability. As a result, significant progress was made in improving financial viability while maintaining aggregate demand, accompanied by a considerable increase in public acceptance of the state due to reforms in the labour market and the tax structure. The following is a description of how shifts in fiscal and monetary policy, competitiveness and employment, involving orchestrated economic policy reforms, may help to reduce economic lag, using Hungary as an example.

Hungary was hit by the financial market turbulence in a particularly vulnerable state, as the country was confronted with a triple internal crisis. First, the economy's growth potential had eroded sharply in the preceding years; second, unsustainable, debt-fuelled economic growth had led to severe indebtedness in all sectors; and third, partly as a result of these two factors, a political crisis was developing in the country.

Essentially, the underlying reasons for the deceleration in the potential growth rate were inherent in the labour market and the structure of fiscal policy. Although the unemployment rate was moderately low in Hungary, this was due to the fact that a major part of the working-age population remained inactive, outside the labour market. Prior to the crisis, the employment rate was the second-lowest in Europe, ahead of Malta only. The unhealthy structure of the labour market was strongly related to the system of taxes and government transfers. The tax wedge was the second-highest (behind Belgium), and aids substituting income were high relative to fiscal sustainability.

Despite the moderate potential growth rate, economic growth was sustained until 2006 by persistently expansionary fiscal policy and household indebtedness. Between 2002 and 2006, the public deficit was on average 7.9

per cent of gross domestic product (GDP), which stimulated growth temporarily, but was unsustainable even in the medium term. The high deficit was not justified by the international economic cycle, since Hungary's main trading partner economies and the European Union as a whole had been growing at a steady rate since 2004. As a result of the high deficit, public debt surged from 51 per cent of GDP in 2001 to 71 per cent in 2008.

In addition to the government budget, increasing household spending was also funded from borrowing to a large extent, and primarily from foreign currency-based mortgage loans. In an economy overheated by the fiscal budget, monetary policy sought to achieve price stability by keeping interest rates high, which drove borrowers towards loans denominated in foreign currency. As a result, households' foreign currency borrowings grew by HUF 3000 billion (about €11.8 billion)[1] between 2004 and 2007, and approximated HUF 6000 billion (about €21.4 billion) by 2009 (Kolozsi et al. 2015). On the one hand, external funds accounted for a growing share of household debt, which significantly increased the external indebtedness of the economy; while on the other hand, foreign currency loans were not backed by a natural foreign currency hedge, making such loans extremely sensitive to exchange rate movements.

The unsustainable path of fiscal policy called for a major adjustment in 2006, which immediately put the brakes on economic growth and led to political instability. The abundance of liquidity in international capital markets and the resulting high-risk appetite allowed for a public deficit of 7 per cent to 8 per cent over a few years; however, in 2006 the European Union (EU) refused to approve Hungary's convergence programme, and requested measures to reduce the deficit. Since its EU entry in 2004, Hungary had been subject to an excessive deficit procedure until 2013. As a result of fiscal restrictions, in 2007 economic growth dropped to 0.4 per cent despite the pick-up in international activity, which, accompanied by a shattered confidence in the legitimacy of the governing parties, led to a political crisis. In 2008, the smaller governing party withdrew from the government, which was followed by the resignation of the Prime Minister in 2009. Public acceptance of, and support for, the government were extremely low, leading to a change of government in the 2010 elections.

As a result of the interrelations between these three crises, the Hungarian economy was in an extremely vulnerable state at the outset of the 2008 financial crisis. Of all the EU member states, Hungary was the first to be forced to borrow from international organizations, signing an agreement for an €18 billion credit line with representatives of the International Monetary Fund (IMF) and the European Commission in autumn 2008. Simultaneously, a second wave of fiscal adjustments started from early 2009. Therefore, in the absence of room for manoeuvre in fiscal policy, unlike the United States (US) and a large majority of EU member states, Hungary was forced to pursue a procyclical fiscal policy. In an economy facing insufficient demand, the fiscal multiplier tends to be above the average (Baum et al. 2012). This sent the country deeper into recession, with an 8.2 decline in GDP compared to its 2007 peak, which in turn led to a further escalation of the political crisis.

The cornerstones of the government's economic policy stabilization programme formed in 2010 were growth-friendly fiscal consolidation, boosting employment and reducing external vulnerability. This enabled significant improvements in financial viability while maintaining aggregate demand, accompanied by a significant increase in public acceptance of economic policy due to reforms in the labour market and the tax structure.

By 2017, Hungary's macroeconomic situation was made significantly more stable. Dynamic GDP growth, increasing employment and a significant rise in real wages, accompanied by a fall in public debt as a percentage of GDP, and by fiscal discipline, provide sound foundations for predictable and steady growth. In 2013, the excessive deficit procedure – which had been launched against Hungary since the beginning of its EU membership – was closed, the country risk premium fell significantly, and Hungary's indicators have also met the nominal Maastricht convergence criteria since 2014.[2] The next section provides a detailed description of how the shifts in Hungarian economic policy starting in 2010 helped to restore economic stability.

11.1 TURNAROUND IN FISCAL POLICY AND EMPLOYMENT

A resolution to the triple internal economic crisis called for a turnaround in the labour market supported by fiscal instruments. Adverse conditions in the labour market contributed to the low employment rate, which also negatively influenced the tax revenues of the budget. Additionally, the weak activity rate also impeded the achievement of balanced economic growth over the long term.

Accordingly, a major part of the reforms implemented were aimed at the labour market. The personal income tax regime was fundamentally reformed. A flat rate personal income tax was introduced; the Job Protection Action Plan was developed; the system of social benefits, which had previously failed to provide sufficient incentives for activity, was reformed; and a public employment scheme was launched to boost activity in the labour market. Additionally, the introduction of the substantial family tax base allowance addressed the demographic challenges as it significantly improved the income situation of families raising children.

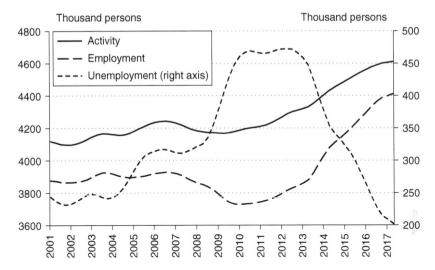

Source: Hungarian Central Statistical Office (HCSO).

Figure 11.1 Activity and employment in Hungary

Due to the measures implemented, between 2010 and 2017 the employment rate increased from 55 per cent to 69 per cent and the number of employees from 3.7 million to 4.4 million (Figure 11.1), while the unemployment rate dropped from 11 per cent to below 4 per cent.

One of the pillars of growth-friendly fiscal consolidation was the transformation of the tax regime. It was found (European Commission 2013; OECD 2010) that, in addition to taxes on capital gains, the greatest distortions resulted from taxes on labour income, which made it reasonable to make efforts to reduce the weight of such taxes during the transformation of the tax regime.

As part of the tax restructuring launched in 2010, the weight of the tax regime started to be shifted from taxes on labour to taxes on consumption, in line with international recommendations (Figure 11.2). Raising consumption taxes improves the external competitiveness of the country, as imports become more expensive while exports become cheaper due to lower wage costs (Baksay and Palotai 2017).

The introduction of the flat income tax rate provided incentives on the supply side of the labour market on both the extensive and intensive margins. In 2010, the Hungarian personal income taxes failed to encourage inactive employees to enter the labour market and those in the labour market to improve their performance; however, it did cause

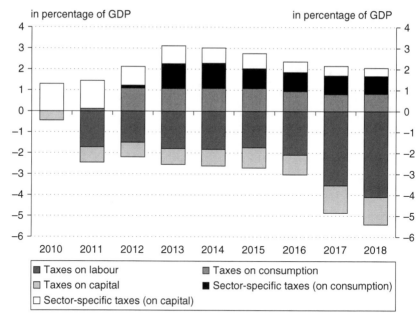

Source: Palotai (2017).

*Figure 11.2   Cumulative budgetary effect of the changes in the tax regime
from 2010*

wage concealment. The introduction of the flat personal income tax
(PIT) regime lowered the marginal tax rate to a regional level, which can
therefore encourage increased labour intensity and investments in human
capital, while reducing the level of income concealment. The static effect
of the tax cut is estimated at approximately HUF 360 billion (about €1.3
billion), while the tax cuts may have increased effective labour supply and
GDP by some 3 per cent in the long term. Consequently, the dynamic
effect of the tax cuts may be much lower, a mere quarter of the static effect,
due to the widened tax bases (Baksay and Csomós 2014).

The reform of the social benefit system also contributed to higher
employment. One of the principles underlying post-2010 economic policy
was 'work instead of aid'. Under that principle, restrictions were introduced
on early retirement, to drive the highest possible percentage of the capable
population from the inactive group to the active group in the labour market.
The expansion and extension of the public employment scheme and the
incorporation of training programmes facilitated the re-entry of the unemployed into the labour market (Matolcsy and Palotai 2016).

In addition to the transformation of the personal income tax regime, the Job Protection Action Plan and the family tax allowance scheme were also introduced. The Plan helps specific groups (under-25s, unemployed people over 55, mothers returning from childcare leave, unskilled workers and permanently unemployed people) to enter the labour market by significantly reducing the employer's contribution payable on their wages. The Job Protection Action Plan was more targeted in terms of household income deciles than the tax credit previously in place, although in the case of the former the allowance was granted to the employer rather than to the employee (Svraka et al. 2014). Additionally, the introduction of the family tax base allowance resulted in a significant improvement in the income situation of families raising several children. Thus, other than labour supply, family tax allowances also affect demographic developments.

After 2010, the Hungarian sector of small and medium-sized enterprises (SMEs) received particular fiscal support again. To improve competitiveness, the threshold for the preferential corporate tax (10 per cent as opposed to the standard 19 per cent rate) was raised to HUF 500 million (c. €1.8 billion), while simple and preferential forms of taxation (small taxpayers' itemised lump sum tax, small business tax) were also introduced and extended. From 2017 the corporate income tax rates were unified and reduced to 9 per cent, which is the lowest in the European Union.

Continued transition to the formal economy was an important means of achieving fiscal balance. Measures targeted at that transition included, in particular, the introduction of online cash registers and the Electronic Public Road Trade Control System (EKÁER), but the establishment of the preferential forms of taxation also contributed to the formalization process. The fact that in recent years value added tax (VAT) revenues have grown at a considerably faster rate than the estimated tax base is an indication of the formalizing effect of the measures. The same is confirmed by the European Commission's estimate, according to which the VAT gap (the difference between theoretical computed tax liabilities and actual tax revenues) dropped by some 7 percentage points between 2013 and 2015, generating extra revenues corresponding to 0.5 per cent of GDP (European Commission 2016).

In order to broaden the fair burden-sharing and improve fiscal balance, sector-specific taxes were introduced in some sectors (finance, retail, telecommunications, energy). The tax burden on households had to be alleviated in order to avoid a further decrease of aggregate demand, especially in household consumption. Thus, it was necessary to involve sectors in fiscal consolidation whose burden-bearing capacity was relatively higher. In 2010, the tax burden on financial institutions amounted to 0.7 per cent of GDP, while revenues from taxes on the rest of the sectors to 0.6 per cent of GDP.

From 2013, the weight of taxes on capital was reduced significantly through a shift towards consumption taxes (telecommunication tax, accident tax, insurance tax, financial transaction duty, utility tax). As of 2016, the sector-specific tax on financial institutions was reduced (Baksay and Palotai 2017).

The reforms implemented resulted in a fiscal turnaround with a major improvement in the position of the public budget. The public deficit fell significantly, reflecting increasing labour market activity, the implementation of tax restructuring, and the introduction of measures to formalize the economy. Since 2012, the deficit of the budget, as a percentage of GDP, has consistently remained below the 3 per cent threshold set out in the Maastricht criteria. The deficit fell to 2.3 per cent of GDP in 2012 and remained around 2 per cent in the following years. For the first time in 12 years, in 2012 the primary balance of the budget (net of interest expenditures) showed a surplus (Figure 11.3). Additionally, a favourable international environment and the central bank's programmes were highly instrumental in significantly reducing

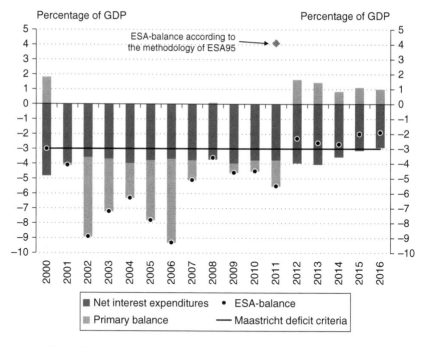

Note: ESA = European System of Accounts.

Source: Eurostat.

Figure 11.3   Government deficit in Hungary between 2000 and 2016

interest expenditures of the budget, making a lower level of primary surplus sufficient to maintain a moderate deficit (MNB 2017c).

A moderate level of public deficit accompanied by robust economic growth resulted in a decline in the public debt ratio. During the financial crisis of 2008, the Hungarian public debt ratio was seen as particularly high by regional standards, which carried significant macro-financial vulnerability risks. However, following fiscal consolidation, public debt as a percentage of GDP fell year by year. This corresponds to an overall decrease of 6 percentage points, that is, the ratio dropped from 80 per cent at the end of 2011 to 74 per cent at the end of 2016. Another indication of the legitimacy of fiscal policy and the commitment to reduce debt is that the decline in debt is also required by the Fundamental Law. This may significantly improve market investors' confidence in Hungary.

The improved fiscal position brought about a major positive shift in the market's perception of the Hungarian economy. In 2013, Hungary exited the excessive deficit procedure after the debt had been put on a downward path and the public deficit had been reduced to below 3 per cent. Simultaneously, both the country's spread on credit default swaps (CDS) and yields on government securities dropped significantly. As a result, in 2014 Hungary was viewed by the market as an investment-grade country in terms of yields in the Hungarian market of government securities. Subsequently, following the example of the market, in 2016 all three leading credit rating agencies again rated Hungary as an investment-grade economy.

11.2   TURNAROUND IN MONETARY POLICY

The turnaround in fiscal policy has created the foundation for the monetary policy turnaround. The Magyar Nemzeti Bank (MNB) intervened in the functioning of the economy with a combination of traditional and unconventional instruments. While preserving the primacy of the core objective – that is, stable and low inflation – it used its measures to support financial stability and the economic policy of the government. With targeted instruments, the central bank aimed to support real economic growth and to strengthen financial stability.

As in other countries across the region, the Magyar Nemzeti Bank also started an easing cycle in 2012, supported by a number of factors. On the one hand, the positive measures of Hungarian fiscal policy significantly improved Hungary's risk rating; and on the other hand, the room for manoeuvre in Hungarian monetary policy was also increased by the accommodating monetary policy stance of the key global central banks (Matolcsy 2015). Subsequently, continued monetary easing was required

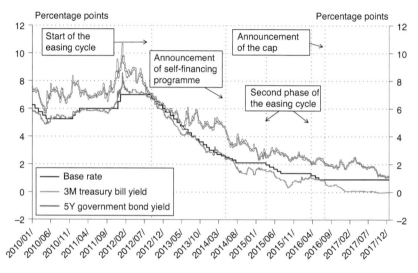

Sources: MNB, Government Debt Management Agency (GDMA).

Figure 11.4   *Central bank base rate and government bond yields in Hungary*

by a strong disinflationary environment, and for the stimulation of economic growth; however, uncertainty observed in international financial markets warranted a cautious monetary policy, as a result of which from August 2013 the easing cycle continued in smaller steps than the previous 25 basis points (bps) (Felcser et al. 2015). The second phase of the easing cycle commenced in March 2015, when increasing downside risks to inflation made it necessary to continue monetary easing. Then, in March 2016, responding to a persistently low-cost environment, the Monetary Council launched the third phase of its easing cycle (see Figure 11.4).

Overall, in the course of the easing cycle, the policy rate fell by 610 bps from 7 per cent to a historic low of 0.9 per cent. In its decisions during the easing cycle, rather than aiming to reach the lowest interest rate level attainable in the short term, the Monetary Council targeted a sufficiently low interest rate level that would ensure the sustainable fulfilment of its primary mandate and the stability of the base rate as regards the effectiveness of monetary easing (Virág 2016).

In the years following the crisis, in 2009–2013, the outstanding amount of corporate loans was shrinking at a rate of 5 per cent a year. Access to credit was particularly difficult for small and medium-sized enterprises, which was a major drag on the recovery in economic growth (Sugawara and Zalduendo 2013). To avoid a credit crunch, in June 2013 the Magyar Nemzeti Bank announced its Funding for Growth Scheme. As part of the Scheme, the Bank granted refinancing loans at 0 per cent to commercial banks, which in turn could lend the funds to SMEs at an interest margin of no more than 2.5 per cent.

As part of the FGS, some 40 000 micro, small and medium-sized enterprises were granted credit at favourable terms, in the total amount of over HUF 2800 billion (c. €9.1 billion). This targeted central bank instrument was therefore a major contribution to the recovery in lending. Following the launch of the Scheme, the sharp decline seen in previous years came to a halt, then from 2015 onwards outstanding corporate loans started to increase. In 2016, the dynamics entered the 5 per cent to 10 per cent range, which is seen as necessary for sustainable economic growth in the long term (MNB 2017d).

In addition, the Magyar Nemzeti Bank adopted several measures addressing the functioning of the Hungarian financial system. In line with international developments, the Hungarian Parliament adopted the draft legislation on the Magyar Nemzeti Bank in the autumn of 2013, thereby integrating the financial supervision function into the central bank. The uniform performance of the monetary policy and financial stability functions (including the macro- and microprudential regulatory and authority functions) integrated into the central bank opened up new horizons for supervisors. The active and proactive use of micro- and macroprudential policy strengthened the stability of the financial system.

As a targeted instrument, the Self-Financing Programme affected all elements of the standard set of central bank instruments, while also supplementing the MNB's instruments by a non-conventional element, the conditional central bank interest rate swap. The Self-Financing Programme can also be considered unique in the sense that it allowed monetary easing while tightening the central bank balance sheet. While numerous leading central banks managed to ease monetary conditions through unprecedented expansions of their balance sheets (that is, quantitative easing programmes), the MNB achieved this goal through a contraction of its balance sheet as a result of the Self-Financing Programme. This is important, because the costs of reserve management declined with the tightening of the central bank balance sheet, while the government securities market became more stable, and interest rate risks borne by banks decreased (Nagy and Kolozsi 2017).

One of the main objectives of the Self-Financing Programme was to reduce the ratio of foreign currency and foreign ownership within public debt. During the 2008 financial crisis, Hungary was made extremely vulnerable by the high ratio of foreign currency and foreign share within public debt. The Government Debt Management Agency set the refinancing of public debt from domestic sources as a strategic target, which received major support from the Self-Financing Programme. As a result, the structure of debt has improved considerably in recent years. The ratio of foreign ownership within public debt declined from 67 per cent to below 40 per cent, while the proportion of foreign currency within central government debt was down from 50 per cent to 22 per cent by end 2017. The total repayment of the EU and IMF loans contributed to both declines considerably. The positive change in the structure of debt played a significant role in the decline in external vulnerability.

The forint conversion of foreign currency loans eliminated the exchange rate risk to the entire national economy, making monetary transmission more efficient. Foreign currency loans to households were of particular risk not only to the financial position of the household sector, but also to the financial system and the Hungarian economy as a whole. Consequently, while phasing out mortgage loans denominated in foreign currency eliminated families' financial positions and exchange rate exposures, a systemic risk was also eliminated. For households, the direct consequence of forint conversion is that their net wealth and monthly disposable incomes are no longer affected by exchange rate fluctuations, that is, they are freed from exchange rate risk. The measure also had a favourable effect on the stability of the banking system, and was accompanied by the increased effectiveness of monetary policy due to the fact that exchange rate movements in the market can again influence the real sector and inflation through conventional channels (Kolozsi et al. 2015).

The MNB's instruments were gradually transformed with the launch of the Self-Financing Programme. The earlier role of two-week bills as the main policy instrument was taken over first by two-week deposits, then three-month deposits. After the easing cycle ended, in July 2016 the Monetary Council announced that it would reduce the frequency of tenders for the three-month policy instrument and limit the quantities accepted in future tenders. For a targeted easing of monetary conditions, the Monetary Council applied quantitative limits on three-month deposits, taking the relevant decisions every quarter. The outstanding amount concerning the limit on three-month deposits declined to HUF 75 billion (€240 million) at the end of 2017 Q4, and the Monetary Council indicated that the quantitative limit would not be reduced further (MNB 2017b).

In order to reinforce the effect of monetary easing through unconventional instruments related to the quantitative restrictions on the three-month deposit facility, the Monetary Council increased the asymmetry of the overnight interest rate corridor by adjusting the spread on its lending instrument in several steps. At its November 2016 rate-setting meeting, fully exploiting the space available to narrow the interest rate corridor, the Monetary Council cut the overnight lending rate and the one-week lending rate to the level of the base rate. In addition, it started to use fine-tuning swaps, in order to handle the uncertainties related to banking sector liquidity developments. In September 2017, the Monetary Council decreased the overnight deposit rate by 10 bps to −0.15 per cent.

Overall, the Magyar Nemzeti Bank's conventional and unconventional measures substantially supported the pick-up of economic growth in recent years, while it also prevented inflation from remaining in negative territory for an extended period, whereby it eliminated deflationary risks and reduced the extent of missing the inflation target. As a result, the inflation rate has risen to the tolerance band. In addition, central bank measures have been responsible for the half of the growth in the past few years, while significantly reducing the fragility of the economy. The stability of the financial system was strengthened by the active and proactive micro- and macroprudential supervision. Central bank programmes contributed greatly to the reduction in public interest expenditures as well (see Figure 11.4), helping the stabilization of the fiscal budget and creating room for tax cuts and the implementation of competitiveness reforms.

11.3   THE NECESSARY TURNAROUND IN COMPETITIVENESS

By means of the implemented reforms, the triple domestic crisis has been successfully overcome, and the Hungarian economy has been placed onto a growth path. Surmounting the structural growth, macrofinancing and political crises following the financial one was indispensable for the persistent and sustainable development of the Hungarian economy. In the first round, the implemented reforms were targeted at the labour market, as the increase in activity and employment contributed to solving all three problems. In parallel with that, a more growth-friendly and more competitive tax system was created. Following that, monetary policy measures that supported the economic recovery and the decline in external vulnerability were taken. As a result of the implemented reforms, the Hungarian economy stepped onto a growth path, fiscal deficit and public debt declined, and inflation was persistently low.

In order to converge to the average of the European Union by means of the aforementioned turns in economic policy, a major improvement in Hungary's competitiveness is necessary (Matolcsy 2017). Competitiveness is examined in detail in various publications of the MNB (Palotai and Virág 2016; MNB 2017a); in addition to comprehensive analyses of the situation, they also contain proposals to increase Hungary's competitiveness.

In terms of the improvement in competitiveness, one of the main tasks is to provide an adequate quantity and quality of human capital for the Hungarian economy, as one of the main obstacles to economic growth at present is the low availability of adequately trained labour. The negative effect of the declining ratio of the working-age population was further amplified by the gradual opening of the opportunities to work abroad following accession to the European Union. The employment rate had risen steadily and steeply since 2010, in which the successful government programmes aiming at the expansion in employment also played a significant role. At the same time, in certain areas the further expansion of companies was hindered by the limited availability of skilled labour.

The activation of domestic and foreign labour reserves could be greatly facilitated by the continuation of the wage convergence. In this respect there are reserves at large companies at present as well, because the difference between the wages paid by them and their employees' productivity is significant. By contrast, a major pay rise in the SME sector is possible through growth in productivity. On the other hand, it is also necessary because the difference between SMEs' productivity and large companies' productivity is greater in Hungary than in the neighbouring countries. In addition, an increase in the productivity of SMEs could contribute to a higher degree of diversification of the rather concentrated Hungarian industrial production and exports.

In terms of the quality of human capital, the performance of education and health care systems is of crucial importance. One of the main challenges of the education system is to prepare students to be able to adapt themselves to the rapidly changing and developing labour market environment. In addition to adaptation, another important aspect is the ability to apply the acquired knowledge. On the basis of the findings of international surveys (the Programme for International Student Assessment, PISA; Trends in International Mathematics and Science Study, TIMSS), Hungarian students sufficiently learn the subject matter of instruction, but cannot adequately apply it in real-life situations.

There is also room in various areas for strengthening the role of the banking sector and the state in supporting economic development. The strengthening of digitalization in the sector would allow the reduction of operating costs, which would create an opportunity for cutting the currently relatively high lending rates (mainly on household loans), for increasing the spread of bank products and for a further simplification of companies' access to loans. The government can primarily facilitate the increase in productivity through creating a supportive business and regulatory environment as well as through reducing the burdens on enterprise and labour (Figure 11.5).

On the whole, with the cooperation of fiscal and monetary policies, the

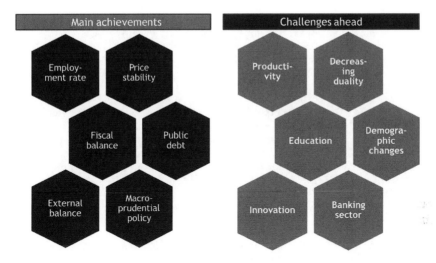

Figure 11.5   Achievements and challenges regarding the convergence of Hungary

changes in economic policy implemented since 2010 successfully treated the symptoms of macrofinancing, growth and political crisis. Nevertheless, dynamic convergence to the average GDP of the EU requires the continuation of the improvement in competitiveness already started.

NOTES

1.   Euro values are calculated at historical exchange rates in the whole document.
2.   Hungary is not a member of the EU's Exchange Rate Mechanism (ERM) II; however, since it has complied with the membership criterion for exchange rate movements since 2012, its entry is only a matter of decision.

REFERENCES

Baksay, G. and B. Csomós (2014), 'Analysis of changes in the tax and transfer system between 2010 and 2014 with the help of a behavioural microsimulation model', *Köz-Gazdaság*, 9 (4), Special issue on tax policy. https://akademiai.com/doi/abs/10.1556/204.2015.37.S.4.
Baksay, G. and D. Palotai (2017), 'Recession management and economic reforms in Hungary, 2010–2016', *Economic Review*, 64 (7), 698–722.
Baum, A., M. Poplawski-Ribeiro and A. Weber (2012), 'Fiscal multipliers and the state of the economy', IMF Working Paper No. 12/286.

European Commission (2013), 'Study on the impacts of fiscal devaluation', European Commission, Taxation Papers, Working Paper No. 36.

European Commission (2016), 'Study and reports on the VAT gap in the EU-28 member states: 2016 final report', TAXUD/2015/CC/131.

Felcser, D. et al. (2015), 'The impact of the easing cycle on the Hungarian macro-economy and financial markets', *Financial and Economic Review*, 14 (3), 39–59.

Kolozsi, P., Á. Banai and B. Vonnák (2015), 'A lakossági deviza-jelzáloghitelek kivezetése: időzítés és keretrendszer' (Phasing out household foreign currency loans: schedule and framework), *Financial and Economic Review*, 14 (3), 60–87.

Matolcsy, Gy. (2015), *Economic Balance and Growth – Consolidation and Stabilisation in Hungary 2010–2014*, Book Series of the Magyar Nemzeti Bank, Budapest: Kairosz Könyvkiadó.

Matolcsy, Gy. (2017), 'Gazdaságtörténeti siker nyolc év alatt, tizenkét lépésben' (Economic history success in eight years, in twelve steps), magyaridok.hu, 16 December. https://magyaridok.hu/velemeny/gazdasagtorteneti-siker-nyolc-ev-ala tt-tizenket-lepesben-2568427/.

Matolcsy, Gy. and D. Palotai (2016), 'The interaction between fiscal and monetary policy in Hungary over the past decade and a half', *Financial and Economic Review*, 15 (2), 5–32.

MNB (2017a), 'Competitiveness Report', Magyar Nemzeti Bank.

MNB (2017b), 'Press release on the Monetary Council meeting of 19 September 2017', Magyar Nemzeti Bank.

MNB (2017c), 'A jegybanki intézkedések hatása az MNB eredményére és a többi szektorra' (The impact of central bank measures on the MNB's profit and the other sectors), Magyar Nemzeti Bank, March.

MNB (2017d), 'A növekedési hitelprogram eredményei' (Results of the funding for growth scheme), Magyar Nemzeti Bank, June.

Nagy, M. and P. Kolozsi (2017), 'The reduction of external vulnerability and easing of monetary conditions with a targeted non-conventional programme: the self-financing programme of the Magyar Nemzeti Bank', *Civic Review*, 13 (Special Issue), 99–118.

OECD (2010), 'Tax policy reform and economic growth', OECD Tax Policy Studies, 20. Paris: OECD Publishing.

Palotai, D. (2017), 'Beértek a 2010–2013 közötti adóreform kedvező hatásai', Magyar Nemzeti Bank, September.

Palotai, D. and B. Virág (2016), *Competitiveness and Growth*, Book Series of the Magyar Nemzeti Bank, Budapest: Válasz Könyvkiadó.

Sugawara, N. and J. Zalduendo (2013), 'Credit-less recoveries: neither a rare nor an insurmountable challenge', Policy Research Working Paper No. 6459, Washington, DC: World Bank. https://openknowledge.worldbank.org/handle/10986/15597.

Svraka, A., I. Szabó and V. Hudecz (2014), 'Employment stimulating tax incentives in the Hungarian labour market', *Public Finance Quarterly*, 58 (4), 401–17.

Virág, B. (2016), 'Tudomány és művészet – stabilan alacsony kamatokkal az inflációs cél eléréséért' (Science and art – with persistently low interest rates for the infla-tion target), Portfolio.hu, 5 May. https://www.mnb.hu/letoltes/virag-barnabas-tudomany-es-muveszet-stabilan-alacsony-kamatokkal-az-inflacios-cel-ele-jo.pdf.

12. Ensuring monetary and financial stability in the Czech Republic

Jiří Rusnok

In this chapter, I would like to share information on key adjustments the Czech National Bank (CNB) has made to its monetary policy framework in the recent period, most recently in 2017. The most important developments in 2017 were related to the exit from the exchange rate commitment[1] and the subsequent step-by-step normalization of the CNB monetary policy. The exit from the commitment was preceded by a rather robust economic recovery and a gradual rise in inflation in 2014–2016.[2] Inflation pressures further accelerated in late 2016 and early 2017, creating the conditions for being able to fulfil the inflation target on a sustainable basis. For quite revealing insights into the underlying inflation dynamics, see Figure 12.1. It compares core inflation (measured as annual harmonized consumer prices index excluding energy, food, alcohol and tobacco prices) in the euro area and the Czech Republic.

While in the euro area core inflation was fluctuating around 1 per cent between 2014 and 2017, core inflation in the Czech Republic was steadily rising over the same period. This illustrates some disconnect between the cycles prevailing in the euro area and the Czech Republic, and provides a justification for the decision to quit the unconventional way of monetary loosening.

At the beginning of 2017, the continuation of exchange rate commitment was no longer necessary in order to fulfil the CNB's primary objective of maintaining price stability. Therefore, the commitment was ended on 6 April 2017. The exit from the commitment was the first step towards normalizing monetary policy, that is, towards using interest rates as the main instrument again. The second half of 2017 witnessed two repo rate increases (by 0.25 percentage points each time), namely at the start of August and November, as is shown in Figure 12.2.

As can be seen, financial market interest rates responded to the increase in the CNB's policy rates by rising at all maturities.[3]

The exit from the exchange rate commitment was quite smooth in terms of exchange rate volatility. A somewhat higher volatility of the koruna

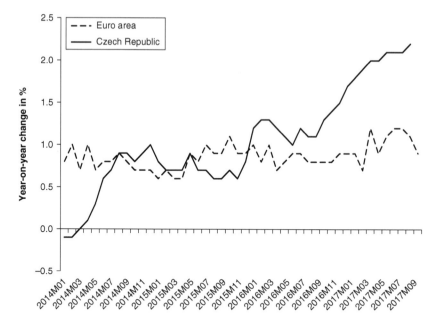

Source: Eurostat.

*Figure 12.1   Core inflation in the euro area and the Czech Republic,
January 2014–October 2017*

vis-à-vis the euro diminished after several weeks, and the koruna started
to follow the appreciation trend. This trend was interrupted temporarily
during the summer of 2017 but recovered afterwards (see Figure 12.3).

In mid-November 2017 the koruna was just above CZK 25.50 to the
euro, thus being around 5.5 per cent stronger than the commitment level of
CZK 27 to the euro. Although the koruna was among the best performers
worldwide, the fact that it was approaching a pre-commitment level hardly
presented any threat to the competitiveness of the exporters.

Actually, the whole economy was doing very well in 2017, possibly
too well. Economic growth rose sharply, from 3 per cent in Q1 to 4.7 per
cent in Q2, and 5 per cent in Q3. The Czech economy (being driven by
manufacturing output) was outpacing potential growth, implying an overheating of some segments of the economy, in particular the labour market.
Unemployment was breaking one historical record after another. The tight
labour market was stimulating wage growth (2017 Q2: 7.6 per cent nominal
and 5.3 per cent real), which fuelled positive consumer sentiment, resulting
in rising household consumption. Credit growth remained high, especially

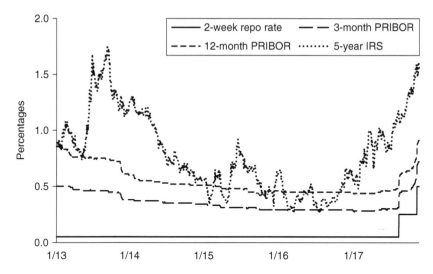

Note: PRIBOR = Prague interbank offered rate; IRS = interest rate swaps.

Source: Czech National Bank.

Figure 12.2   Interest rates

for housing loans. Public finances were in surplus throughout most of 2017. Also, the trade balance and current account remained in surplus. Inflation peaked near the upper limit of the CNB's inflation target, namely at 2.9 per cent in October, but declined afterwards. All of the above indicators witnessed the Czech business cycle to be ahead of the euro area cycle.

There is one more reason for optimism with respect to the Czech economy, namely a very promising evolution of the public budget during 2007–2019 (see Figure 12.4).

Figure 12.4 shows that while the government debt-to-GDP ratio was 27.5 per cent in 2007 and peaked at 45 per cent in 2013, it is projected to fall to 30 per cent in 2019. This is a substantially better performance than in the majority of euro area countries. It may indicate that Czech public finance will be ready to act effectively as a shock absorber in the future.

To conclude, let me list the macro-prudential policy instruments the CNB has adopted in recent years to cope with financial risks. Those enhancing the resilience of the banking sector are as follows:

- A capital conservation buffer: 2 per cent (since 2014).[4]
- A systemic risk buffer: 1–3 per cent in place for four banks since 2014, and five since 2017.[5]

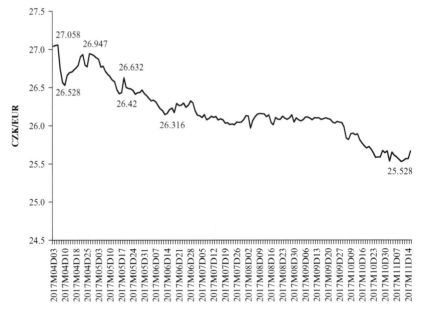

Source: Eurostat.

Figure 12.3   CZK/EUR exchange rate

- A countercyclical buffer, which was activated in Q4 2015: 0.5 per cent applicable as of January 2017 and 1 per cent from July 2018.[6]

Instruments mitigating the risks of residential real estate credit exposures are as follows:

- Loan-to-value limits for mortgages (applied since 2015):
  - upper loan-to-value limit on individual loans of 90 per cent, and aggregate limit of 15 per cent of new loans with loan-to-value limits of 80–90 per cent (since April 2017);
  - institutions should apply a loan-to-value limit of 60 per cent to investment-type loans (buy-to-let mortgages) should they bear characteristics of higher riskiness;
  - institutions that do not comply materially can be (and in some cases are) subject to a Pillar 2 add-on.
- Providers should monitor borrowers' debt-to-income and debt service-to-income ratios, and set internal limits for them: a debt-to-

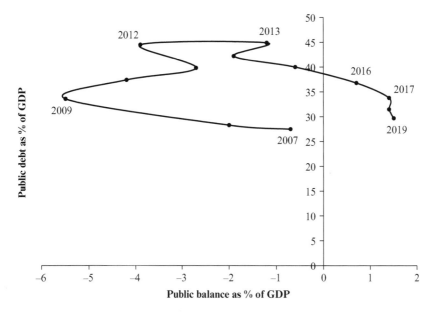

Note: Data for 2017–2019 as forecast by the CNB.

Sources: Eurostat, Czech National Bank.

Figure 12.4   Public finance in Czech Republic, 2007–2019

income ratio of over 8; a debt service-to-income ratio of over 40 per cent.[7]

What I can share as a particularly useful approach with the benefit of hindsight is that the macro-prudential policy started to tighten several years before the monetary policy tightening occurred.[8] This enabled the risks of overheating of particular financial market segments to be mitigated at a time when monetary policy was still preoccupied with dealing with overly low inflation.

My overall assessment of the current economic situation is positive on all fronts: the Czech economy is doing very well, CNB monetary policy has embarked on a path towards normality, and inflation is under control. Financial conditions are gradually getting more restrictive, not only through the increasing interest rates and appreciating koruna, but also through macro-prudential tightening. Policies are thus quite consistent and not only act countercyclically, but also safeguard financial stability.

NOTES

1. The reasons for adopting the exchange rate commitment in November 2013 are elaborated in Franta et al. (2014).
2. Brůha and Tonner (2017) provide an *ex post* assessment of the effects of the exchange rate floor on the Czech economy: inflation and the main real aggregates. They conclude that the introduction of the floor was a correct policy action that has retrospectively been successful.
3. For more details on the development of interest rates see CNB (2017a).
4. http://www.cnb.cz/en/financial_stability/macroprudential_policy/capital_conservation_buffer/index.html.
5. http://www.cnb.cz/en/financial_stability/macroprudential_policy/systemic_risk_buffer/index.html.
6. http://www.cnb.cz/en/financial_stability/macroprudential_policy/countercyclical_capital_buffer/index.html.
7. http://www.cnb.cz/miranda2/export/sites/www.cnb.cz/en/legislation/official_information/vestnik_2017_07_20717180_en.pdf.
8. For a detailed overview of CNB's macro-prudential policy see the CNB Financial Stability Report 2016/2017 (CNB 2017b).

REFERENCES

Brůha, J. and J. Tonner (2017), An Exchange Rate Floor as an Instrument of Monetary Policy: An Ex-post Assessment of the Czech Experience. CNB WP, 4/2017.

CNB (2016/2017a), Financial Stability Report 2016/2017. Czech National Bank.

CNB (2017b), Inflation Report I/2018. Czech National Bank.

Franta M., T. Holub, P. Král, I. Kubicová, K. Šmídková and B. Vašíček (2014), The Exchange Rate as an Instrument at Zero Interest Rates: The Case of the Czech Republic. CNB RPN 3/2014.

13. Sustainable pension reforms: what can we learn from the experiences of Poland and other EU countries?

Paweł A. Strzelecki

The advancement of the ageing process can be measured by two indicators: the old age dependency ratio (OADR), which is defined by the relation of persons aged 65+ to persons aged 15–64; and the total dependency ratio (TDR), whose nominator includes also children aged 0–14. Since the mid-1980s, old-age dependency ratios have been increasing in all European countries as a result of population ageing (United Nations 2017). In the countries of Western Europe population ageing was more advanced, and the total dependency ratios increased in parallel with old-age dependency ratios. At the same time, the majority of the countries of Central and Eastern Europe experienced a period of demographic dividend (Bloom et al. 2003), given a rise in the share of the most productive persons (aged 40–49) in the population. In addition, in many of these countries economic growth improved on the back of the increasing proportion of highly educated persons – the educational dividend (Crespo Cuaresma et al. 2014). However, also in these countries the total dependency ratios started to increase after 2010 as a sign of changes in the near future. Facing the challenge of population ageing, pension systems in the European countries have been reformed in many directions (Whiteford and Whitehouse 2006). Due to the less advanced ageing process, some countries (for example, Poland) had an opportunity to introduce major reforms before the end of the demographic dividend period. In some other countries, the economic crisis seemed to be a trigger for significant reforms (OECD 2013). According to population projections the current differences in the advancement of population ageing among countries of the European Union (EU) should disappear in the next decades. Central and Eastern Europe countries are going to converge to the countries of the Western part of the continent not only in terms of economic development but also in terms of the increasing share of older persons in society (European Commission 2015). It means that in countries such as, for example, Poland or Slovakia the dynamics

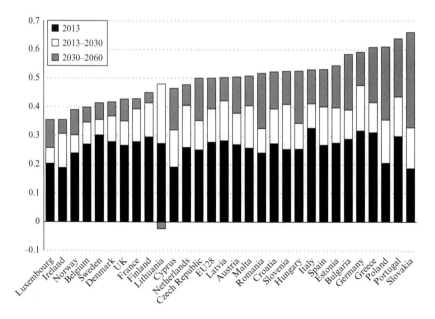

Source: Own elaboration of the data from European Commission (2015, p. 24).

Figure 13.1 *Dependency rates (population 65+ / population 15–64) in 2013 and their predicted changes until 2030 and 2060 in the EU countries*

of the change of the age structure will be much higher than in the rest of the European continent, and the OADR is expected to triple (Figure 13.1) until the year 2060.

The inevitable changes in the size of the older and younger generations will create pressure not only on public finances, but also on the relation between aggregate consumption and savings in the economy, and the organization of the societies and labour markets. These changes are likely to happen because the patterns of labour income and consumption are relatively stable. Analyses using National Transfer Accounts (NTAs) data show that despite some differences between countries the shape of the private consumption and labour income profiles (Figure 13.2) is universal for countries with less and more advanced population ageing (Lee and Mason 2011). At the same time, it is also evident that countries where population ageing is more advanced are under pressure to raise the average exit age from the labour market. The pension reforms can counterbalance the consequences of population ageing by, for example, extending work careers or

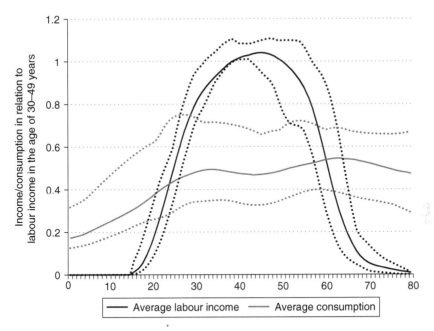

Note: Dotted lines present minimum and maximum in the 25 European countries.

Source: Own elaboration of the data from National Transfer Account project, www. agenta-project.eu.

Figure 13.2   *The average, minimum and maximum lifecycle profiles of labour income (LY) and consumption (C) as proportion of the average earnings of person 30–49 years old*

delaying the moment when, on average, the individual consumption of one generation needs to be financed by other generations.

After the financial and economic crisis in 2008, there was also a return of the discussion about the possible consequences of the ageing process for the economy. From the view of central banking, the secular stagnation hypothesis (Summers 2016) has been of particular importance. This hypothesis predicts a global slump in productivity growth, with empirical analysis suggesting also possible headwinds to asset prices resulting from population ageing (Takats 2010). A review of other important concepts can be found in Furnkranz-Prskawetz (2015). In this chapter, population ageing is the starting point of the discussion – the process that requires pension systems to be adjusted. Introducing pension reforms and maintaining the effects of reforms is difficult. The aim of this chapter is to present changes made to the pension systems in Poland and selected EU countries, and the perception of their effects as observed through the lens of subsequent pension projections prepared by the Working Group on Ageing Populations and Sustainability by the European Commission in the period 2009–2018. An analysis of the experiences derived from introducing changes in the pension systems, and a comparison of the projections, seems to be useful in answering questions such as:

- Is population ageing still a challenge for EU pension systems taking into account pension projection results?
- When and why do governments introduce costly reforms and how is sustainable reform to be introduced?
- Are there any differences between declared and actual channels of adjusting pension systems to population ageing?

The chapter first analyses the possible ways of pension system adjustment to population ageing and the possible trap of dynamic inconsistency. It then considers the circumstances under which pension reforms have been introduced in Poland since 1999, and the long-term consequences of these measures. After that it seeks to establish to what extent the changes in the expected expenditures on pensions are determined by the changing macroeconomic assumptions of the pension projections. The chapter sums up by presenting main conclusions.

13.1 HOW DO EUROPEAN COUNTRIES PLAN TO ADJUST PENSION SYSTEMS TO POPULATION AGEING?

Regardless of the type of pension system, there are three possible ways of adjusting pension systems to the increasing proportion of the number of persons who receive pension benefits compared to those who pay contributions. The first method is to move the frontier between economic activity and inactivity. This includes increasing the retirement age, but covers also the efforts of the state to increase labour force participation of persons in later stages of their labour market careers. To some extent this process can be reinforced by increasing healthy life expectancy or increasing the human capital of the younger generations that are replacing older generations on the labour market. The second method of adjustment is to reduce the level of pension benefits. The simplicity of this solution is self-evident but the level of the pensions is often a part of the promise given by the state. Another limitation is the adequacy of the future pensions. The system can become politically unsustainable if the benefits are too small to prevent massive poverty. The third option is to gradually increase the burdens on the working age population. This can be done by increasing contributions to the public pension system, increasing taxation to cope with the poverty of elderly persons, or to motivate people to increase their own retirement savings. Despite important differences, these solutions assume that the costs of adjustment to ageing are attached to generations active on the labour market.

What is perceived as automatic, and what remains a policy decision, depends on the type of pension system. The principle of the defined contribution pension systems is actuarial fairness between generations that should lead to adjustment of the pension benefits and then, as a result, behavioural adjustment of the retirement age or savings. On the other hand, population ageing in systems with defined benefits create a direct pressure on government expenditures and thus force decision-makers to introduce limitations regarding eligibility for benefits, or to increase financing by tax or through the contribution channel.

The problem with necessary adjustment of the pension systems to the ageing process is the fact that what is optimal and profitable in the long-term horizon (higher retirement age, adjustment of the retirement benefits to the actuarially fair level, higher long-term savings) can be perceived as not optimal in the short-term perspective. In economics, this is a well-known problem of dynamic inconsistency (Kydland and Prescott 1977). In such a situation there are permanent short-term temptations to abandon the commitment to optimal long-term enhancements. Unfortunately there is no ultimate answer to this paradox, but economists propose some ways to overcome this problem using the mechanisms of commitment to solutions optimal in the long term. For example, in monetary policy this problem was addressed by creating the institution of an independent central bank which is focused on building its own reputation and uses inflation targeting.

The results of the pension system projections made by the Working Group on Ageing Populations and Sustainability (AWG) by the European Commission show that in the different countries various combinations of the adjustment methods are expected to be observed in the future (Figure 13.3). In the countries where the impact of the ageing process on the relation between public pension expenditures and gross domestic product (GDP) is projected as being most severe (for example Poland, Slovakia and Austria) the decrease of the coverage of the pension benefits plays a significant role in the adjustment of pension expenditures in the future. The decreasing coverage usually means an increase of the exit age from the labour market, and an increase of labour force participation, which increases GDP growth.

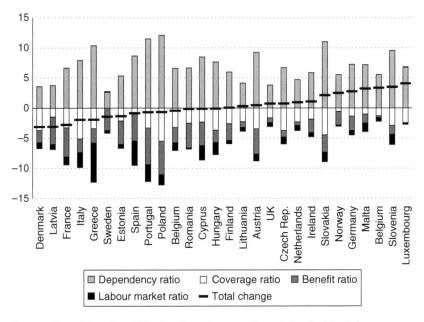

Source: Own elaboration of the data from European Commission (2015, p. 87).

*Figure 13.3   The decomposition of the changes in the relation of public
                expenditures on pensions to GDP in the period 2014–2060*

This last effect is described as the labour market contribution to the changes
of the relation of pension expenditures to GDP.

Beside countries with typical flat rate defined benefit pension systems
(classification based on European Commission 2015, p. 54), in most
countries the crucial part of the projected adjustment to ageing is through
the reduction of the level of pension benefits. So, in principle, the pension
systems are reformed to offer less and less generous promises about future
pension benefits. However, the next section of this chapter analyses to what
extent this was observed in reality from the mid-2000s to the mid-2010s.
The most important message that comes from Figure 13.3 is that in all
EU countries the projected burden of additional expenditures due to the
demographic structure has already been addressed in the pension systems
to some extent. Even in the countries with relatively high projected growth
of pension expenditures (such as Slovenia and Luxembourg) some adjustments have reduced the increase in costs caused by population ageing. In
the majority of countries the implemented pension reforms should prevent
the relation of pension expenditure to GDP from increasing in the future.

This suggests that, due to the current regulations, the problem of the influence of population ageing on pension expenditures has been already addressed. The problem that remains is: what is the commitment to abide by these regulations in the future? Below are presented some findings regarding this problem on the basis of comparing past projections with the actual data.

13.2 SHORT HISTORY OF REFORMING THE PENSION SYSTEM IN POLAND: WHAT CAN WE LEARN FROM THE PAST?

This section presents some stylized facts from the history of contemporary reforms of the Polish pension system. The aim of this analysis is to collect findings about the factors that influenced the implementation of the pension reforms and their sustainability.

The major reform of the Polish pension system was introduced in 1999. It reshaped the pension system for generations born after 1948, from the typical defined benefit system to the defined contribution pension system. The system introduced in 1999 consisted of two pillars: notional defined contribution, and obligatory financial investment into pension funds. This reform was preceded by the analysis of the long-term unsustainability of the pension system (Góra and Rutkowski 1997). However, it was quite clear that the direct reason for this reform was the avalanche increase of pension expenditures due to the huge post-transformation unemployment of persons in pre-retirement age. The reform of the pension system was considered as a first step to address this problem. However, further steps were relatively spread out in time. The next big effort to align the pension system with increasing life expectancy was introduced in 2009, by ceasing to make early pension accessible five years before the statutory retirement age. The third major reform designed to cope with population ageing was the gradual increase of the statutory retirement age to the age of 67 for both men and women in 2040. This reform was introduced in 2013 but later reversed in 2017, bringing the current retirement age in Poland back to 60 years for women and 65 years for men (European Commission 2018, p. 56). It should be also mentioned that since 1999 the views on the role of the financial part of the pension system in Poland have also changed. After the global financial and economic crisis, in many CEE countries the funded components of their mandatory pension schemes have been downscaled or even cancelled (Bielawska et al. 2018). A significant reduction of the mandatory funded pillar was also introduced in Poland, in two steps in 2011 and in 2014.

From the three main reforms introduced to adjust the pension system to the ageing process that were mentioned above, only the two reforms introduced in 1999 and 2009 appeared as sustainable. However, it should be mentioned that the construction and share of the funded mandatory component have changed in comparison to that introduced in the initial reform from 1999. The third reform, introduced in 2013, has been reversed, even though experts have argued consistently that the reform was necessary.

What decides that the reform is sustainable or not? Let us analyse that problem from two perspectives: the calendar of elections and the effects of the reforms on expenditures. One can notice that two initial reforms were introduced two years after the elections (in 1997 and in 2007) by the new governments. The second similarity of the circumstances is that governments were forced to undertake reforms by the tight budget constraints. The reform in 1999 was introduced under pressure created by the fast growth of government expenditures on pension benefits in the previous pension system, amplified by the economic crisis in 1998. The reform introduced in 2009 brought on the changes first announced in 1999; but it took the government a decade to become determined enough. Also in this case the decision made in 2008 was influenced by the expected pressure on public finances due to the economic crisis that also preserved this decision afterwards.

The gradual increase of the retirement age was introduced under different circumstances. First, it was introduced in the sixth year of the same government. It was also introduced a few years after the problems caused by the economic crisis, so it was perceived as a voluntary austerity measure. The reasons for the reform were clear for the experts, but their communication to the voters was rather parsimonious, as policy-makers were convinced that the reason for reform was obvious and widely accepted. The reform started to work during the recovery and amid decreasing unemployment rates, so the required longer labour market activity seemed not to be onerous for persons covered by the reform. However, it appeared that the lack of consensus in this field between the ruling party and the opposition resulted in a lack of commitment to this reform. In the parliamentary election in 2015 the reform became one of the main topics and, what was even more important, the party that won the elections committed itself to cancel this reform. As a result the new government was determined to show that the reform introduced in 2013 was useless. What is even more important is that the relatively good budget situation after 2015 made the reversal of the reform feasible. To conclude, this finding shows that the business cycle, the political calendar, good advertising and the search for wider commitment are important factors for the sustainability of the reforms, even if they are blessed by experts.

The assessment of the consequences of the reforms can be also illustrated by the changes in the projections of the pension system prepared by Poland for the European Commission for the purposes of the AWG. Since 2009 it has been possible to decompose the changes in the relation of pension expenditure to GDP into two parts: first, changes related to reforms of the pension system; and second, changes that reflect the updated path of macroeconomic assumptions and improvements in the models used to prepare the projections (Table 13.1).

The first projection presented was prepared before the crisis, but published in 2009. It assumed that despite population ageing, pension expenditures to GDP would decline from 13.7 percent to about 8 percent in 2060 due to the future dynamic economic growth. The future fast GDP growth was a result of the assumption of the continuation of the vigorous productivity growth observed before the crisis. The increase of the path of pension expenditures in 2012 reflected mainly the rapid adjustment of the macroeconomic assumptions after the crisis. However it also reflected the first major reform that reduced the role of the obligatory financial part of the pension system and increased the responsibility of the state for the future pensions. This reform also reflected the erosion of the reliance on the financial markets after the crisis. There was also a sharp decline in pension contribution revenue due to the consequences of the economic crisis, that needed to be compensated from the short-term gains from the reform.

In the period 2012–2015 two major changes in the pension system were introduced. First was the gradual increase of the statutory retirement age from 65 for men and 60 for women to 67 for both sexes in 2040. According to the projection this reform contributed to the substantial decrease of the expenditures in the short and medium term, but not in the long term, as it led to a greater accumulation of average pension liabilities. The second major reform involved the state taking over most of the capital collected by the pension system for future payments. It greatly improved the level of public debt in the short run, but it also contributed to the increase of the burden of public implicit liabilities.

Between 2015 and 2018 the major change was the reversal of the gradual increase of the retirement age. The estimated costs of this reform were close to the gains from the introduction of the reform in 2013, but in the same period the changes in the level of the minimum pension and favourable pension indexation improved the adequacy of the pensions, but significantly increased future expenditures.

Another dimension of analysis is the projected and real changes of the adequacy of pensions (Table 13.2). The experiences of reforming the pension system in Poland suggest that the average replacement rate in the general system remained remarkably stable, despite all the pension

Table 13.1 *The comparison of the changes in the relation of the public expenditures on pensions to GDP in the projections of the Polish pension system in the years 2009, 2012, 2015 and 2018*

	2005	2010	2020	2030	2040	2050	2060
Projection 2009	13.7	10.8	9.6	9.1	8.7	8.5	8.0
Changes 2009–2012		1.0	1.4	1.8	1.6	1.5	1.6
Policy related changes (reforms)		0.0	0.0	0.2	0.4	0.8	1.1
Changes in macro assumptions and model		1.0	1.4	1.8	1.6	1.5	1.6
Projection 2012	13.7	11.8	10.9	10.9	10.3	10.0	9.6
Change 2012–2015			−0.1	−0.4	−0.2	0.6	1.2
Policy related changes (reforms):							
– gradual increase of the retirement age to 67			−0.6	−0.6	−0.7	−0.3	0.2
– other reforms (including reduction of the capital part of the system)			0.1	0.3	0.6	1.0	1.2
Changes in macro assumptions and model			0.4	−0.1	−0.1	−0.1	−0.2
Projection 2015	13.7	11.8	10.8	10.5	10.1	10.6	10.8
Change 2015–2018			0.3	0.5	0.7	0.6	0.3
Reforms (mainly decrease of the retirement age)			0.8	1.0	1.0	0.7	0.4
Changes in macro assumptions and model			−0.5	−0.5	−0.3	−0.1	−0.1
Projection 2018	13.7	11.8	11.1	11.0	10.8	11.2	11.1

Source: Own elaboration based on the pension system projections of the AWG by the European Commission and Polish projections.

predictions that had expected this indicator to drop sharply. The expectations were justified by the defined contribution formula of the pension system. However it appeared that a lower replacement level was relatively hard to accept. At first the introduction of the payment phase of the

Table 13.2   *The comparison of the observed (bold numbers) and*
              projected replacement rates in the Polish pension system in the
              subsequent pension projections

	2005	2007	2010	2013	2020	2030	2040	2050	2060
Projection 2009	**46.3**	45.4	46.3	47.1	48.8	39.1	32.2	28.8	27.7
Proejction 2012	**46.3**	**47.7**	51.7	43.8	43.6	37.5	28.6	24.5	23.5
Projection 2013	**46.3**	**47.7**	**51.7**	46.9	46.2	45.5	41.2	31.1	28.5
Projection 2015	**46.3**	**47.7**	**51.7**	**53.0**	53.8	47.9	39.4	31.2	28.7

Source: Own elaboration based on the pension system projections of the AWG by the
European Commission.

pensions from the new, defined contribution system was postponed. Then,
the level of the minimum pension was increased because of lump sum
valorisation in 2012. And 2013 saw the introduction of a gradual increase
of the retirement age.

As a result, in 2013 the average replacement level was significantly
higher than in all previous projections. These observations suggest that the
decrease of the level of future pensions can be relatively difficult for people
to accept, even though such a decline seems to be the automatic method of
adjustment in a system with defined contributions.

13.3   FINANCIAL AND ECONOMIC CRISIS AND PENSION REFORMS IN THE EUROPEAN UNION

Times of economic crisis with very high unemployment rates and expanding poverty among households can be perceived as the worst possible
times for long-term reforms. However the experiences of the years before
and after the crisis show something completely different. An analysis for
the Organisation for Economic Co-operation and Development (OECD)
countries (Beetsma et al. 2017) has shown that the year 2008, when the
last financial and economic crisis had started, was followed by the three
years with the highest number of pension reforms targeted on long-term
fiscal sustainability in the OECD countries in the whole analysed period of
1970–2013. What is also important is that the relatively very high number
of reforms that led to higher financial and fiscal sustainability was also
observed after 2011.

According to the data from AWG reports, the pension reforms after
the economic and financial crisis that appeared in 2008 were the most

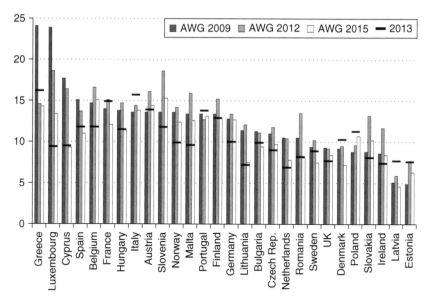

Source: Own elaboration based on European Commission (2009, 2012, 2015).

Figure 13.4   *The evolution of projected pension expenditures to GDP in 2060 in the three projections of the AWG in comparison to the level observed in 2013*

significant in the group of countries with the highest projected increase of pension expenditures, due to the lack of reforms in the past (European Commission 2009). This fact is consistent with the findings of Beetsma et al. (2017). Greece, Cyprus and Spain were at the top of the list with a projected increase of annual pension expenditure to GDP of between 6.7 percentage points and 12.4 percentage points in the period 2007–2060.

A comparison of the AWG projections illustrates the adjustment of the long-term expenditures on pensions in the time of crisis after the year 2008. The level of pension expenditures to GDP in different EU countries amounted to between 7 and 17 per cent of GDP (Figure 13.4). The projected levels of expenditures in 2060 were in most of the countries higher than the current level, but in the countries with the highest expected expenditures before the crisis (such as Greece, Luxembourg, Cyprus and Spain) a sharp reduction was observed in both periods 2009–2012 and 2012–2015. However, it should be noted that in other countries the changes were more connected with changing assumptions of macroeconomic projections than with the pension reforms.

The general trend is that the predictions of the expenditures in the future are close to recently observed values. This may suggest that the preferences regarding the accepted level of pension expenditures also play an important role in pension reforms that shape the future level of pension expenditures.

It can be also noticed that countries where the earlier predictions showed a significant decrease of the pension expenditures in comparison to the recently observed values were usually less eager to adjust pension expenditures further. Three out of four countries with an increase of pension expenditures by 2060 between the projections of 2009 and 2015 (excluding 2012 because of the sharp macroeconomic changes) were countries with relatively high recent expenditures and low future expenditures. This may suggest that in countries such as Poland, Estonia and Italy changes in the pension system can reflect preferences of the decision-makers who perceive the current level of expenditures as optimal, and relatively easily decide for reforms that increase expenditures if the long-term predictions show potential reductions of expenditures.

Economic crisis also changed the perception of the future changes of the macroeconomic variables. This was reflected in the significant changes of the macroeconomic assumptions between the pension projections in AWG 2009 (European Commission 2009) and AWG 2012 (European Commission 2012) projections. Three years later, the projection of AWG 2015 (European Commission 2015) was based on improved macroeconomic assumptions not only regarding short-term but also long-term developments. The comparison of the available decompositions of the factors driving changes of the pension projections in 2015 and 2012 prepared by the countries shows that in most of the countries the effects of pension reforms were relatively much less important than the changes in the macroeconomic assumptions of the projections (Figure 13.5). This suggests that changes in the macroeconomic outlook accepted by experts played a key role in the changes of the long-run projections of pension expenditures. In almost all countries the macroeconomic outlook had improved in comparison to the previous projection, so the predicted GDP growth was higher, contributing to the decline in the relation of the pension expenditures to GDP even without major pension reforms. Why was this improvement observed in most countries in the period 2012–2015? It can be explained by a certain overreaction of the long-term macroeconomic expectations in the times of economic crisis. In the projections prepared during the crisis (AWG 2012 in comparison with AWG 2009) the perception was far more pessimistic.

The changes in pension projections that reflect the vision of the future are an additional explanation as to why long-term pension reforms were

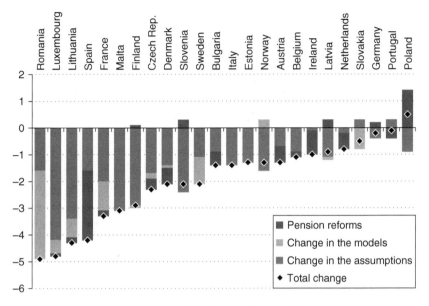

Figure 13.5   The decompositions of the changes between the AWG projections in 2015 and in 2012 of the pension expenditures to GDP in 2060

introduced during or just after economic crisis. Such moves are based in the psychology of experts and decision-makers. In this explanation the perception of the future expenditures is much more pessimistic in the downturn than in the upturn, despite the fact that in theory the current business cycle position should be independent from the long-term economic outlook. AWG projections are used by the European Commission to make long-term assessments of the financial sustainability of the countries. The conclusions from the comparison of the subsequent AWG projections support the idea that a pressure to introduce reforms from the international organization appeared precisely in the time of economic downturn. The pressure was reduced once the short-term macroeconomic indicators improved. These findings add an extra dimension to the already presented model (Beetsma et al. 2017) where the decisions about reforms are made in periods when public budgets are under pressure.

13.4 CONCLUSIONS

This chapter has presented some stylized facts from the historical data that can be useful in the discussion about reforming pension systems. The sustainability of the introduced pension reforms depends on their efficiency in solving important social problems. For example, the switch from defined benefit to defined contribution pension systems in Poland and some other Central and Eastern European countries was instrumental in hampering the expansion of the social expenditures. The reform also created clear incentives for labour force participation of elderly persons. So, two major problems of the countries in transition to market economy were tackled at the same time.

The second hint in the political economy of pension reforms is that achieving democratic consensus for the reforms is of the essence. Experiences of the reforms of the Polish pension system suggest that reforms introduced by the new governments in the two first years after the elections that changed the government (such as a move to a national defined contribution pension system in 1999, and cancellation of early pensions in 2009) were relatively sustainable. The reform of the gradual increase of the retirement age introduced in 2013, and the reversal of this reform introduced in 2017, is a visible example of how an efficiently introduced reform with positive labour supply effects can be later abandoned because of the lack of political consensus. This observation also supports previous research on sustainability of pension reforms (Hinrichs 2000). The way to avoid this trap of dynamic inconsistency in the future is to seek consultation and advertise the need for reform, as well as to develop strong institutions, thus increasing the independence of the main long-term principles of the system from current policy choices, or at least increasing the cost of a potential reversal of already implemented rules.

One should also be aware that if the formulas of the pension systems do not reflect the preferences of potential voters, the agreed solutions can be bypassed by other policy decisions. A typical example was the expected and observed average replacement rate in the pension system in Poland in the period 2007–2013.

The valuable lesson that can be learned from comparing the factors driving changes of the AWG pension projections is that there are mechanisms that make it easier to introduce major and long-lasting pension reforms in periods of economic downturn, whereas introducing the reform in times of prosperity is usually hard, not only because of the costs of reform but also because of the cyclical fluctuations of the vision of the future that, as shown in this chapter, was reflected in the assumptions of the pension projections. Thus, this chapter has identified that the pressure for structural reforming of the pension systems is a result not only of the budget constraints faced during the crisis, but also of procyclical fluctuations in the expected long-term economic outlook of both governments and international institutions.

Adjusting pension systems to the major contemporary problem of demographic transition is an important change that has required and will continue to require the introduction of many reforms. However, new challenges are ahead, such as robotization and the next technological revolution. In this context the discussion about the optimal way of providing income to people who cannot work because of their age can turn into a discussion about providing income to people who cannot find any work because of technological change. The discussion about the advantages of introducing universal basic income has already started, and it may be a next trigger of future social security and pension reforms.

REFERENCES

Beetsma, R., E. Wart and R. van Maurik (2017), 'What Drives Pension Reform Measures in the OECD? Evidence Based on a New Comprehensive Dataset and Theory', CEPR Discussion Paper 12313.

Bielawska, K., A. Chłoń-Domińczak and D. Stańko (2018), 'Retreat from Mandatory Pension Funds in Countries of the Eastern and Central European in Result of Financial and Fiscal Crisis: Causes and Effects', https://www.aeaweb.org/conference/2018/preliminary/paper/RS2ZtRF2.

Bloom, D., D. Canning and J. Sevilla (2003), *The Demographic Dividend: A New Perspective on the Economic Consequences of Population Change*, Santa Monica, CA: Rand.

Crespo Cuaresma, J., W. Lutz and W. Sanderson (2014), 'Is the Demographic Dividend an Education Dividend?', *Demography*, **51** (1), 299–315.

European Commission (2009), 'The 2009 Ageing Report. Economic and Budgetary Projections for the EU 27 Member States (2008–2060)', European Economy 2/2009.

European Commission (2012), 'The 2012 Ageing Report: Economic and Budgetary Projections for the EU-27 Member States (2010–2060)', European Economy 2/2012.

European Commission (2015), 'The 2015 Ageing Report: Economic and Budgetary Projections for the EU-28 Member States (2013–2060)', European Economy, 3/2015.

European Commission (2018), 'The 2018 Ageing Report: Economic and Budgetary Projections for the EU Member States (2016–2070)', European Economy, Institutional Paper 079/2018.

Furnkranz-Prskawetz, A. (2015), 'Demographic Change and the Economic Growth', *Proceedings 43rd Economics Conference*, Oesterreichische Nationalbank.

Góra, M. and M. Rutkowski (1997), *Bezpieczeństwo Dzięki Różnorodności* (Security through diversity), Biuro Pełnomocnika Rządu ds. Reformy Zabezpieczenia

Społecznego (Office of the Government Plenipotentiary for Social Security Reform).

Hinrichs, K. (2000), 'Elephants on the Move: Patterns of Public Pension Reform in OECD Countries', *European Review*, **8** (3), 353–78, https://doi.org/10.1017/S10627 98700004956.

Kydland, F.E. and E.C. Prescott (1977), 'Rules Rather than Discretion: The Inconsistency of Optimal Plans', *Journal of Political Economy*, **85** (3), 473–91.

Lee, R. and A. Mason (2011), *Population Aging and the Generational Economy: A Global Perspective*, Cheltenham, UK and Northampton, MA, USA: Edward Elgar Publishing.

OECD (2013), 'Pensions at a Glance 2013: OECD and G 20 Indicators', Paris: OECD Publishing.

Summers, L.H. (2016), 'Secular Stagnation and Monetary Policy', *Federal Reserve Bank of St Louis Review*, Second Quarter 2016, **98** (2), 93–110.

Takats, E. (2010), 'Ageing and Asset Prices', BIS Working Papers, 318, Bank for International Settlements, https://ideas.repec.org/p/bis/biswps/318.html.

United Nations (2017), 'World Population Prospects 2017', Online Database, https://esa.un.org/unpd/wpp/.

Whiteford, P. and E. Whitehouse (2006), 'Pension Challenges and Pension Reforms in OECD Countries', *Oxford Review of Economic Policy*, **22** (1), 78–94.

14. Europeanization meets transformation: a political economy approach to transition

Alina Mungiu-Pippidi[1]

There are two radically different versions of the post-communist narrative. One tells the triumphal tale of the only world region in which the reforms recommended by the 'Washington Consensus' worked, where democracy quickly consolidated and the transition came to completion; a model for transformations in the rest of the world that Western policy-makers and development agencies seek to transplant to the broader Middle East and other places.

The other and more realistic account speaks of a historic window of opportunity that lasted for only a quarter-century, during which efforts by the West and patriotic Central and Eastern European (CEE) elites managed to drag the region (including the Baltic and Balkan countries) into Europe proper, leaving Europe and Russia pitted against each other along the old 'civilizational' border between them.

Both accounts have their attractions and their risks. But they cannot both be right. They might seem like mere caricatures, but they have been shaping policy arguments and people's lives for many years, and their widely divergent practical consequences are deadly serious. In the former 'end of history' scenario in the spirit of Fukuyama, human agency is everything and building a critical mass in favour of change is the essential factor. This was so, for example, in the struggle against Serbian strongman Slobodan Miloševic in 2000 (when he finally lost a national election), and in the 'colour revolutions' that began erupting in parts of the former Soviet Union a few years later. In the second 'border of civilizations' scenario in the spirit of Huntington, by contrast, a critical mass can be built to some effect only on the right side of the geopolitical border: On the wrong side, you can have countless Orange Revolutions without putting a country on the right path.

For the European Union (EU), the choice between these scenarios is important. If the first one is true, then all that we need to do is to help any willing country make progress along the path of reforms until it comes close enough to EU standards on all counts, economic and political. Integration will follow as a logical consequence, and every country has an equal chance on the basis of merit (Verheugen 2003).

But if the second scenario is the valid one, then all countries that are located within the border of Europe need to be offered enlargement as quickly as possible as a means to stabilize them and the whole geopolitical area, and there is no point in complaining afterwards that it was all a mistake, as we often hear today about Romania and Bulgaria. After all, Lithuania and Latvia were admitted at the same time as Estonia, even though they lacked Estonia's merit as the only Baltic country that had managed by the time of its EU accession to bring corruption under control. Was this fair? Why should a stronger anticorruption performer such as Estonia have been treated no better than such anticorruption laggards as Latvia and Lithuania? This can be rendered understandable only by the logic of the second scenario, invoked by former German Foreign Minister Joschka Fischer in a famous speech (Fischer 2000).

14.1 VARIETIES OF TRANSITION

The term 'transition' has been used loosely over the past quarter-century in relation to Eastern Europe, and it expanded to mean almost anything once it was applied to Afghanistan or the countries of the Middle East and North Africa. Its initial meaning – an exit from political authoritarianism – was lost when the economic dimension was added so as to take account of the specific post-communist context, the passage from a command to a market economy. The 'what' in the menu of reforms was the Washington Consensus, to use the term originally coined by economist John Williamson in 1989 (the Bretton Woods institutions also 'sold' to some indebted Latin American countries this menu of structural adjustment policies, hence the 'universalization' of transition). But this 'what' mattered less in the end than did the 'who' of the transition: who was in charge of these reforms. This is another way of saying that the key factor was the balance of political power in post-communist countries, as this balance manifested itself in the early years of the transition. This was what I argued as part of a set of essays marking the twentieth anniversary of the fall of the Berlin Wall (Mungiu-Pippidi 2010).

Structural adjustment policies were applied differently across the successful countries (so more than one path to success existed), and thus do not in the end explain much. To read the World Bank's *Transitions* newsletter over the years was to discover a changing list of champions.

Poland and Hungary replaced each other quite a few times as the 'ideal reform country', the Baltic states caught up with the early transition achievers and rose to the top of the list, only to see their respective gross domestic products (GDPs) shrink by up to 25 per cent in the economic crisis that began in 2008. Slovenia, the number one economic performer during the first decade after communism, initially seemed like an especially 'good fit' for economic transition, but its reforms were rather modest. The Slovenian state sector remained largely unreformed until late in the transition and so proved vulnerable when the economic crisis came. Harvard economist Dani Rodrik, joined by many European economists, believes that reforms in South and East Asian countries, where the state retains a large role, have proved far more successful than have reforms made in countries where the Washington Consensus reigned (Rodrik 2006).

It was not only economic reforms that differed widely across successful transition countries. De-communization policies varied as well. Hungary made low compensation payments to former owners of nationalized property, while the Czechs restored all nationalized property to its former owners. Poland managed to build a new market economy without dealing with formerly nationalized property at all. Romania and Bulgaria saw internal struggles over restitution for nationalized assets that lasted throughout the whole length of their respective transitions. Lustration, the banning of former communists from political life, was introduced in its most radical form in the Czech Republic and the former East Germany, but was discarded nearly everywhere else. The former Communist Party came in first in the 1993 election in Poland, the most radically anti-communist country, after having dramatically lost the first free (or, more accurately, partly free) election only four years before. Communists pushed ahead with market-based reforms in Hungary and Slovenia; radical populists in Serbia and Slovakia turned in favour of European integration once in office.

14.2   THE ROLE OF NATIONALISM

The difficulty of understanding a region as complicated as Central and Eastern Europe by focusing on institutional or policy variables rather than path-dependent, complex individual country trajectories becomes apparent when we consider the role played by nationalism. Along with the bankruptcy of communist economies, nationalism was the main driver of communism's demise. Nationalism had played a positive role in preventing the total communization of Poland and Yugoslavia (where even the ruling communist parties had nationalist factions), and hence barred the Soviets from gaining a total victory over Central and East European societies. But nationalism was also used as a survival strategy by ex-communist parties in countries – primarily Romania and Serbia – where demands voiced by assertive minorities seemed to pose a threat to the state.

In the late 1980s, nationalism also mobilized people in the Soviet republics, where movements for language rights would become movements for national self-determination. Nationalism inspired the successful transitions undertaken by the Baltic states, where Russian-speaking minorities were denied the vote. Moldova allowed Russian-speakers to vote, and had a far less successful transition. In Central and Eastern Europe's most successful country, Estonia, nationalist centre-right coalitions have governed for more than 20 years. All the while, Moldova has seen struggles – most of which have failed – to defeat the Communist Party in elections. Mart Laar, the genial Estonian Prime Minister who promoted the most liberal economic reform package in Eastern Europe (the famous flat tax, which never featured in the recommendations of international financial institutions), was a nationalist historian who later became the chief inspiration for Georgian President Mikheil Saakashvili.

The first generation of CEE leaders were all patriotic intellectuals (there were many historians among them) with long-standing anti-communist and anti-Russian sentiments who embraced freedom and the West as an anti-Russian national project. In their own words, 'A "Return to Europe" was what our citizens voted for in the first free elections' (*Irish Independent* 2002). Liberals such as Václav Havel always objected to the inclusion of Russia in Europe or the European Union (Havel 2001).

Liberalism and nationalism were also strongly intertwined in Ukraine and remain so today; only the package was far less successful there. In all countries occupied by the Soviet Union, liberalism was successful where it was joined with nationalism. But where liberation from communism could not take the form of national emancipation – as was the case in Albania, Romania and the former Yugoslavia, none of which had Soviet troops on their soil by 1989 – a blended national-communist ideology delayed liberalism's success by ensuring that liberal forces would need six or ten years to gain a feeble majority. Liberal ideology thus had a hard time triumphing wherever it lacked the assistance of this nineteenth-century combination of liberalism with nationalism.

Yugoslavia's bloody post-communist civil war led to the creation of several new states. All are peaceful today, and all (aside from Bosnia, the only 'stuck' case) enjoy reasonably good prospects of European integration. Russian-speaking Crimea, by contrast, changed national allegiance overnight from Ukraine to Russia in 2014, and frozen conflicts along the Dniester and in the Caucasus will keep countries such as Armenia, Georgia and Moldova hostage to Russia indefinitely. It seems likely that these differing outcomes – peace and gradual EU integration in the Balkans versus protracted conflicts in the former USSR – are due, in the end, simply to differing circumstances rather than differing policies. As Barrington Moore Jr once put it, small East European countries should not even be included in discussions on social and political change, as 'the decisive causes of their politics lie outside their own boundaries' (Moore 1966).

14.3   THE EU AND THE 'RETURN TO EUROPE'

It is the influence of the two great geopolitical blocs that has shaped the post-Cold War politics of the small East European countries, which had all been part of the communist system for many years. The 'demonstration effect' that had been present during late communism (for example, West Germany doing so much better than East Germany) continued: East Europeans wanted to be free and prosperous like their Western neighbours, and transition 'laggards' wanted to be transition 'achievers'.

Throughout the decades of the 'return to Europe', including the more formal EU accession process, public support for EU integration ran very high in the CEE countries. This crucial variable explains the conversion of nearly all their post-communist elites into opportunistic pro-Europeans, who adopted pro-accession policies even in national-communist countries such as Romania and Serbia. Driven by rising poverty and the stark contrast between their economic performance and that of the other CEE countries, publics in Bulgaria and Romania badly wanted to join Europe. Owing to the mismanagement of their early transition years, neither country had attracted much foreign direct investment in the 1990s; Europe was needed as much for its money as for any regime legitimacy and security benefits that it might happen to provide.

After securing domestic dominance for themselves (in business, as well as in politics and the judiciary), communist-successor parties in Romania, Bulgaria, Serbia and Albania made European accession their next important objective. The advance toward Europe was undertaken with and not against the former power establishment; otherwise, it would not have been possible at all. The process of 'democratization without de-communization', a characteristic of transitions in South-Eastern Europe, was followed by a similar one of 'Europeanization without de-communization'.

Current patterns of political trust and participation in the region reflect these paradoxes. East Europeans distrust their national political elites, whom they consider poor at handling the problem of corruption. East European voters do not turn out for European elections to elect their nationals to become members of the European Parliament (MEPs).[2] Within the EU, confidence in the Union and its institutions is higher in post-communist Europe than it is anywhere else (whether within or outside the Eurogroup), and such trust is particularly high in poorer countries. Moreover, the preference for populists is smaller in Eastern than in Western Europe. But in the East, this European preference is not, as in Western Europe, an extension of the trust that the public places in national elites to enhance national fortunes through membership in the EU. Instead, it is the same old geopolitical preference: the identification of Europe with the West and freedom versus Russia and communism. In the East but not in the West, trust in the EU has always been strongly correlated with trust in the North Atlantic Treaty Organization (NATO).

Not only popular opinion but also government policies prove the staunchness of favourable CEE attitudes toward the EU. Slovakia, Estonia and Latvia joined the euro after the 2008 crisis (in 2009, 2011 and 2014, respectively) in a deliberate attempt to show their continuing confidence in the European project. What they hoped to receive from Brussels was some paternalistic, objective and benevolent rule from outside and above.

14.4 THE ROLE OF GOVERNANCE

Measures of good governance in a country are significantly associated with its score on the Human Development Index of the United Nations (UN). Central Europe, the Baltic states and the Balkan countries thus are not spectacular achievers, but simply have levels of effective governance that their social and economic situations would predict. Only Estonia and Georgia are doing slightly better than they should, so evidence of any virtuous circle should be sought there.

But while virtuous circles in the relationship between human development and governance are scarce, there are many vicious ones: Russia, Ukraine, Azerbaijan and all five Central Asian countries are doing far worse in terms of 'state capture' by private interests, for instance, than their human development statistics would suggest should be the case.[3] Most accounts of political and economic reforms in the region that put institutions at centre stage stumble by failing to take into account the importance of the endogeneity of such institutions themselves. This endogeneity overshadows whatever independent effects institutions might have, and relegates the causal question to the original choice of institutions themselves (Kitschelt and Malesky 2000). In other words, countries chose presidential systems or 'partial' reforms because the power balance at the time gave leaders the hope that they could control the transition process. When the European Bank for Reconstruction and Development (EBRD) titles its report looking back at the last quarter-century *Stuck in Transition?*, we might well ask if 'transition' is the right word at all (EBRD 2013).

The main policy goal during these 25 years varied across countries; comparing them as if that goal were the same is misleading. Some elites wanted to emulate West European countries, and succeeded. Others wanted to transform the vast public assets of communist times into their own property and thus to consolidate their control of society, and they succeeded as well. In some in-between cases, such as Albania, Bulgaria, Kyrgyzstan and Romania, the two camps were fairly equal in power, with the upshot being highly disputed transitions that resembled civil wars. What mattered was whether the rulers were able to control the social allocation of public resources, or chose to allow free economic competition and equal treatment by the state. The difference lay not in the sequence and types of reforms, but simply in the objectivity and impartiality of those who were directing the reforms.

The process is not finished. In 2014, several high-ranking Romanian politicians went to jail after being convicted of corrupt behaviour while in office. In Bulgaria (where the judiciary is weaker), there have been two parliamentary elections in two years (in May 2013 and October 2014) amid massive street protests against the capture of the state by corrupt elites. Ivo Sanader, who was Croatia's pro-EU Prime Minister from 2003 to 2009, landed in jail in 2011 after being extradited from Austria. Bosnian Serb leaders received harsh convictions at the Hague tribunal dealing with war crimes in the former Yugoslavia. Although there was no shortage of rent-seeking elites anywhere, their trajectories and lifespans seemed quite different in the closer-to-Europe half (as opposed to the closer-to-Russia half) of Eastern Europe.

By 2000, about a decade into the post-communist era, I reported an individual model of support for democracy based on the World Values Survey 2000 for the Central European countries (including Romania and Bulgaria, but excluding the Baltics). An important determinant of support for democracy was state dependence, which I defined both in objective terms (in one form or another, the individual received public funds, whether as a public sector worker or as the beneficiary of some social allocation or pension) and as a matter of attitudes (individuals who believed that the state is responsible for people's welfare were more inclined to favour autocracy; Mungiu-Pippidi 2006). Both the original social basis of democracy and the ways in which that basis changed varied greatly across the region. In bivariate regressions associating state capture with democracy, civil society, media freedom and individual empowerment, we see a high degree of determinism. Only Albania and Georgia were stranded between the two worlds or geopolitical blocs.

The evidence is clear and stands out strongly even in the pages of the EBRD's *Stuck in Transition?* report: in the CEE countries, the key thing has been the balance between the old elites and the new, between the rulers and civil society. This determined the fate of economic reforms, which could have been and were used as instruments either to control society or to set it free. Economic success in the short or medium term is not necessarily associated with either path (that of continued control by old elites, or that of freedom), but long-term development – the ability to 'catch up' to the West – can only be found associated with real economic freedom. This means not only the freedom of trade, but also free internal economic competition under a state that acts impartially as an honest referee of market relations.

That means that students of transition should accord no more than a secondary role to the Washington Consensus, even in its 'augmented' form (the later version that came to the fore after 'shock therapy' failed in Russia, when economists discovered that 'institutions' matter and indeed shape transitions). What should be foremost in our analyses? I would say political modernization combined with geopolitics. Warnings about the intellectual dangers of the term 'transition' are not new. Writing in 1992, Robert A. Nisbet warned that transition is a synonym for change, but that we should be aware that change is not necessarily necessary (and therefore is not inevitable). In 2003, Charles Tilly cautioned that while histories may be comparable, paths are not reproducible, making historical institutionalism quite limited as a tool for analysing policy. A year before that, Thomas Carothers in the *Journal of Democracy* had announced 'The End of the Transition Paradigm', noting that change is not unidirectional or identically sequenced (Nisbet 1992; Carothers 2002; Tilly 2003).

If the account that hinges on geopolitical factors is closer to the observed facts, we should not be surprised to find great variation within the 'successful' half of post-communist Europe. Each country has its own narrative, shaped by domestic contingencies that make themselves felt within the broader geopolitical story. Nationalism has always been strong in Hungary, a reality that its charismatic Prime Minister, Viktor Orbán, has used to his profit, leading his Fidesz party to an overwhelming majority in the National Assembly in 2010 elections. Hungarian voters may harbour less solicitude for the rule of law than some of their Western European counterparts, but their views are not out of line with the still quite young age of Hungarian democracy. In most new democracies, public opinion believes that democracy is about majority rule; building respect for minority opinion, and the idea of valuing procedures above results, takes time.

Yet the CEE's high achievers as well as its laggards defy Western notions of democracy. These Europeanizations have met unfinished transformations which defy textbook democracy. After all, Estonia's neoliberal consensus was made possible by the exclusion of non-Estonian speakers from the franchise; about a third of Estonia's population consists of Russian speakers who settled in the country during the Soviet period. According to the World Values Survey 2000, the members of this group differed from their Estonian-speaking neighbours by expressing higher support for collectivism and lower support for the market economy and democracy. Excluding Russian speakers from the political decision-making process probably helped Estonia's swift advance toward reform. The key to Estonia's successful reform was anti-communism: Estonia remains the country that carried out the most radical purge of Soviet-era judicial and administrative personnel. All its other successful reforms derived from that.

As the EU considers plans to enforce democracy better within EU borders, legitimate doubts can be raised as to what yardstick will be used and whether double standards can be avoided. It may be safer to defend democratic standards within the various national political spaces using the EU framework, rather than to seek the creation of an EU police agency tasked with enforcing democracy and cutting EU funds. In 2012, a forceful EU intervention in Romania to defend besieged President Traian Băsescu (whom Parliament had impeached) backfired, as an electoral majority first endorsed the impeachment in a referendum and then empowered Băsescu's enemies by giving them two-thirds of the vote in the legislative elections held in December of that year. In the November 2014 presidential election, purely by means of a domestic mobilization of civil society, Romanians managed against the odds to elect challenger Klaus Iohannis, a political outsider from the country's ethnic-German minority, because the internal dynamics of the competition had not been affected by an EU intervention. EU tried to intervene in Hungary and Poland to support rule of law, but its interventions seem to mobilize nationalist constituencies more than help rule of law supporters. The EU should always avoid prompting leaders in its member states to resort to nationalist appeals, for even where nationalism is dormant, it has not said its last word in Europe. The EU framework should be enough to favour certain tendencies; beyond that, a nation's internal politics should remain its own business.

NOTES

1. This chapter draws on Mungiu-Pippidi (2015).
2. See Special Eurobarometer 397, 2014, http://ec.europa.eu/public_opinion/archives/ebs/

ebs_397_en.pdf; Standard Eurobarometer 80, 2013, http://ec.europa.eu/public_opinion/archives/eb/eb80/eb80_publ_en.pdf.
3. I prefer predicting not democracy but good governance, understanding the latter as a mixture of formal and informal institutions that explains who gets what. A focus on governance is preferable because it does a better job of explaining each country's transition-era 'choices' (or better put, lack of choice, since the initial reforms made as the transition era began were determined by the relative power that rulers held over societies at the time). As a proxy measure for governance, I use the World Bank's figures showing how well or poorly a country does at controlling corruption.

REFERENCES

Carothers, T. (2002), 'The End of the Transition Paradigm', *Journal of Democracy*, **13** (1), 5–21.

EBRD (2013), *Stuck in Transition? Transition Report 2013*, London: European Bank for Reconstruction and Development.

Fischer, J. (2000), 'From Confederation to Federation: Thoughts on the Finality of European Integration', Humboldt University, Berlin, 12 May.

Havel, V. (2001), 'Europe's New Democracies: Leadership and Responsibility', speech at the conference Europe's New Democracies: Leadership and Responsibility, Bratislava, 11 May.

Irish Independent (2002), 'Use This Historic Chance, Leaders Implore', A. O'Connor and M. Kearns reporting on a joint statement issued by V. Havel, A. Kwasniewski, R. Schuster and F. Mádl, then presidents of the Czech Republic, Poland, Slovakia and Hungary, 16 October.

Kitschelt, H. and E. Malesky (2000), 'Constitutional Design and Postcommunist Economic Reform', prepared for presentation at the Midwest Political Science Conference, Chicago, IL, Panel on Institutions and Transition, 28 April.

Moore, B., Jr (1966), *Social Origins of Dictatorship and Democracy: Lord and Peasant in the Making of the Modern World*, Boston, MA: Beacon Press.

Mungiu-Pippidi, A. (2006), 'Romania: Fatalistic Political Cultures Revisited', in H.-D. Klingemann, D. Fuchs and J. Zielonka (eds), *Democracy and Political Culture in Eastern Europe*, London: Routledge, pp. 308–35.

Mungiu-Pippidi, A. (2010), 'Twenty Years of Postcommunism: The Other Transition', *Journal of Democracy*, **21** (1), 120–27.

Mungiu-Pippidi, A. (2015), 'The Splintering of Postcommunist Europe', *Journal of Democracy*, **26** (1), 88–100.

Nisbet, R.A. (1992), *Social Change and History: Aspects of the Western Theory of Development*, New York: Oxford University Press.

Rodrik, D. (2006), 'Goodbye Washington Consensus, Hello Washington Confusion? A Review of the World Bank's Economic Growth in the 1990s: Learning from a Decade of Reform', *Journal of Economic Literature*, **44**, 973–87.

Tilly, C. (2003), *Contention and Democracy in Europe, 1650–2000*, New York: Cambridge University Press.

Verheugen, G. (2003), 'Let Us Not Hesitate in Seizing This Opportunity', Plenary Session of the European Parliament, Strasbourg, 9 April.

PART V

Reforming EU frameworks or EU countries?

15. Reforms in the EU: the interface of national and Community levels[1]

László Csaba

There are few issues more contested in the literature on European studies than the question pertaining to the architecture of the European Monetary Union (EMU) as it exists today. Opinions revolve around two basic propositions. In one powerful line of thought, gathering momentum in both academe and policy studies, but also in electoral campaigns and discussions in the European Parliament, the whole construction is wrong. First, because it does not take into account the structural disequilibria in the trade and financial positions of the member states, emanating from their different levels of development and also from their different socio-economic models and the lack of political union. Therefore the arrangements are conducive to regular reoccurrence of structural surpluses and structural deficits that cannot be managed via the exchange rate mechanism or monetary policy in general. Thus, as argued, *inter alia* by Nobel laureate Joseph Stiglitz (2016), the single currency, owing to its misconstruction, is the problem rather than the solution.

Second, as explicated by analysts taking a broader analytical perspective and echoing the concerns of the southern member states, the EMU framework fortifies the inherited core–periphery relations, imposing an overly stringent set of policies on the weaker economies without actually providing the usual benefits via fiscal transfers and allowing for delayed and managed structural adjustment, by allowing for lax fiscal and monetary policies (Magone et al. 2016). The latter no longer counts as an extreme or non-professional viewpoint, as we would have had it a decade ago: sustaining negative real rates of interest, sustaining coexistence of lax fiscal and monetary policies, are often presented as inherent features of the 'new normal' (Blanchard et al. 2016, Chapters 2 and 3).

I have always taken a different position, which seems to have been borne out by the facts. The EMU has proven to be a great success if measured in its own terms. The phrase originally introduced by Helmut Kohl, namely that the single currency is to be 'as strong as the German Mark', has proven right. Perhaps even too much so, judging from the policy-makers at the European Central Bank (ECB), who have adopted a set of policies, not originally envisaged by the mandate of the ECB, to provide liquidity and avoid the threat of a depression, especially since President Mario Draghi famously remarked in July 2012 that the 'ECB will do whatever it takes to save the euro'. This included a series of non-conventional measures of monetary easing, without actually pushing up inflation, as measured by the Harmonized Index of Consumer Prices anywhere close to 2 per cent, the inflation target of the ECB since 2003.

This is not to dispute away or belittle the series of challenges faced at both the Community and national levels, be they in the sphere of environment, unemployment and low labour market participation rates, sluggish innovation and secularly low rates of macroeconomic growth in Europe, let alone the series of problems of a purely political nature that have led to grave consequences, from the Brexit vote in June 2016 to the referendum in Catalonia in October 2017. Also, classical EU policies such as those on cohesion and agriculture, environment and global trade relations, face a series of unmet challenges. However, if we take the classical assignment problem of economics and public administration seriously, it is certainly wrong to ascribe all tasks to a single player, in this case the ECB. As labour markets in the European Union (EU) are nationally segmented, and fiscal policies are also managed nationally, with no structural policies at the Community level, growth as a synthetic indicator of economic success can and should not be measured on the performance of any single player, and vice versa. The result is an outcome of interaction of several policies, with monetary management being only one of many tools, even if a quite powerful one. Therefore I continue to agree with those who appreciate the performance of the ECB and joint monetary policy in securing one of the fundamental side conditions for lasting economic growth: price stability, that is, neither an inflation nor a deflation environment (Brunnermeier et al. 2016; Dallago et al. 2016).

One of the fundamental arguments supporting my view is that several members of the euro zone have been performing quite well in terms of international standards, from Luxembourg to Estonia, and from Slovakia to Germany, and more recently Ireland. Therefore it seems to be a fallacy of overgeneralizing the Greek, French and Portuguese experience if claims about the alleged EMU-induced austerity and the ensuing national-level secular stagnation are being theorized. If we take into account the very broad array of new monetary instruments applied by the ECB since July 2012, and if we are aware of the extensive liquidity provision which has ensued ever since – that is, over a period of five years, thus exceeding the time span of the Great Depression of 1929–33 – the claims advanced about the alleged excessively restrictive stance of the ECB following German economic thinking seem unfounded and misplaced.

In one of the classical debates ever since the classical paper of Martin Feldstein (1997) doubting the viability of EMU on both theoretical and policy grounds, two big questions have been looming – like the proverbial elephant in the room – in the professional debates globally. Number one is: if EMU is infeasible, how did the euro survive, and in good shape, a period of more than 15 years, which is already a respectable time span in economic history terms? Number two, if Feldstein and his countless followers were right, has there been any benefit of non-participation in EMU, and for whom, and why? With the spread of political Euroscepticism and inspired by Brexit, the doubters' voice has become more vocal than, say, it was in the 2000s.

Looking from the economic angle it is hard to find relevant arguments against euro membership for any small open economy. The debate might well have been sidetracked by the fact that English is the lingua franca for the economics and European studies communities. Thus the influence of British positions tends to be magnified by the single language domination in the profession. The United Kingdom (UK) has never been enthusiastic about the single currency, and with good reason. Having been the centre for global capital markets since the late eighteenth century, the City of London easily survives without the complex and also in part politically motivated arrangements of the European Union in general and the ensuing monetary model of integration, and thus also the practical arrangements of the single currency in particular. It is common knowledge that UK capital markets are deep and sophisticated, while Continental capital markets are shallow and segmented; the Capital Market Union is in its planning stage only, with a series of preconditions missing. Banking in the UK is more extensive and sophisticated than on the Continent. The UK financial sector has always been global, transacting more with the rest of the globe than within Europe. The British business cycle has never been synchronized to that of continental Europe (particularly Germany). The UK never traded more with Europe than with the rest of the globe, while continental Europe and the euro zone tend to be a relatively closed economy, on a par with the United States (with trade accounting for 18 to 20 per cent with the non-EU world, measured in terms of the gross domestic product). In short, the UK has never been a serious candidate for monetary union,[2] let alone forming an optimal currency area with the rest of the EU.

Once we abstract away the special situation of the United Kingdom and return to continental Europe, none of the above arguments hold. The euro zone is a relatively closed economy, with synchronized business cycles and a long history of learning-by-doing that culminated in the establishment of a special construct (Issing et al. 2004). The two fundamental arguments have been, first, the need to avoid currency fluctuations, which make retaining a separate currency a luxury good for any small open economy, but even for medium-sized economies; and second, importing the stability originating from the Bundesbank and complementing the single market with a single currency entailed a plethora of obvious and hardly disputable palpable benefits for the vast majority of actors, corporations, banks, households and policy-makers alike. If we exclude currency traders and central bank board members, very few individuals lose out, even in theory, from 'giving up the exchange rate instrument', as long as they joined a stability club with interest rates way below the accustomed historical levels.

Once we consider the experience of crisis management in Europe we find that no country actually benefited from big devaluations or from applying interest rates which would not have shadowed those of the ECB. Therefore neither theory nor policy provides sound arguments for the theoretically conceivable position arguing in favour of a nationally separate, arbitrary or old-fashioned monetary policy and its instruments in any real-world scenario.

The study of various adjustment programmes (most recently, Costa Cabral et al. 2017; Ódor 2017) has underscored the great and fundamental diversity in the member states' coping with the crisis. In other words: there is neither a cookbook to go by that would follow from abstract academic insights, nor do we observe the EMU framework acting as a straightjacket on the options taken by the member states.

This is by no means a trivial observation. On the one hand there is a newly emerging consensus on the features of the 'new normal' set of policies, including the lastingly negative real rates of interest and a relatively lasting application of lax monetary conditions. Furthermore the reliance on fiscal policy tools, including some discretionary elements, is no longer anathema, although as the volumes cited above highlight, the rules-based arrangements still prove superior to ad hoc measures, especially in the medium and longer run.

Meanwhile institutional arrangements have proven to be less crucial than was previously theorized. The availability of complex and highly institutionalized arrangements at the EU level, such as the two-pack, the six-pack, the fiscal compact, and the fines introduced for trespassers, failed to stop the notorious non-compliance of traditional violators of fiscal discipline, such as France and Italy.

Complex national arrangements in Belgium, for instance, failed to impose austerity. By contrast, in some countries the low level of institutionalization has not proven to be a major obstacle to fiscal solidity. As a matter of fact, some of the best performers, such as the Baltics and Slovakia, until very recently, have been operating with a very low level of institutionalizing solid fiscal practices by way of independent fiscal councils or budgetary guidelines anchored in the Constitution. Even in Hungary, abolishing the independent fiscal council with an independent analytical apparatus of its own in 2010 has not led to major derailment. Except for the crisis year of 2011, the government made an effort and managed to keep headline deficits under the Maastricht level; and the reported public debt to GDP ratio, the more relevant indicator for assessing fiscal sustainability in the medium run, has also declined, from 81 per cent in 2010 to 74 per cent by end 2016. While the latter is much less than stipulated in the debt brake framework written in the 2011 new Basic Law – that replaced the 1989 Constitution, negotiated during the round table talks leading to peaceful transition – the improvement is non-trivial and rather exceptional among the EU countries, and EMU countries in particular.

What is the explanation for this paradox? It is less of a novelty to claim that the basically intergovernmental nature of the EU, that is a legal-political setting anchored in the 2009 Lisbon Treaty on the European Union, puts severe limits on any supranational practice that would directly interfere with the economic practices of the member states. At least as important are the precedents, set *inter alia* in 2003–2004 on non-punishment of flagrant fiscal trespassing by Germany and France. This allowed smaller states to replicate, and not only in years of deep recession. The most obvious case has been Greece (Visvizi 2014), but other countries such as Hungary also managed to allow practices that are out of line with the Community financial framework in philosophy and implementation alike.

On the national level the explanation lies in the nature of the polity in each country. In the well-performing countries there is a wide professional and also social consensus over the basic issues, for example about what is the right way to follow. In Ireland, for instance, big political changes have not prevented the successful continuation of the adjustment programme and of financial consolidation of the banking sector. In Slovakia a hectic political scene never translated into a derailment in the fiscal and monetary fields. In short, broad consensus – both professional and political – was able to fill the institutional gaps with success.

By contrast, the only commonality in the varieties of political complexities shared by the trespassing countries is the lack of consensus and the weak implementation capacity of formal institutions. This sounds like a platitude in some cases, such as Greece and Portugal.[3] It is less trivial but equally important in countries such as Spain, where fiscal improvements seem to have been making headway since the early 2000s or so. However, as the 2008–2009 crisis has revealed, local finance revolving around the local savings institutions, the *caixas*, has sustained an intimate and unhealthy relationship with local political structures, thus undermining the efforts of the central government and the central bank alike.

From the above it follows that the euro zone framework cannot and should not be blamed for what has been, in essence, poor national crisis management. The framework, to be discussed in the next point, has not been perfect, but did not constitute a barrier to successful adjustment. True, it has also proven ineffectual in pressing for deep changes and adjustment in the countries in difficulty, most importantly in France, Spain and Greece.

It would be grossly unfair to skip the question of whether and to what degree the euro zone framework has been able to cope with the financial crisis of the past, and to what extent has it been upgraded to forestall similar events in the future. As far as the past is concerned, the answer is rather negative. The crisis has uncovered the improvised and unfinished nature of the EMU framework, lamed by a large degree of national egoism and unwillingness to confer power to the Community-level regulators even in cases where the logic of the internal market would have called for it. What emerged in 2016 as the Single Resolution Mechanism is basically the implementation of the Lámfalussy proposals dating back to 2001 (more on that in Kudrna 2016). The ECB could not play the role of lender of last resort within its original mandate, which has proven to be a problem during crisis management. In a single market with many cross-border transactions, banking supervision is bound to be transnational (that happened only in 2014). Last but not least, the insight over the need to create a standing buffer to avert and pre-empt speculative attacks took a long time to emerge in the form of the European Stability Mechanism.

It is difficult to assess whether those new arrangements – somewhat overambitiously termed as the Fiscal and Banking Union – will prove waterproof in the case of the next crises. This is so not least because of the ever-growing expansion of private finance and globalization. If, back in 1994, a US$50 billion dollar bail-out for Mexico was considered to be a jumbo deal, by now a 'normal' Greek rescheduling – which is unlikely to be a singular, one-shot action as was the case with Mexico – involves similar or bigger sums without calling for headlines in the news. Monthly asset purchases in the range of €80 billion – twice nominally the sum mentioned[4] – and targeted discretionary measures, as well as liquidity provision without upper limits, constitute an integral part of the unconventional monetary policy instruments lavishly used by the ECB since 2014 (see Alvarez et al. 2017). Financial innovation implying market actors' ability to circumvent rules is unlikely to come to a halt. Also, in times of crisis the cohesiveness of the Community is crucial for efficient and swift action; this may or may not be forthcoming.

What seems to be a fundamental unresolved problem, as I have argued earlier (Csaba 2016), is the fact that all the institutional and policy innovations of the Fiscal and Banking Union, as well as the transformation of the ECB into a fully fledged central bank with the respective function of lender of last resort, have all taken place outside the framework of the Treaty on the Functioning of the European Union. This is problematic in its own right, and even more so in terms of the democratic legitimation of technically necessary measures of improvement. With the United Kingdom leaving the EU in 2019, the major player which opposed any changes to the Treaty has gone. On the other hand, even elementary familiarity with German, French, Italian and Spanish politics indicate that far-reaching changes, as indicated in the White Paper and the Commission paper on the financing options for the next pluri-annual framework, are unlikely to receive the kind of political backing which is needed for such bold initiatives to materialize. Thus further deepening of the Fiscal and Banking Union through issuance of sovereign-backed securities, without this leading to the unconditional mutualization of public debt obligations, looks both technically feasible and economically desirable (Demarry and Matthes 2017). Still, the likelihood of this to happen is sub-minimal, for the very reason mentioned above: the lack of political momentum in the big states in the driving seat. This bleak outlook may change, though, if the political impasse is overcome with the new European Parliament and Commission coming in by mid-2019. Should the domestic political situation come to appeasement, the chance of a Treaty revision, allowed for by the conclusion of Brexit by that time (Fabbrini 2017), could settle this weighty strategic question. Still, the latter seems a highly optimistic reading of events against the sad reality, namely that the weakness of the governance in the large member states is structural rather than ephemeral, ad hoc in nature.

Finally, who should reform, and in what way? (Taking into account that the answer can only be partial, owing to the open-ended nature of the processes analysed.) As far as the Community level is concerned, much of the improvements that are technically necessary as a minimum have been realized. The €705 billion managed by the technocratic team of the European Stability Mechanism (ESM) constitutes a respectable sum to deter playful market actors from speculating against the single currency and the governments of the euro zone. The quasi-unlimited liquidity provision of the ECB and its intervention in favour of ailing economies allows to pre-empt the replication of sudden stops and the drying out of money markets for them. Stress tests conducted by the joint banking supervisions serve as an early warning system to induce capital adequacy improvements and structural upgrading in banks of systemic relevance.

On the other hand, the paradox I discussed in terms of national economies survives at the EU level. As a matter of fact, owing to the de facto two-speed Europe it is likely to intensify. Member states which de facto opted out from the euro zone for reasons of retaining their political room for manoeuvre and freedom to choose any option they deem appropriate – not constrained by the joint framework – are unlikely to get along with the majority, especially not in a quasi-automatic fashion. Consensus-building thus is likely to remain fragmentary and inadequate, with the unreformed system of decision-making in the European Council and the European Parliament causing any decision to come late.

In turn, national reforms supportive of competitiveness cum financial solidity remain key. Possibilities for such measures vary by country. In France, for instance, newly elected President Macron has faced the first strikes against his labour market measures already in the prime time of his taking office. By contrast, the Baltic states continue with their tough line without encountering serious opposition. In much of Central Europe the ambition as well as the ability to change seems to have ebbed. These countries are thus likely to stay out of the euro zone, though the broader and palpable economic benefits of doing so remain unclear to any informed observer. Keeping all policy options open against a rules-based framework is a conceivable stance, but one burdened with high risks for any small open and financially vulnerable economy.

NOTES

1. This chapter is a significantly revised version of a paper prepared for a conference of the Oesterreichische Nationalbank entitled 'A Modern Take on Structural Reforms', Vienna, 20–21 November 2017. Useful comments of conference participants on the preliminary version are appreciated, with the usual caveats.
2. The 'five economic tests' promulgated by then Chancellor of the Exchequer, Gordon Brown, in June 2003 was a clear admission of the United Kingdom not being ready for the single currency 'any time soon'.
3. Compare, extensively, Kotios et al. (2017) and Bongart and Torres (2017).
4. At the time of writing American tapering of these is over, while ECB communication to date shows no sign of replicating the United States practice, despite expectations of many market participants to this end.

REFERENCES

Alavarez, I., F. Casavecchia, M. De Luca, et al. (2017), 'The use of Eurosystem's monetary policy instruments and operational framework since 2012'. ECB Occasional Paper, Frankfurt am Main, no. 188/May.

Blanchard, O., R. Rajan, K. Rogoff and L. Summers (2016), *Progress and*

Confusion: the State of Macroeconomic Policy. Cambridge, MA and London, UK: MIT Press.

Bongart, A. and F. Torres (2017), 'EMU as a sustainable currency area'. In: N. Costa Cabral, J.R. Gonçalves and N. Cunha Rodrigues (eds), *The Euro and the Crisis: Perspectives for the Eurozone as a Monetary and Budgetary Union*. New York: Springer, pp. 17–32.

Brunnermeier, M.K., H. James and J.-P. Landau (2016), *The Euro and the Battle of Ideas*. Princeton, NJ: Princeton University Press.

Costa Cabral, N., J.R. Goncalves and N.C. Rodrigues (eds) (2017), *The Euro and the Crisis: Perspectives for the Eurozone as a Monetary and Budgetary Union*. New York: Springer.

Csaba, L. (2016), 'Fiscal and banking union in the EU: a solution or a trap?'. In: A.B. Atkinson, P.M. Huber, H. James and F.W. Scharpf (eds), *Nationalstaat und Europäische Union: eine Bestandsaufnahme*. Baden-Baden: Nomos Verlag, pp. 109–22.

Dallago, B., G. Guri and J. McGowan (eds) (2016), *A Global Perspective on the European Crisis*. London: Routledge.

Demarry, M. and J. Matthes (2017), 'Can a reliable framework for sovereign-backed bonds be established?'. *Intereconomics*, **52** (5), 308–15.

Fabbrini, F. (2017), 'Brexit and EU treaty reform: a window of opportunity for constitutional change?'. In: F. Fabbrini (ed.), *The Law and Politics of Brexit*. Oxford, UK and New York, USA: Oxford University Press, pp. 267–91.

Feldstein, M. (1997), 'The political economy of the European economic and monetary union: political sources of an economic liability'. *Journal of Economic Perspectives*, **11** (4), 23–42.

Issing, O., I. Angeloni and V. Gaspar (2004), *Monetary Policy in the Euro Area: Strategy and Decision-making in the European Central Bank*, 2nd edition. Cambridge, UK and New York, USA: Cambridge University Press.

Kotios, A., G. Galanos and M. Kotoulakis (2017), 'How Greece's systemic weaknesses limited the effectiveness of the adjustment programs'. *Intereconomics*, **52** (5), 293–301.

Kudrna, Z. (2016), 'Financial market regulation: crisis-induced supranationalization'. *Journal of European Integration*, **38** (3), 251–64.

Magone, J., B. Laffan and C. Schweigert (eds) (2016), *Core–Periphery Relations in the European Union: Power and Conflict in a Dualist Political Economy*. London: Routledge.

Ódor, L. (ed.) (2017), *Rethinking Fiscal Policy after the Crisis*. Cambridge, UK and New York, USA: Cambridge University Press.

Stiglitz, J.E. (2016), *The Euro and Its Threat to the Future of Europe*. London: Allen Lane.

Visvizi, A. (2014), 'From Grexit to Grecovery: the paradox of the Troika's engagement with Greece'. *Perspectives on European Politics and Society*, **15** (3), 335–45.

16. Reflections on a public risk-sharing capacity for the euro area

Hubert Gabrisch

The series of banking and sovereign debt crises since 2008 have challenged the existing architecture of the European Union (EU). Political inertia and popular anti-EU resentments in many member states resemble the 'Euro-pessimism' phase in the 1970s and 1980s, which the Single European Act from 1987 could finally overcome.[1] Its substantial reforms prepared the present architecture of the EU, which is now in trouble. The feeling that 'something must be done' is again widespread among politicians, the press and the academic world.

This chapter offers reflections on one substantial reform proposal, namely the introduction of a 'central fiscal capacity' to the euro area (EA). My perspective is its risk-sharing function in contrast to the fiscal discipline regime imposed by the Maastricht Treaty, the cornerstone of the existing architecture. This regime contains no common provision to deal with spillover effects of national fiscal adjustment programmes. Everything is left in the hands of individual countries. The reader might imagine the analogy of a city fire department. House owners are responsible for appropriate protection against fire. But this is no reason for a community to abstain from having a fire department. Its task is not only to extinguish the fire in a burning building, but also to prevent the fire from spreading to the neighbourhood. Similar to the transformation of privately organized fire departments into publicly organized ones in the eighteenth century, the introduction of a central fiscal capacity would be a substantial transformation of the euro area's present architecture.

In view of this line of reasoning, the next section provides an overview of cross-border risk-sharing in the EU, reform concepts and the academic literature. It is followed by a critical review of the Maastricht framework, asking why individual country responsibilities are not only unable to protect the euro area against shocks, but may even amplify them. The third section discusses the criteria for designing a central fiscal capacity. The final section concludes.

16.1 PRIVATE VERSUS FISCAL RISK-SHARING IN THE EU: AN OVERVIEW OF RESEARCH LITERATURE AND POLICIES

In a monetary union, full cross-border income risk sharing is given when consumption growth rates are equalized across all countries. The standard approach to test and estimate the size and channels of risk-sharing is the methodology proposed by Asdrubali et al. (1996). This approach identifies three channels:

- Capital markets: internationally diversified portfolios smooth income shocks in the issuer economy for the holder economy; more integrated capital markets reinforce risk-sharing.
- Credit markets: international banks could continue to supply credit to a country with an idiosyncratic output shock if they can mobilize funds saved in other countries.
- Government channel: fiscal transfers and grants through integrated fiscal systems would protect private consumption (for example, via an unemployment insurance scheme) or government consumption against an output shock.

In a study published by the International Monetary Fund (IMF), Allard et al. (2013) summarize some empirical studies on the EU, the euro area and single-state federations of a similar economic level before the year 2010 (Figure 16.1). This figure illustrates what makes the EU and the euro area distinct:

- Less overall insurance. While federations such as the United States (US), Canada and Germany managed to smooth about 80 per cent of local income shocks on private consumption, the euro area only managed to insulate half of that amount; in other words, when the gross domestic product (GDP) contracted by 1 per cent in one of the euro area countries, households' consumption in that country was depressed by as much as 0.6 per cent (as opposed to 0.2 per cent in the US, Canada and Germany.
- Less market-based insurance. Capital markets in the euro area played much less of an insurance role than elsewhere, in part because cross-border ownership of assets within the euro area remained more limited than, for example, across states of the US or across German *Länder*, despite the single market.
- Little fiscal risk-sharing. Cross-country fiscal risk-sharing was almost non-existent, both in the EU and the euro area, compared

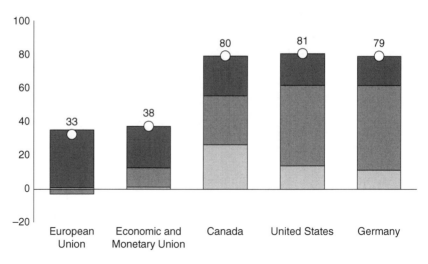

Note: Fiscal transfers = government channel; factor income and capital depreciation = capital market channel; saving = credit market channel.

Source: Allard et al. (2013) and references therein.

Figure 16.1   Risk-sharing in different federations, different periods before 2010

to the cross-state transfer and grant schemes in the US, Canada and Germany.

Other studies that go beyond the year 2010 (Furceri and Zdzienicka 2013, p. 9; Ferrari and Picco 2016; Poncela et al. 2016) confirm the picture. Cimadomo et al. (2017) obtain somewhat different results. The authors find a slight rise in consumption smoothing in the aftermath of the euro crisis, due to credits by the European Financial Stability Facility (EFSF) and the European Stabilization Mechanism (ESM) to Greece and other euro economies after 2010. Notice here that the fiscal conditionality of these credits might have contributed to drastic interruptions in consumption, for example in Greece, while their size may have only partly offset these negative effects.

Many commentators argue that the lack of an appropriate fiscal risk-sharing instrument at the euro area level may have contributed to aggravating the severity of the economic downturn in the euro periphery and delayed the recovery in the entire area. This view is behind many proposals to insert a fiscal risk-sharing tool into the euro area framework. However, the response of the official EU – the Four and Five Presidents reports (EU Commission 2012, 2015a), and recently the EU Commission's 'Reflection Paper' (EU Commission 2017a) – remains vague. The official EU favours stronger private risk-sharing mechanisms in the euro area as documented by the banking union and the recent proposal of a capital markets union (EU Commission 2015b, 2017b). This preference for more private risk-sharing is backed by the Maastricht Treaty, which provides for a fiscal discipline regime for member countries in the monetary union under the condition of a single monetary policy and sovereign fiscal policies in the countries.

In the academic literature, the superiority of private risk-sharing was modelled starting with the seminal paper of Allen and Gale (2000), who formally showed that with increasing connectivity in a credit network (= risk-sharing) individual and systemic risks are shrinking. In this tradition, some academic commentators advocate the restoration of decentralized responsibilities of government debt and financial sector reforms (Fuest and Peichl 2012; Feld and Osterloh 2013), and would accept only central solutions, which integrate the function of private cross-border risk-sharing and conditional financial support; examples of these solutions are the ESM and its possible transformation into a European Monetary Fund (EMF). Others argue that the implementation of a capital markets union would completely ensure cross-border risk-sharing (e.g., Brühl et al. 2015).

Yet, experience seems to show that the private risk-sharing idea does not work under all circumstances. After 40 years of financial market liberalization and increasing cross-border trade with securities it has become fairly evident that systemic financial fragility is not on the retreat; the best example is the financial crisis of 2007–2008 in the US, the world's possibly most integrated financial market. A second generation of financial network models attempts to explain why the first-generation idea of increasing risk-sharing might fail. In contrast to Allen and Gale (2000), authors have modelled situations in which more complete networks may raise systemic fragility. Battiston et al. (2012) argue with the dynamic effects of financial stress, induced by the work of the financial accelerator. The propagation of an idiosyncratic shock today makes each network member more vulnerable to a further liquidity shock tomorrow, even when the initial shock has been absorbed. The presence of dynamic effects may lead to a systemic crisis, not despite but because of more individual risk-sharing. Acemoglu et al. (2013) show how the fragility of a network depends on the architecture of the network. Networks are able to absorb minor daily shocks to one of their nodes. However, a complete network might fail in the case of severe shocks (like the US real estate shock) in the absence of excess liquidity of at least one node or of external creditors.

These second-generation models are the economic rationale behind the various proposals to establish a fiscal risk-sharing instrument at the euro area level.

16.2 WHY FISCAL DISCIPLINE IS NOT A COMPLETE SUBSTITUTE FOR FISCAL RISK-SHARING

Most single states and large federations have public risk-sharing instruments at their disposal. This is the result of a historically long process of power centralization combined with intra-state fiscal federalism (Germany) or inter-regional compensation (France, Italy). Economics justifies a fiscal federal system with the argument that in the absence of exchange-rate prerogatives and with highly open economies, 'local governments simply have very limited means for traditional macroeconomic control' (Oates 1999) when they are hit by a shock.[2] 'Traditional macroeconomic control' means the use of anticyclical monetary and fiscal policies, mostly through coordination between the central bank and the treasury.

The euro area was built from the outset on the principle that shock absorption requires structural reforms and fiscal adjustments at the country level. The fiscal framework that was adapted to the monetary union is laid down in the EU Treaties of 1997 (the principle of no bail-out and the ban of central bank financing), the Stability and Growth Pact (SGP) and its later reforms, the Two-Packs for increased surveillance from 2011, and the Fiscal Compact (FC) from 2012. Its substance is fiscal discipline, not risk-sharing. The underlying idea is the prevalence of asymmetric shocks, caused by expansionary policy discretion and non-competitive economic structures. Therefore, the later reforms underline the relevance of eliminating structural budget deficits as the result of policy discretion. Another belief is that many shocks have a cyclical component, and the EU fiscal framework provides all the rules to use national fiscal policies to deal with them. Sound fiscal policies use the automatic stabilization function of revenues and expenditures to ensure a balanced budget over the cycle. Finally, in the case of common macroeconomic shocks and a common business cycle, the centralized monetary policy is adequately equipped to deal with them, too.

However, the analysis of data from the mid-1990s to the mid-2010s revealed some striking shortcomings of this approach. There is, firstly, the observation that more trade and financial integration transforms an idiosyncratic shock into a common shock via the trade and financial multipliers, as in my analogy of a fire department the spreading of a fire

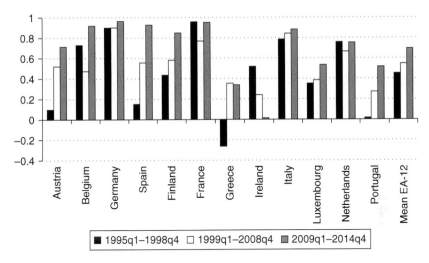

Note: HP trend-adjusted quarterly real GDP growth rates.

Sources: Own calculations and illustration based on Eurostat quarterly GDP data [namq_10_gdp].

Figure 16.2   Business cycle synchronization in the euro area, coefficients of correlation with the EA-12

to the close neighbours. Figure 16.2 underlines why asymmetric shocks, justifying a country-specific reform approach, lost their earlier importance. The figure shows the Hodrick–Prescott (HP) trend-adjusted real gross domestic product (GDP) rates of change for each of the 12 original euro area countries (EA-12), and their correlation with the euro area business cycle on a quarterly basis for three periods since 1995. A coefficient of 1 depicts complete synchronization of the national business cycle with the euro area business cycle. As a result, the synchronization increased continuously since 1995. In the last period, a 1.00 percentage point deviation from the trend rate of GDP in the euro area is correlated with a 0.65 percentage point deviation on average in each country. With respect to Germany and France, a euro area-wide shock is almost completely transferred to both countries, and vice versa.

Accordingly, a fiscal consolidation in one country would trigger negative spillover effects to other countries. Poghosyan (2017, p. 26) estimates that a fiscal consolidation of 1.0 per cent of GDP in Germany would reduce the GDP in ten euro area countries by 0.3 per cent after five years. Hence, the more the cross-country business cycles are correlated, the higher is the

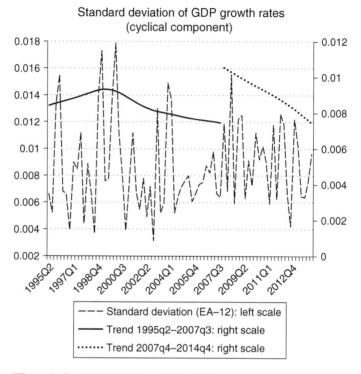

Note: HP trend-adjusted data for the original EA-12.

Sources: Own calculations and illustration based on Eurostat quarterly GDP data [namq_10_gdp].

Figure 16.3   Standard deviation (SD) of GDP rates of change, cyclical component and the (polynomial) trend

need for a common fiscal instrument, which protects country A against losses caused by unilateral fiscal adjustments in country B.

Another matter of concern, secondly, is the rising divergence of the business cycles' amplitudes (a measure for the degree of consumption smoothing) in turbulent times. Figure 16.3 depicts the standard deviation (SD) of the cyclical component of the GDP rate of change for the EA-12 countries for each quarter between the second quarter of 1995 and the fourth quarter of 2014, and the trend lines for two periods: the calm and the turbulent ones. The first, solid trend line shows a declining divergence between countries after the introduction of the euro until the end of 2007. The second, dotted trend line reveals a jump in the SD at a substantially higher level in the following quarters, and a return to the calm period level since about the second quarter of 2013. Seemingly, less cross-border consumption smoothing in turbulent times is the combined effect of country-specific fiscal adjustment programmes and strong feedback from spillover effects on the other euro area countries.

Thirdly, a centralized monetary policy does not dispose of all instruments to deal with common shocks. In the euro area, it turned out that monetary and fiscal policies are not complete substitutes, particularly when conventional monetary policy nears the zero lower bound. Figure 16.3 illustrates that the divergence in cycle amplitudes returned to its pre-crisis level only after the ECB became active in summer 2012, when it announced the Outright Market Transactions (OMT) programme. The unconventional monetary policy stopped the acute phase of the crisis, however, with 'diminishing returns' (Begg 2017; Carnot 2017): quantitative easing increasingly contributed to an increase of financial asset prices, thus probably increasing the financial fragility of the system.

And finally, the cyclical component of the fiscal budget should work via the automatic stabilization function of revenues and expenditures. The working of automatic stabilizers is meaningful only when the cyclically adjusted budget is sufficiently sensitive to income shocks. When governments were recently forced to reduce their structural deficits by social and tax system reforms, this had the displeasing property of also reducing the sensitivity of the cyclical budget. I calculated the cyclical sensitivity of the budget as the ratio of the percentage point changes of the cyclical component in terms of GDP to a 1 per cent rate of change of the GDP for the 28 EU countries in the period from 2008 to 2016 (Figure 16.4). A positive value means the stabilizers act in the normal direction: a decline in GDP leads to a higher deficit and vice versa. The grey bars illustrate the large differences in the cyclical sensitivity among the countries due to country traditions and recent reforms of the social and tax systems. This includes substantially different income multipliers of automatic adjustments. The dark bars shed a light on the years of reinforced fiscal consolidation (2013 and 2014). There are many cases of an automatic destabilization, that is, a negative GDP rate of change is related to a positive change (improvement) in the cyclical component.

One should not be surprised that euro area countries might want to protect themselves against negative spillover effects of reform actions unilaterally undertaken by one or more other countries. This can happen unilaterally, through coordination by the EU Commission, or through a central fiscal capacity. The first method might lead to economic disintegration and is not further discussed. The second option – coordination of fiscal measures – is fraught with technical problems. The corpus of

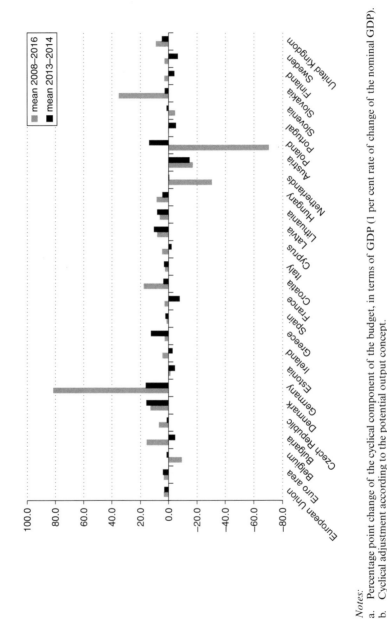

Notes:
a. Percentage point change of the cyclical component of the budget, in terms of GDP (1 per cent rate of change of the nominal GDP).
b. Cyclical adjustment according to the potential output concept.

Sources: Author's compilation and presentation based on Ameco (GDP) and Eurostat (cyclically adjusted general government net lending) data.

Figure 16.4   Income sensitivity[a] of the cyclical component of national budgets, 28 EU countries, 2010–2016[b]

national and common fiscal rules in the EU has become very complex. Today, there is a plethora of different national rules entailing resource-intensive methodological work by the European Commission for surveillance and coordinated action; and many departments, sub-departments, committees and working groups are engaged to analyse, to diagnose and to recommend. All this might lead to a significant time lag in fiscal actions, and runs the risk of procyclical effects. A common fiscal instrument would help to simplify rules and regulations.

16.3   CRITERIA FOR AN EU-SPECIFIC DESIGN OF A CENTRAL FISCAL RISK-SHARING CAPACITY

As a substantial transformation of the existing euro area architecture, the introduction of a central fiscal capacity reaches far beyond purely economic considerations: it enters into the realm of member countries' self-conception of being sovereign states. This is one reason why various EU reports and reflection papers underline the needs for such a reform, but never cross the Rubicon of precise concepts, despite an already considerable collection of proposals in the arena (for an overview, see Iara 2015). The following considerations focus on four proposals: a full-fledged euro area budget, a European unemployment benefits system (EUBS), a stabilization or 'rainy day' fund, and an EMF. They are evaluated with the help of three selective criteria: sovereignty, institutional efficiency and economic effectiveness.

Sovereignty

The EU is not a single state or a federation like the US or Canada, and probably will never be one. The EU is a confederation of states at best. And the introduction of a central fiscal risk-sharing capacity is closely related to the sensitive issue of member countries' sovereignty. A solution of the problem might be the creation of a new 'European sovereignty' (as was broadly explicated in Emmanuel Macron's Athens speech in September 2017[3]). Seen from the constitutional perspective, a European sovereignty might mean the establishment of new legal entities within the borders of a confederation of national states: the constituent entities (the national states) retain the right to withdraw from the supranational body (the EU or the euro area), but in a federation member states do not hold that right. And the creation of such a new European sovereignty does not necessarily mean the taking away of national competences and their transfer to the new entity. A central fiscal capacity would be an overlay on the existing system, completing it according to the distinct features of the euro area, instead of replacing it. The European Treaties stipulate rather precisely where member states delegate some segments of their sovereignty, with additional segments requiring a revision of the Treaties, which is in the present state of the union a rather heroic assumption. Among the proposals mentioned above, a full-fledged euro area budget would probably necessitate a new division of power between the new entity and the participating countries and, hence, a change of the Treaties. All other proposals could be established within European secondary law, simply through a Council regulation or directive.

Efficiency

According to the Tinbergen rule, each achievable policy goal needs at least one linearly independent instrument, otherwise a trade-off may emerge between them. That might be the case when the central risk-sharing instrument is unduly combined with the goal to also enforce fiscal discipline. If so, the risk-sharing function would have to fully compensate the negative effects stemming from the disciplinary arm of the instrument – clearly reducing the efficiency of the instrument. The EMF proposal of the Commission (EU Commission 2017b) is an example of an inadequate mix between stabilization and disciplinary functions. A more efficient solution would be the separation of the functions into two instruments and entities. Two separate instruments – one at the national level, one at the central level – would make both of them more efficient. The disciplinary arms of the existing fiscal framework – including the principle of no bail-out – would become more reliable; while the stabilizing arm at the central level would mitigate the spillover effects of country-level consolidation programmes.

Effectiveness

A risk-sharing capacity may address cyclical shocks and soften the cross-border spillovers induced by the different national systems of automatic stabilization. An EUBS would compensate for spillover effects from different national unemployment benefit systems (Vandenbroucke 2017) and have a direct smoothing influence on private consumption. Because the system would work in combination with national systems, the size of common funding would be less in terms of the common GDP compared to the national systems. However, a substantial problem is to identify what is cyclical and what is not. In the case of persistent shocks with long-term unemployment, the system would change from risk-sharing into redistribution by transfers (Allard et al. 2013), which is generally unwished-for among European politicians and the population. A stabilization fund is an alternative concept, when dedicated to compensating for discretionary cuts of national budgets' investment expenditure (about 3 per cent of GDP), which is the first victim when governments are requested to consolidate according to the rules of the existing fiscal framework. Activated only in cases of large country-specific and common shocks, it is most similar to my analogy of a fire department, where national governments remain responsible for sound fiscal policies in the same way as house owners remain responsible for appropriately protecting their homes against the outbreak of a fire. The fund would support infrastructural and private investment overwhelmingly not through transfers but through grants that create an equivalent through future income. Finally, and through its discretionary interventions, the stabilization would become a fiscal partner and counterpart to the European Central Bank (ECB) on a level playing field; a prerequisite to return some control over the euro area macroeconomy in cooperation with the ECB that would be less prone to exceed its power.

16.4   CONCLUDING REMARKS

There is a need for substantial reforms of the EU. The present institutional architecture does not address the challenges stemming from shock proliferation due to increased trade and financial integration. Substantial parts of this architecture are questioned by governments and the public. What Europe needs is a new project, a vision, based on a new understanding of sovereignty. Following the analogy of a modern fire department, I have argued that a fiscal risk-sharing capacity in the euro area would not necessarily create a super-state. It would be an overlay on the existing framework, complementing it according to the distinct features of the monetary union. The capacity should be strictly separated from the disciplinary function of the given fiscal framework, which will only apply to the member countries. It would make the fiscal stipulations of the Maastricht Treaty reliable. But it would unconditionally balance the common risks from different country systems. This approach goes with a stabilization fund dedicated to investment, or a European unemployment insurance system, directly dedicated to consumption smoothing.

NOTES

1. The term 'Euro Pessimism' was coined by Baldwin and Wyplosz (2004).
2. Oates published his essay on fiscal federalism in the year of the euro introduction, and some passages read like addressing this event.

3. https://de.ambafrance.org/Staatsprasident-Macron-in-Athen-Vorschlage-fur-eine-Neugr
    undung-Europas.

REFERENCES

Acemoglu, D., A. Ozdagla and A. Tahbaz-Salehi (2013), 'Systemic Risk and Stability in Financial Networks', MIT Working Paper 1303.

Allard, E., P.K. Brooks, J.C. Bluedorn, F. Bornhorst, K. Christopherson, F. Ohnsorge, T. Poghosyan and an IMF Staff Team (2013), 'Toward a Fiscal Union for the Euro Area', IMF Staff Discussion Note SDN 13/09.

Allen, F. and D. Gale (2000), 'Financial Contagion', *Journal of Political Economy*, **108** (1), 1–33.

Asdrubali, P., E. Bent, B.E. Sørensen and O. Yosha (1996), 'Channels of Interstate Risk Sharing: United States 1963–1990', *Quarterly Journal of Economics*, **111** (4), 1081–110.

Baldwin, R. and Ch. Wyplosz (2004), *The Economics of European Integration*, New York: McGraw Hill.

Battiston, S., D. Delli Gatti, M. Gallegati, B.C. Greenwald and J.E. Stiglitz (2012), 'Liaisons Dangereuses: Increasing Connectivity, Risk Sharing, and Systemic Risk', *Journal of Economic Dynamics and Control*, **36** (8), 1121–41.

Begg, I. (2017), 'Fiscal Rules and the Scope for Risk Sharing', *Intereconomics*, **52** (3), 131–7.

Brühl, V., H. Gründl, A. Hackethal, H.-H. Kotz, J. P.v. Krahnen and T. Tröger (2015), 'Comments on the EU Commission's Capital Markets Union Project', White Paper Series 27, Research Center SAFE, Universität Frankfurt a. M.

Carnot, N. (2017), 'European Fiscal Governance and Cyclical Stabilisation: Searching for a Lasting Arrangement', *Intereconomics*, **2017** (3), 148–54.

Cimadomo, J., O. Fortuna and M. Giuliodoro (2017), 'Private and Public Risk Sharing in the Euro Area', *Tinbergen Institute Discussion Papers* 2017-064/VI.

EU Commission (2012), 'The Four Presidents' Report: Towards a Genuine Economic and Monetary Union', https://ec.europa.eu/priorities/sites/beta-political/files/5-p residents-report_en.pdf.

EU Commission (2015a), 'The Five Presidents' Report: Completing Europe's Economic and Monetary Union', http://ec.europa.eu/priorities/sites/beta-political/ files/5-presidents-report_de_0.pdf.

EU Commission (2015b), 'Green Paper Building a Capital Markets Union', http://ec.europa.eu/finance/consultations/2015/capital-markets-union/docs/ green-paper_en.pdf.

EU Commission (2017a), 'Reflection Paper on the Deepening of the Economic and Monetary Union', https://ec.europa.eu/commission/sites/beta-political/files/ reflection-paper-eu-finances_en.pdf.

EU Commission (2017b), 'Proposal for a Council Regulation on the Establishment of the European Monetary Fund', https://ec.europa.eu/info/sites/info/files/econ omy.../com_827.pdf.

Feld, P. and S. Osterloh (2013), 'Is a Fiscal Capacity Really Necessary to Complete EA?', *Freiburg Discussion Papers* 13/5.

Ferrari, A. and A.R. Picco (2016), 'International Risk Sharing in the EA', *European Stability Mechanism Working Paper* 17/2016.

Fuest, C. and A. Peichl (2012), 'European Union Fiscal Union: What Is It? Does It Work? And Are There Really "No Alternatives"?', *CESifo Forum*, **13** (1), 3–9, Munich.

Furceri, D. and A. Zdzienicka (2013), 'The Euro Area Crisis: Need for a Supranational Fiscal Risk Sharing Mechanism?', *IMF Working Paper* WP 13/198.

Iara, A. (2015), 'Revenue for EMU: A Contribution to the Debate on Fiscal Union', *Working Paper* 54-2015, European Commission, Brussels.

Oates, W.E. (1999), 'An Essay on Fiscal Federalism', *Journal of Economic Literature*, **37** (3), 1120–49.

Poghosyan, T. (2017), 'Cross-Country Spillovers of Fiscal Consolidations in the Euro Area', *IMF Working Paper* WP 17/140.

Poncela, P., F. Pericoli, A.R. Manca and M. Nardo (2016), 'Risk Sharing in Europe', *JRC Science for Policy Report*, European Commission, Brussels.

Vandenbroucke, F. (2017), 'Risk Reduction, Risk Sharing and Moral Hazard: A Vaccination Analogy', *Intereconomics* **52** (3), 154–9.

17. Reviving convergence: making EU member states fit for joining the euro area

Lúcio Vinhas de Souza, Oliver Dreute, Vladimir Isaila and Jan-Martin Frie[1]

> If we want the euro to unite rather than divide our continent, then it should be more than the currency of a select group of countries. The euro is meant to be the single currency of the European Union as a whole. All but two of our Member States are required and entitled to join the euro once they fulfil the conditions. Member States that want to join the euro must be able to do so. This is why I am proposing to create a euro accession Instrument, offering technical and even financial assistance.
> (European Commission President Jean-Claude Juncker in his State of the Union Address, 13 September 2017)

Aside from Denmark and the United Kingdom, which both negotiated opt-out arrangements in the Maastricht Treaty, all member states of the European Union (EU) are required and entitled to adopt the euro. Today, however, seven member states are subject to a derogation as they have not yet fulfilled the necessary conditions. These are: Bulgaria, the Czech Republic, Croatia, Hungary, Poland, Romania and Sweden.

Yet, taking a closer look, it becomes clear that most of these countries would in fact not have great difficulty in complying with the euro adoption criteria, regardless of their different economic and political contexts. Hence, if one of them intended to adopt the euro, it could, in principle, proceed without significant further adjustments. What, then, is holding them back?

The fallout from the 2008 financial crisis has slowed the impetus of member states to join the euro area and cast doubts on the ability of the euro area both to maintain fiscal discipline and to promote convergence among its members. Indeed, significant divergences persist among member states today, both within the euro area and outside it, even where the euro convergence criteria are met.

Accession to the euro area formally depends on the fulfilment of five

Table 17.1   The five convergence criteria

What is measured	Price stability	Sound public finances		Durability of convergence	Exchange rate stability
How it is measured	Consumer price inflation rate	Government deficit as per cent of GDP	Government debt as per cent of GDP	Long-term interest rate	Deviation from a central rate
Convergence criterion	Not more than 1.5 percentage points above the rate of the three best-performing member states	Reference value: not more than 3 per cent	Reference value: not more than 60 per cent	Not more than 2 percentage points above the rate of the three best-performing member states in terms of price stability	Participation in the EU's Exchange Rate Mechanism (ERM II) for at least 2 years without severe tensions

Note: GDP = gross domestic product.

Source: European Commission.

convergence criteria (Table 17.1) laid down in Article 140(1) of the Treaty on the Functioning of the European Union (TFEU).

In addition to the Treaty convergence criteria, national legislation must be compatible with Economic and Monetary Union (EMU) rules set out in Articles 130 and 131 TFEU, relating to the independence of national central banks, the prohibition on monetary financing, and compatibility with the statutes of the European System of Central Banks (ESCB) and of the European Central Bank (ECB). The current situation of the seven member states with a derogation is as indicated in Table 17.2.

All seven countries are thus generally compliant with the convergence criteria and none are under threat of an excessive deficit procedure.[2]

Given that the convergence criteria relate mainly to countries' macroeconomic environment, it is not surprising that this good overall compliance is reflected in a macroeconomic performance that is roughly on par with the euro area average (Figure 17.1). Notwithstanding this, some also perform well above average (Sweden and the Czech Republic in particular),

Table 17.2   Convergence criteria as fulfilled by non-euro area member states with a derogation

Convergence Criteria

	Consumer price inflation rate	Government deficit as % of GDP	Government debt as % of GDP	Long-term interest rate	Deviation from a central rate	Legal convergence
	Reference Value: 0.7%	Reference Value: Not more than 3%	Reference Value: Not more than 60%	Reference Value: 4%	Participation in ERM II for at least two years without severe tensions	Adaptation to requirements under Article 131 of the Treaty
Bulgaria	−1.3	0.0	29.5	2.3	NO [NOTE a]	NO
Croatia	−0.6	−0.8	84.2	3.5	NO	NO
Czech Republic	0.6	0.6	37.2	0.4	NO	NO
Denmark	0.0	−0.9	37.8	0.3		
Hungary	0.4	−1.8	74.1	3.1	NO	NO
Poland	−0.2	−2.4	54.4	3.0	NO	NO
Romania	−1.1	−3.0	37.6	3.3	NO	NO
Sweden	1.1	0.9	41.6	0.5	NO	NO

Note:

a Bulgaria is not a formal part of the EU's Exchange Rate Mechanism (ERM), but the Bulgarian lev has been pegged to the euro since 1999.

Sources: Eurostat; ECB (2016).

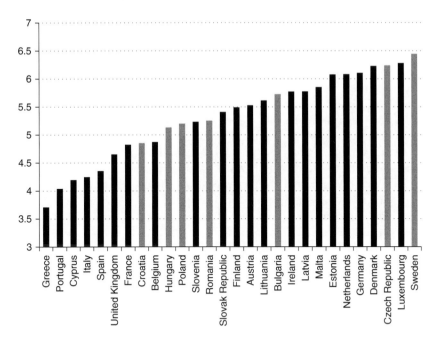

Notes: The macroeconomic environment index is a composite indicator of the Global Competitiveness Index 2017 consisting of single indicators measuring: government debt levels, savings, inflation, and country credit. Values range from 1 (low) to 7 (high).

Figure 17.1 Macroeconomic Environment Index 2017

while others show room for improvement, also reflecting the very different economic and political contexts of each country.

Thus, while as a first step it may be worth recalling the benefits of adopting the euro, as a second step it will also be important to further strengthen the ability of the euro area to act as a lever for convergence. The benefits of adopting the euro are wide-ranging:

- Stable prices. Since the introduction of the euro, inflation has averaged just below 2 per cent, contributing to price stability in the euro area.
- Transparency. The single currency has enabled price transparency across the single market, creating a downward pressure on prices, more competition between suppliers, and more competitive markets.
- Lower travel costs. The cost of exchanging money at borders has disappeared in the euro area, making it cheaper and easier to travel.

- More cross-border trade. The elimination of exchange risks or costs facilitates cross-border trade within the euro area. At the same time, the 'home market' gets larger, both for those selling goods and services, and for those seeking out suppliers offering better services or lower costs.
- More international trade. A large and open euro area is attractive to other trading nations, which can access a large market using one currency. Euro area companies also benefit because they can export and import to and from the global economy using the euro.
- Better access to capital. Investors can move capital to those parts of the euro area where it can be used most efficiently, because exchange rate risks have disappeared, reducing the cost of loans for citizens and companies.
- In addition to all these benefits, belonging to the euro area is about belonging to a community based on responsibility, solidarity and mutual benefits.

Of course, the benefits of the euro are not unconditional, and depend on member states' capacity to operate smoothly inside the Monetary Union, based on sound policies. This is why thorough preparation for euro area membership is essential.

17.1   BEYOND NOMINAL CONVERGENCE

The current criteria for adopting the euro refer to nominal variables relating to the macroeconomic environment – the inflation rate, the long-term interest rate and the exchange rate – and to the budget deficit and debt ratios. However, these criteria do not necessarily reflect developments in the real economy, which can also pose challenges on the road to adopting the euro.

The European debt crisis, multiple euro area accession experiences, academic analyses, as well as evidence from the ground have shown that fulfilling the existing convergence criteria does not necessarily lead to long-term, sustainable economic performance. Other factors also matter: namely, a number of member states that joined the euro area had serious problems due to lack of competitiveness, shortcomings in their public administration and weaknesses in their banking sector. A weak macroeconomic environment added to the negative impact. Therefore, as already emphasized by the European Central Bank (2016) and by the European Commission, it is also important to look at member states in terms of their overall competitiveness and institutional capacity.

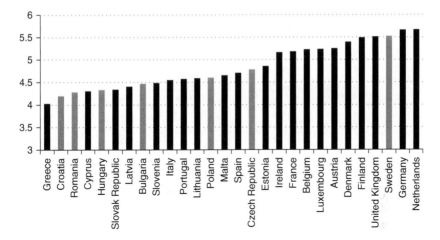

Note: Values range from 1 (low) to 7 (high).

Source: World Economic Forum

Figure 17.2   Global Competitiveness Index 2017

Competitiveness

Competitiveness and high productivity are key elements to ensuring a smooth transition into the euro area. Otherwise, risks of asymmetries and divergences will remain. Currently, six of the non-euro member states with derogations are under the EU-28[3] average of 4.8 out of 7 on the Global Competitiveness Index (Figure 17.2; World Economic Forum 2017).

Institutional Capacity

Institutional capacity is essential with respect to several dimensions. First of all, an optimal investment environment requires swift and efficient administrative procedures, reliable and accessible data, legal certainty and planning capacity. Secondly, the efficient functioning of domestic markets is dependent on variables such as the rule of law, the quality and efficiency of institutions, public and corporate institutional cultures, the level of training and expertise of civil servants, the agility and capacity of institutions to react to shocks and economic evolutions, and attitudes to corruption. Inadequacy in any of these areas can result in capital flight or a lack of investment, domestic and foreign. Currently, six of the non-euro member states with derogations are under the EU-28 average of 4.5 out

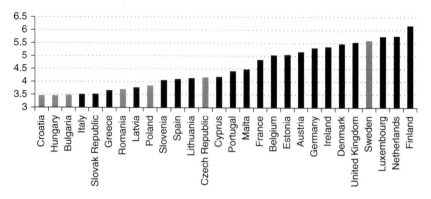

Notes: Within the Global Competitiveness Index, the Institutional Capacity is a composite indicator consisting of single indicators measuring: property rights, ethics and corruption, undue influence, government effectiveness, security and accountability. Values range from 1 (low) to 7 (high).

Figure 17.3   Institutional Capacity Index 2017

of 7 on the Global Competitiveness Index (Figure 17.3) (World Economic Forum 2017).

Without going into a detailed analysis, one necessary conclusion is that there are economic convergence needs that go beyond the nominal convergence criteria as laid down in the Treaty. Meeting the nominal convergence criteria alone does not guarantee permanent successful participation in the euro area.

Member states should also – as a bare minimum – have the capacity to manage their budgets in accordance with the principle of sound public financial management, and be institutionally ready to participate in the Banking Union. Beyond this, properly functioning labour and product markets and an efficient public administration are also indispensable. And, ideally, any necessary reforms and adaptations should take place before the euro adoption.

However, further legally binding convergence criteria could only be established by EU law. Even if this is considered feasible, such a step could be regarded as discriminatory, creating unjustified obstacles for non-euro area member states in adopting the euro. Therefore a new joint effort is needed to ensure that non-euro area member states are able – and willing – to join the euro area, while avoiding the shortfalls other member states have suffered from. The emphasis should be on enhancing competitiveness, building up the needed institutional capacities and, where necessary, reinforcing the macroeconomic environment, as the basis for real and lasting convergence.

17.2   A ROLE FOR A NEW EURO ACCESSION INSTRUMENT

The new euro accession instrument, proposed by President Juncker in his 2017 State of the Union address, offers a framework to operationalize this joint effort. Although there already exist various European instruments[4] and technical assistance programmes[5] aimed at boosting competitiveness, modernizing financial administrations[6] and building administrative capacity, it would be useful to complement ongoing activities with a coherent set of measures, specifically aimed at preparing non-euro area member states with a derogation towards a successful and sustainable participation in the euro area.

Better coordinating or blending existing programmes and instruments would allow for greater synergies and a scaling-up of efforts, without creating new bureaucracies, and while minimizing costs. It would also enable the preparation and implementation of tailor-made reform programmes, aimed at helping member states with a derogation to comply with the broader legal and economic requirements of being part of the euro area.

Such assistance programmes should be based on an agreement between the member state and the European Commission, clearly establishing the member state as co-owner of the process. They should build on a thorough and comprehensive analysis of the particular strengths and weaknesses related to competitiveness and administrative capacities of the member state in question. And they should draw on the experiences of current euro area member states after they adopted the euro, and especially during the crisis. It should also be clear that the proposed euro accession instrument would be voluntary. Participation would neither be a precondition for adopting the euro, nor a guarantee for joining the euro area.

Only if the target (that is, a sustainable adoption of the euro), the path (that is, increasing competition and stepping up administrative capacities) and the conditions are transparent, publicly explained and debated, as well as politically endorsed, will the necessary impetus towards accession to the euro area be created and maintained. This means there should be clarity on the mid-term economic policy of the member state; agreement on the policy areas that should be subject to convergence; and an understanding that convergence efforts will have to continue beyond the term of the assistance. Any weaknesses should be tackled using a set of coherent and combined actions in the relevant fields, with clearly fixed targets and an achievable timeline to create a realistic path for the member state towards euro adoption.

The type of support offered would be mostly of a technical nature. Currently, similar technical support is provided to EU member states by the European Commission through the Structural Reform Support Programme (SRSP) managed by the Structural Reform Support Service (SRSS).[7] One option, among others, could thus be for the proposed euro accession instrument to build on the wide expertise of this service in the relevant fields.

If the existing financial resources in the SRSP were insufficient to cover all the needs and accompanying investments, member states could be offered the possibility to make use of Article 11 of the Structural Reform Support Programme Regulation, which allows for the transfer of unspent amounts from the technical assistance lines under the European Structural Investment Funds (ESIF).[8]

17.3   CONCLUSIONS

Although, at present, most of the non-euro area member states would not have great difficulty in complying with the convergence criteria laid down in the Treaty for the adoption of the euro, it is clear, after the crisis, that successful membership to the euro area also requires real economic convergence that goes beyond the nominal convergence criteria. This real convergence is primarily an issue of competitiveness and institutional capacity.

The euro area accession instrument proposed by President Juncker in his 2017 State of the Union speech, as one of the initiatives to be launched and/or completed by the end of 2018, should therefore focus on enhancing competitiveness and institutional capacity-building. Based on an analysis of the strengths and weaknesses of individual member states, it should provide tailor-made, coherent and combined assistance, with clearly fixed targets and an achievable timeline to create a realistic path for the adoption of the euro.

Such a voluntary instrument could also help to foster a relaunch of the economic convergence process in the Union, which is indispensable to achieve shared prosperity among all EU members and to ensure the resilience of the Economic and Monetary Union. For lasting convergence, and to secure permanent support by citizens and member states, the convergence process needs a revived political narrative that includes the accession of all member states to the euro area.

NOTES

1. Disclaimer: views expressed represent exclusively the positions of the author and do not necessarily correspond to those of the European Commission.
2. With the exception of Romania, to which the Commission addressed a warning, on 22 May 2017, on deviating from the convergence criteria.
3. EU-28 = Austria, Belgium, Bulgaria, Croatia, Cyprus, Czech Republic, Denmark, Estonia, Finland, France, Germany, Greece, Hungary, Ireland, Italy, Latvia, Lithuania, Luxembourg, Malta, Netherlands, Poland, Portugal, Romania, Slovak Republic, Slovenia, Spain, Sweden, United Kingdom.
4. To bridge the gap in competitiveness, investment and productivity across the continent, but especially in euro area accession countries, the EU has put forward multiple initiatives such as the European Regional Development Fund (ERDF), European Social Fund (ESF) and Cohesion Fund (CF), as well as Investment Funds aiming to spur investment in regions that need it the most such as the European Fund for Strategic Investments (EFSI), the Horizon 2020 Framework Programme for Research and Innovation, and the programme for the Competitiveness of Enterprises and Small and Medium-sized Enterprises (COSME) and others. These funds can be of very high granularity, targeting specific regions, actors or sectors; aiming, on the one hand, to bring added value and, on the other, to rescue ailing regions or sectors. Although not directly targeting pre-accession countries, these tools can greatly improve real convergence by improving economic competitiveness.
5. Technical Assistance Programmes from the European Commission through its Directorate-General for Regional and Urban Policy (DG REGIO) aim towards institutional strengthening and administrative capacity-building, and propose measures to identify, prioritize and implement structural and administrative reforms in response to economic and social challenges. These programmes target administrative capacity-building in the broadest sense possible, both private and public, in almost all sectors. The 2016 budget managed by DG REGIO for technical assistance through the ERDF, ESF and CF, among others, is €104 million, according to DG REGIO estimates. In addition, the European Stability Mechanism provides technical assistance to countries upon request. This, however, is very limited and has only been carried out in Cyprus. The European Central Bank also provides some technical assistance to member states.
6. The European Commission's Directorate-General for Financial Stability, Financial Services and Capital Markets Union (DG FISMA) assists member states in the transposition of EU directives, and assesses the completeness and correctness of national transposition measures, while monitoring how EU law is applied in practice, handling complaints and launching cases on possible breaches of EU law by member states. It works in partnership with the European Central Bank (ECB), Single Supervisory Mechanism (SSM), Single Resolution Mechanism (SRM), Single Resolution Board (SRB) and European Systemic Risk Board (ESRB) to provide this type of technical assistance.
7. See the list of possible actions in Article 5 of Regulation (EU) 2017/825 on the establishment of the Structural Reform Programme for the period 2017 to 2020 and amending Regulation (EU) 1303/2013 and (EU) 1305/2013, OJ L 129/1.
8. Depending on the country-specific situation, this could be done either by implementing the planned programme as such; by adjusting the scope of some of the projects; by reprogramming the European Structural Investment Funds (ESIF) envelope; or by making use of the performance reserve. The modifications under 'ESIF 2' will already contribute to a better use of the funding possibilities in those member states that did not benefit very much from the ESIF so far.

REFERENCES

European Central Bank (ECB) (2016), *Convergence Report*, Frankfurt am Main.
Juncker, J.C. (2017), *State of the Union 2017*, Brussels: European Commission.
World Economic Forum (2017), *The Global Competitiveness Report 2016–2017*, Geneva.

Index